The Hemingway
Short Story

Also by George Monteiro
and from McFarland

Reading Henry James: A Critical Perspective on Selected Works (2016)

Robert Frost's Poetry of Rural Life (2015)

Elizabeth Bishop in Brazil and After: A Poetic Career Transformed (2012)

The Hemingway Short Story

A Critical Appreciation

GEORGE MONTEIRO

McFarland & Company, Inc., Publishers
Jefferson, North Carolina

ISBN (print) 978-1-4766-6988-5
ISBN (ebook) 978-1-4766-2918-6

LIBRARY OF CONGRESS CATALOGUING DATA ARE AVAILABLE

British Library cataloguing data are available

© 2017 George Monteiro. All rights reserved

No part of this book may be reproduced or transmitted in any form or by any means, electronic or mechanical, including photocopying or recording, or by any information storage and retrieval system, without permission in writing from the publisher.

Front cover: portrait of Ernest Hemingway, 1940 (Photofest); image of Kilimanjaro © 2017 Stanislav Glushko/iStock

Printed in the United States of America

*McFarland & Company, Inc., Publishers
Box 611, Jefferson, North Carolina 28640
www.mcfarlandpub.com*

For Brenda, once again

The blue-backed notebooks, the two pencils and the pencil sharpener (a pocket knife was too wasteful), the marble-topped tables, the smell of early morning, sweeping out and mopping, and luck were all you needed.—*A Moveable Feast* (1964)

Contents

Acknowledgments viii
Preface 1
Introduction 5

1. Home Delivery   27
2. This House Is Not a Home   36
3. The Jungle Out There   42
4. An Angler's Art   50
5. Italian Grammar   60
6. The Wages of Love   68
7. The Hit in Summit   72
8. Writer on Vocation   75
9. Winner Take All   81
10. The Mercenary's Call   138
11. Memory and Experience   148
12. Standing Alone   153
13. The Hemingway Ending   155

Chapter Notes 159
Bibliography 173
Index 179

Acknowledgments

First of all, I wish to thank all those teachers and critics who have taught me how to read literature, and particularly those who introduced me to Ernest Hemingway's writing.

Secondly, I want to acknowledge the editors and publishers who have consented to the use in this book of material previously published in their journals and books. They are the Ernest Hemingway Foundation, Springer Publishers, University of Alabama Press, University of Nebraska Press, Wayne State University Press, Washington State University Libraries, and Wiley Global Permissions.

Preface

"Much, though not too much, has been written about Cervantes' master novel," it was once noted, "yet, we are still far from understanding it in its general plan and its details."[1] Pretty much the same thing can be said about Ernest Hemingway's fiction, work that, according to Ford Madox Ford, is composed in words that "strike you, each one, as if they were pebbles fetched fresh from a brook."[2] This book is about Hemingway's stories, work that set the standard for much of the short fiction in his time and since.

Hemingway published his first fiction collection in Paris with the Three Mountains Press in 1924. A small book of 30 pages, *in our time* is made up of 18 separately numbered chapters. It can be argued plausibly that this book, with its lower-case title, constitutes the first minimalist work by an American realist. To fill out his first collection of short stories, *In Our Time*, brought out in New York by Boni and Liveright in 1925, he incorporated these bits of experimental realist writing but printed them in italics to differentiate them from the individually titled short stories that comprise the bulk of the book. Yet even those 14 stories, while not as radically succinct as the best of the "Chapters," can be described as minimalist when compared with the typical American short stories of the day, particularly those of his immediate predecessor O. Henry, and his contemporaries, Ring Lardner and F. Scott Fitzgerald. Probably not until the appearance of Raymond Carver's first story collections did Hemingway's readers begin to see in him the progenitor of American minimalist fiction. It would not surprise me to learn that Carver's editor, Gordon Lish, consciously applied Hemingway's theories of fiction—the iceberg theory and the related notion of the thing left out—to Carver's stories, radically revising and cutting up the prose, such that Carver turned into something of a Hemingway follower or disciple. Lish acted as if he thought that the minimalist style he was "inventing" for Carver was the next step in the evolving logic of the American short story.

Hemingway's "minimalism" led him to talk about the things he omitted from his stories, insisting that they were made stronger by those omissions. He offered an example. "It was a very simple story called 'Out of Season,'" he explained, "and I had omitted the real end of it which was that the old man hanged himself. This was omitted on my new theory that you could omit anything if you knew that you omitted and the omitted part would strengthen the story and make people feel something more than they understood."[3] To omit this "fact" in "Out of Season" is an aesthetic decision. It sacrifices a fact for the sake of a mystery about the guide's future, a mystery growing out of the resonance for the reader who has become interested in the fate of the individual to whom his young American patrons deny a final chance to prove himself a worthy hire. Take another instance. There has always been a controversy over whether Margot Macomber's killing of her husband is an accident or a murder. When Hemingway was asked about this, he answered that perhaps he could find out if he thought about it long enough. But he wasn't about to do that. What the story said was that Margot "had shot at the buffalo … and had hit her husband about two inches up and a little to one side of the base of his skull" (28).[4] In both stories—"Out of Season" and "The Short Happy Life of Francis Macomber—the omission of crucial information has a basis in Hemingway's conviction about the good story. It exemplifies "the principle of the iceberg": "there is seven-eighths of it underwater for every part that shows. Anything you know you can eliminate and it only strengthens your iceberg."[5]

Hemingway boasted that critics had great difficulty in determining which of his stories reflected actual experience closely and which were entirely imaginary. This distinction begs the question that both kinds of story relied on imagination to turn them into fully realized stories. A second way to get at what is left out or the part of the whole that is submerged (withheld from the reader, so to speak) is through what might still be usefully called symbolism. All sorts of things in a story resonate figuratively—plot, incident, character, image et al.—but there is danger here of over-reading on the part of the critic or interpreter and over-determination by the writer. For as Hemingway warned, symbolism grows naturally in a story; the symbols are not, like raisins in dough, stuck in by the writer after he has written his story. He complained about the scholar-critic Carlos Baker's readings of his work. "Do you suppose he can con himself into thinking I would put a symbol into anything on purpose"?[6] Yet his opposition to such symbols was not itself foolproof. For an instance in which he violates his own principled practice, consider the frozen leopard epigraph that precedes the narrative of "The Snows of Kilimanjaro." It is apparent that Hemingway saw something in the "aspiring" leopard that he was unable to make part of the story proper, and so he stuck it in—adopting the device re-popularized in his own time in Modernist poems by the likes of T. S. Eliot, Ezra Pound and their followers. Far more successful is the symbolism of the cafe in "A Clean, Well-Lighted Place" or of the world as hospital permeating "In Another Country." As he confided to his wife Mary (in 1952, just when *The Old Man and the Sea* was published), "nobody really knows or understands and nobody has ever said the secret. The secret is that it is poetry written into prose and it is the hardest of all things to do."[7] Yet the symbol-hunting critic was his enemy. "Then there is the other secret," he wrote. "There isn't any symbolism (mis-spelled). The sea is the sea. The old man is an old man. The boy is a boy and the fish is a fish. The shark[s] are all sharks no better and no worse."[8] Clear enough, so far; but he then concludes: "What goes beyond is what you see beyond when you know. A writer should know too much."[9] Only then can he fulfill his "obligation to invent truer than things can be true."[10] This paradox, which made perfectly good sense to him, had little or nothing to do with whether he engaged in the common practice of the writer who writes up his actual experiences or whether he invented the experience dramatized in a story out of whole cloth. But it has a great deal to do with what Hemingway expected his readers to get out of his best stories. Of course, with stories like his, no reader can know enough to get at a full understanding of what is hidden below the one-eighth of the narrative that shows on the page. But he can add what he knows to the pool of available knowledge, a contribution thus to the continuing effort to enhance our understanding of the literature that continues to speak to us.

Introduction

In a 1950 front-page review of Ernest Hemingway's *Across the River and Into the Trees* in the *New York Times Book Review* the writer John O'Hara proclaimed that the book's author was the most important writer in the English language since the death of Shakespeare in 1616. The reaction to O'Hara's statement was immediate and loud in its objections. In fact, O'Hara's opinion achieved such notoriety, and was so long-lasting, that a full ten years later O'Hara himself was still trying to explain what he had meant in insisting on Hemingway's great historical importance.

> The various circumstances that have made him the most important are not all of a purely literary nature. Some are anything but. We start with a first-rate, original, conscientious artist, who caught on because of his excellence. The literary and then the general public very quickly realized that a great artist was functioning in our midst. Publicity grew and grew, and Hemingway helped it to grow, not always deliberately but sometimes deliberately. He had an unusual, almost comical name; he was a big, strong, highly personable man. He associated himself, through his work, with big things: Africa, Italy, Spain, war, hunting, fishing, bullfighting, The Novel, Style, death, violence, castration, and a teasing remoteness from his homeland and from the lit'ry life. All these things make you think of Hemingway, and each and all of them add to his importance, that carries over from one writing job to another. I have a theory that there has not been a single issue of the Sunday Times book section in the past twenty years that has failed to mention Hemingway; his name is a synonym for writer with millions of people who have never read any work of fiction.[1]

Born in 1899, in Oak Park, Illinois, Ernest Hemingway was the son of Clarence and Grace Hall Hemingway. He was educated in the public schools of Oak Park, where, in addition to his studies, he played football and wrote for school publications. Upon graduation he was hired as a cub reporter for the *Kansas City Star*. In May 1918 he joined the Red Cross ambulance corps, arriving in Italy a few weeks later. Wounded at the front in early July, he returned to Oak Park a war hero. After the war he worked for a time in and around Chicago and later for a Toronto newspaper. On September 3, 1921, he married Hadley Richardson. His commitment to a literary career can be considered to have begun at that time, starting out, mainly, with short stories.

That he would commit himself fully to the task of becoming a professional writer was the single great choice behind Hemingway's decision in 1921 to leave for Europe. He was 22 years old, and he was eager to try Paris, the home then of such famed exiled writers as Gertrude Stein, James Joyce and Ezra Pound. In December 1921, Ernest and Hadley sailed from New York on the *Leopoldina*. He was to spend most of the decade in Europe; by the time he returned to the United States he had become famous, mainly as the author of the novels *The Sun Also Rises* and *A Farewell to Arms*. In 1927 he had divorced Hadley and married Pauline Pfeiffer. He had also published *In Our Time* (1925) and *Men Without Women* (1927). Five years after publishing *Winner Take Nothing* (1933), he collected the three separate volumes of stories and added to them a handful of other pieces—four stories written after 1933: "The Snows of Kilimanjaro" (1936), "The Short Happy Life of Francis Macomber" (1936), "The Capital of the World" (1936), and "Old Man at the Bridge" (1937); one early story previously bypassed for commercial publication, "Up in Michigan" (1923, *Three Stories & Ten Poems*); and *The Fifth Column*, a play set in Civil-War Spain—to make up *The Fifth Column and The First Forty-Nine Stories* (1938), the only collective gathering of his stories to appear during his lifetime. After Hemingway's death, on July 2, 1961, in Ketchum, Idaho, there appeared two other collections of his short fiction, *The Fifth Column and Four Unpublished Stories of the Spanish Civil War* (1969), containing previously published but uncollected stories, and *The Nick Adams Stories* (1972), containing stories previously published in the three collections, *In Our Time*, *Men Without Women* and *Winner Take Nothing*, along with unpublished stories and fragments. Still subject to debate is whether or not *A Moveable Feast* (1964), the first of Hemingway's works to appear after his death, is more profitably read as a memoir of Hemingway's Paris years or as a collection of stories and sketches in which the names of characters and places are real—a story cycle that melds fact and fiction.

Hemingway's apprenticeship as a serious writer of short stories cannot be fully traced, let alone documented. It is known that upon arriving in Europe late in 1921, he began to write fiction that he tried assiduously to publish, with little success. Then nearly all of his early short stories were lost in December 1922. A valise containing nearly all the stories he had written to that date was stolen from his wife while she was carrying them to Hemingway, who was in Lausanne. Just how many stories were lost has never been determined. Three stories from that period that did survive—"Up in Michigan," "Out of Season" and "My Old Man"—achieved print in Hemingway's first book, *Three Stories & Ten Poems*, issued in 1923 in Paris by Contact Publishing Company in a print run of only 300 copies.

As Hemingway's earliest known work in the genre, these three stories deserve more than passing attention. "My Old Man," among the most derivative of Hemingway's stories, parodies, in an honorific way, the style and subject matter of characteristic stories by Sherwood Anderson and Ring Lardner. It is written from the point of view of a boy who never fully understands the nature or the import of his "autobiographical" tale about his life with his father, a jockey, at the European racetracks. The father's true character reveals itself in the story the callow youth tells in the familiar puzzled style defined and nurtured by Anderson in his racetrack stories and elsewhere. Like Anderson, Hemingway follows a pattern of initiation that leaves the boy more experienced in the raw ways of the world but barely more perceptive. Like Lardner, Hemingway chooses to center on an adolescent "tough," one living in a know-it-all world, and speaking that world's language, but knowing very little, and, at the end, having what he started out knowing brought into doubt. "Up in Michigan," a story that Hemingway's first trade publisher would not permit him to include in the first collection, *In Our Time*, tells the story of a young woman's first sexual experience. The story again deals with an initiation that leaves the central character seemingly more experienced but actually less knowledgeable and in greater confusion. She never realizes the extent to which she has romanticized the young blacksmith, or that the rough sex on the hemlock planks of the dock is tantamount to the rape others would see in it. The word "it"—in definite and indefinite senses—appears throughout the story, often standing for "sex." This substitution/omission works aesthetically, however, because sex is precisely what the young woman, given her background, would repress. The way she displaces her own sexual attraction in favor of other details is rendered in the following passage, foreshadowing as it does, the much later statement, "She was frightened but she wanted it. She had to have it but it frightened her": "Liz liked Jim very much. She liked it the way he walked over from the shop and often went to the kitchen door to watch for him to start down the road. She liked it about his mustache. She liked it very much that he didn't look like a blacksmith.... One day she found that she liked it the way the hair was black on his arms and how white they were above the tanned line when he washed up in the washbasin outside the house. Liking that made her feel funny" (59). Horace Liveright, Hemingway's first trade publisher, was not the only one to find "Up in Michigan" too "outspoken" for publication. Gertrude Stein thought so too, telling its author that the story was "inaccrochable," meaning that it was the equivalent of a painting that could not be "hung" for public display. That it was Stein who admonished Hemingway is somewhat surprising, for in its stylistic rhythm and repetition of words in only slightly varied sentences, "Up in Michigan" epitomizes the early influence of Stein's writing, notably in *The Making of Americans* and *Three Lives*, on Hemingway's short fiction.

"Out of Season," set in Italy, is a story of a small world in which everyone is out of sorts and everything is out of sync. The old guide drinks so much that he cannot fulfill what is required to ensure the success of the fishing venture on which the young couple embarks. To start with, the fishing, out of season, is illegal. But because they have forgotten the lead sinkers the fishing itself goes awry. Yet this, superficially the guide's mishap and misfortune, merely reflects the true burden of the story, which is to show just what the couple's spiritual weather is like. The woman is out of sorts, as is the man, and their relationship is out of sync. The story ends with the drunken guide's promise that things will go better the next day. It's a fond hope, though, for the young man has the last word: "I may not be going, said the young gentleman, very probably not. I will leave word with the padrone at the hotel office" (139).

Hemingway's second book, with a printing of 170 copies, appeared in 1924. Brought out by the Three Mountains Press in Paris, *in our time* (the contents of which, a year later, would be incorporated into *In Our Time*) consists of eighteen prose chapters. The book was one volume of "The Inquest" (1923), a series of avant-garde titles edited by Ezra Pound, which included work by Pound, Ford Madox Ford, and William Carlos Williams, among others. Manuscript material now in the Hemingway Collection at the John F. Kennedy Library shows that Hemingway was trying to name the subgenre to which these pieces belonged. Before he settled on the rubric "chapter" for the pieces included in the early volume *in our time*, he tried out "episodes" and "unwritten stories." Later readers, responding more directly to their inclusion in the 1925 *In Our Time*, have chosen to call them by different names, for example, "inter-chapters," "vignettes," and "miniatures." Probably begun as exercises in condensing the raw materials of narrative, most of them attempt to convey the emotional and spiritual ambience of a single incident. For its value as an example of Hemingway's early realistic prose, it is instructive to look at one of them. Here is the whole of chapter 1.

> Everybody was drunk. The whole battery was drunk going along the road in the dark. We were going to the Champagne. The lieutenant kept riding his horse out into the fields and saying to him, "I'm drunk, I tell you, *mon vieux*. Oh, I am so

soused." We went along the road all night in the dark and the adjutant kept riding up alongside my kitchen and saying, "You must put it out. It is dangerous. It will be observed." We were fifty kilometers from the front but the adjutant worried about the fire in my kitchen. It was funny going along that road. That was when I was a kitchen corporal [65].

It is a piece of naturalistic prose, told in the first-person, in which nothing seems to happen. Years later, in 1935, Hemingway would publish *Green Hills of Africa*, a book of travels in which he "attempted to write an absolutely true book to see whether the shape of a country and the pattern of a month's action can, if truly presented, compete with a work of the imagination" (v). In both instances, in the chapters of *In Our Time* and the experimental narrative of *Green Hills of Africa*, Hemingway was working toward stretching fiction in the direction of actuality. In chapter 1, as elsewhere—initially in the first *in our time* and then at intervals throughout his career (see, for example, the motives and incidents that run through the hero's mind in "The Snows of Kilimanjaro")—Hemingway tests the dramatic possibilities of what might be termed a *memorate*: an image or sensation or a small complex of the two that seemingly persists in the author's or his narrator's memory. Here, in chapter 1, we find many of the familiar characteristics of Hemingway's early prose: short sentences; simple, ordinary language; repetition and redundancy; the occasional use of a foreign phrase, the general meaning of which is clear from the context. And, of course, there is war as subject. Other chapters focus on bullfighting and crime as well as war. Chapter 10 treats, in a radically foreshortened way, materials that Hemingway later developed into his war novel of depression and spiritual numbness, *A Farewell to Arms*. When he included it in the 1925 *In Our Time*, presenting it no longer as a chapter but as a story, he titled it "A Very Short Story." He also turned chapter 11 into a story, entitling it "The Revolutionist." Such conversions may have resulted from Hemingway's recognition that they were different from the other sixteen untitled chapters incorporated into *In Our Time* or, more likely, from his need to expand his first full collection of short stories. In any case, to put together *In Our Time*, Hemingway was compelled to gather all of his available fiction from his two previous books, along with the stories he had written since the loss of that notorious suitcase. For "Up in Michigan" he was able to substitute "The Battler," written for the volume and not previously published.

Besides the fifteen chapters referred to above, *In Our Time* includes thirteen stories, one of which is presented in two parts. Beginning with the 1930, second edition of the book all subsequent editions begin with an introductory piece, at first labeled "Introduction by the Author" but subsequently given the permanent title "On the Quai at Smyrna." But in the 1925 edition the book had begun with "Indian Camp." Few writers have opened a first collection of stories with a more powerful or characteristic piece. "Indian Camp" can be looked at, from one point of view, as an overture of themes that both permeate the rest of volume and announce the concerns of much of Hemingway's subsequent work. It presents as a child the Nick Adams who had already appeared briefly in Hemingway's work as a soldier wounded on the Italian front (chapter 7 of *in our time*). The narrative, although in the third person, reveals the central consciousness of the child, the reader usually seeing only what the child sees. The boy's rite of passage takes place when his father, a physician, takes the boy along to attend an Indian woman in labor and has the boy "assist" him (he jokes that the boy is his "interne"). Under primitive conditions and using rudimentary implements, the father delivers the baby, a boy. Exhilarated, he boasts that this one is "for the medical journal," only to discover that the baby's father, lying quietly in the upper bunk, has cut his throat from ear to ear. O. Henry, still very much in vogue at the time, might well have ended the story here at the moment of the shocking discovery that the "proud" father has committed suicide. Hemingway does not. He follows the doctor and his son out into the dawn as they row across the water away from the camp and back home. Nick continues to ask questions—about women, suicide, and death—and his father continues to answer those questions as best he can. And what does Nick, who has witnessed such pain and suffering, finally conclude? "In the early morning on the lake sitting in the stern of the boat with his father rowing, he felt quite sure that he would never die" (70). Nick will live on to learn to accept the fact that he, too, will suffer the common doom; but at this moment it is his child's belief of personal immortality that quiets him before the act of violence to which he has just been exposed.

Nick as child, adolescent, and adult appears in six other stories in the Boni & Liveright *In Our Time*: "The Doctor and the Doctor's Wife" (*Transatlantic Review*, 1924), which focuses on the character of Dr. Adams as revealed in unpleasant encounters with a workman and with his own wife and a concluding meeting with his son; "The End of Something," which dramatizes the end of a young love relationship over which hovers the competing claim of adolescent male companionship; "The Three Day Blow" ("the greatest drunk story in the language," John Berryman once said in conversation), which shows two boys taking themselves seriously and self-importantly at a time when Nick is depressed having broken up with his girl friend; "The Battler," a brief tale in which Nick, while riding the rails, runs into a punch-drunk ex-prizefighter traveling with a black man who acts as his keeper; "Cross Country Snow" (1925), which presents Nick, recently married, on a skiing vacation in Europe with a friend, lamenting that the responsibilities attending marriage and imminent parenthood will bring to an end the pleasures of "bumming" around at will; and "Big Two-Hearted River" (1925), a story of the adult Nick fishing alone in Michigan's Upper Peninsula.

"A Very Short Story" and "The Revolutionist" were first published as chapters in the first *in our time*; "My Old Man" and "Out of Season" had appeared in *Three Stories & Ten Poems*; "Mr. and Mrs. Elliot" (1924), which also caused Hemingway problems with his publisher, satirizes the domestic life and sleeping arrangements of a desiccated poetaster given to drinking white wine in the evening and writing reams of poetry during the night. The satirical mode of this story is uncharacteristic of Hemingway's early fiction. "Soldier's Home" treats with simple power the theme of the returning war veteran's disgust and despair. Returning too late to receive even the hero's fleeting welcome, he drops, depressingly, into a world in which nothing works for him. Everything causes him more trouble than it is worth. Home from the war, the soldier discovers, is no longer home as he had known it.

More subtly than does "Up in Michigan," "Cat in the Rain" presents a crisis in the emotional needs of a young woman. The story is set in Europe. On vacation, presumably, a young American man reads in bed, while his wife (presumably) looks out at a cat caught in the rain. She leaves the room intending to get the cat, but by the time she gets outside, the cat is gone. Later the hotelkeeper, having witnessed her unsuccessful search, sends her another cat, "a big tortoise-shell" one. The woman's need for a cat, while her husband lies in bed, suggests what is missing in their relationship; so too does her attraction to the hotelkeeper, expressed in the author's characteristic style of repetition and syntactical variation in short sentences: "He stood behind his desk in the far end of the dim room. The wife liked him. She liked the deadly serious way he received any complaints. She liked his dignity. She liked the way he wanted to serve her. She liked the way he felt about being a hotel-keeper. She liked his old, heavy face and big hands" (130).

An early reader of "Big Two-Hearted River" called it a purely naturalistic story in which nothing happens; there is no action. No one did more than Hemingway to teach readers to see the drama inherent in the telling of such stories in which "nothing happens." On the surface, the narrative tells of one man's journey over familiar terrain to a place where he will pitch his tent for a few days of fishing for trout in a stream he has fished in the past. In focused detail Hemingway unfolds his story of a man returning to a place and an activity that is deeply meaningful to him. Everything Nick Adams does he does carefully, exactly as it should be done, from pitching his tent and cooking his food to threading a grasshopper to bait his hook. Nick places great value on technique and expertise, but things do not go as smoothly as he would like. Just as he finds the land around him burnt and the grasshoppers scorched black from the fire, he too finds himself spoiling his immediate pleasures by thinking thoughts he had tried hard to repress. Indeed, there is tension running through the narrative which is intended to orchestrate the theme of tension threatening the psychological balance of the young man returning to old haunts and finding that they seem to harbor new and unnamed ghosts he has brought with him. Not for nothing, apparently, does he put off going into the swamp, rejecting the place where fishing would be "a tragic adventure." Nick's world is a world of pressure. Even from the bridge over the river Nick sees tension and quiet force in each trout's holding itself fast in the stream: "Nick looked down into the clear, brown water, colored from the pebbly bottom, and watched the trout keeping themselves steady in the current with wavering fins. As he watched them they changed their positions by quick angles, only to hold steady in the fast water again. Nick watched them a long time." And he took a long, long look. "He watched them holding themselves with their noses into the current, many trout in deep, fast moving water, slightly distorted as he watched far down through the glassy convex surface of the pool, its surface pushing and swelling smooth against the resistance of the log-driven piles of the bridge" (163).

 D. H. Lawrence was the first critic to suggest that *In Our Time* was unified in a unique way. He called it "a fragmentary novel"—"a series of successive sketches from one man's life." If the book does "not pretend to be about one man," it is nevertheless exactly that, he insists; for "these few sketches are enough to create the man and all his history: we need know no more."[2] A related critical idea that has affected the on-going publication of Hemingway's stories involves the life of Nick Adams, boy and man. Eleven years after Hemingway's death, *The Nick Adams Stories* appeared. This volume reprints all previously published Nick Adams stories (including chapter 7 of *In Our Time*), several unfinished and or rejected fragments from manuscript, and two previously unpublished stories, "Summer People" and "The Last Good Country," that were determined to be in more-or-less finished form. The sequence of the stories follows, insofar as his age can be determined, Nick's life from childhood to his mid-to-late thirties. The book adds little to Hemingway's reputation as a short-story writer, a fact indirectly acknowledged by the publisher's blurb, which says only that the collection includes "Eight New *Additions* Hitherto Unpublished" (emphasis added).[3]

 After the favorable critical reception of *In Our Time*, Hemingway chose to follow up his triumph with *Torrents of Spring*, a work that not only parodies the novel form but satirizes contemporary fiction, particularly Sherwood Anderson's. It was published in 1926 by Scribner's, which became Hemingway's regular publisher. *The Sun Also Rises*, a second novel, was published later in the same year. By 1927 Hemingway had in hand enough new short stories to warrant a second collection. Echoing the titles of Robert Browning's *Men and Women* and Ford Madox Ford's *Women and Men* (Ford's book appeared in Pound's "Inquest" series, as did the 1924 *in our time*), Hemingway called his book *Men Without Women*, explaining wryly to his editor, after he had listed the stories he proposed to include in the volume, that the title was meant to indicate that "in all of these" stories, "almost, the softening feminine influence through training, discipline, death or other causes [is] absent" (*Letters* 245).

The first story in the volume is "The Undefeated," a more complex treatment of the material on bullfighting appearing in the chapters of *in our time* and a complementary back-story for the Pedro Romero episodes of *The Sun Also Rises*. It is the first of his stories to probe deeply into the limits of professionalism, a theme that interested Hemingway all his life. The aging professional, still recovering from a goring, is given the chance to perform in a nocturnal, a nighttime bullfight. He requests the services of an experienced picador, a friend who will help him. The performance goes well enough at first (though the fighter's efforts are not appreciated by the third-string newspaper critic). But the bullfighter runs into difficulties, not of his own making, and he is severely gored. And in the final scene, as he lies in the infirmary waiting for surgery, he implores his friend, the picador, not to cut off his pigtail. It is the symbol of his profession.

"The Undefeated" dramatizes the tragic situation in which the bullfighter, weakened through wounding and aging, is not able to overcome his bad luck in drawing bulls he can no longer master. Hemingway finds pathos and poetry in the bullfighter's desperate attempts to meet his standards as a torero and preserve his personal integrity. At the end the bullfighter breathes deeply into the anesthesia, ready for surgery. He is the first of those heroes who are destroyed but not defeated—a theme that Hemingway returns to often, most famously in *The Old Man and the Sea* (1952).

The human value of performing professionally—being "pretty good in there" (272)—is the major theme of "Today is Friday," which is included in this collection as a story in the form of a one-act play. Hemingway sets his piece historically in Jerusalem on the first Good Friday. The characters, besides a tavern keeper, are the Roman soldiers who have carried out the execution of Jesus and now, at the end of their working day, stand around talking over the day's events. Not yet suffused with historical Christianity, mythology or legendry, Jesus emerges in the eyes of some of the Romans, not as an outlaw or a man obsessed by a vision but as a courageous performer under extreme duress. In "Fifty Grand" (1927) Jack Brennan breaks with the code of fairness in prize-fighting in asserting his own personal, largely implicit, sense of morality. Knowing he cannot win an honest fight, he bets heavily against himself only to have his opponent deliberately foul him in an attempt to throw the fight. The old fighter, double-crossed, fouls his opponent and is disqualified, thereby losing both the fight and his championship. But through crossing and double-crossing, the outcome of the fight is the same as it would have been had it been fought squarely; besides, the old fighter has won his bet. The complex issue of "outlaw" morality reappears in *To Have and Have Not* (1937), a novel developed out of two narratives, "One Trip Across" (*Cosmopolitan*, 1934) and "The Tradesman's Return" (*Esquire*, 1936), both published originally as short stories.

Hemingway's working title for "The Killers" (1927) was "The Matadores," linking the story to bullfighting. Set in a town outside of Chicago, it tells the story of two hit-men waiting in a lunchroom for their victim, and can be seen as a particularly sardonic parody of the professional's performance of an ugly, ritualized killing that misfires—if only for the time being. Nick Adams is the link between the two parts of the story: he witnesses the visit and the departure of the hit-men, after which he hurries off to warn the intended victim of his danger. Because of his presence at these events, the point of the story is often seen to be that he has been affected by what he has experienced. As such, the story becomes, like the earlier "Indian Camp" and "The Battler," the rendering of still another milestone episode in Nick Adams's worldly education. Still other milestones in that journey, both earlier and later ones, appear in *Men Without Women*, including: "Ten Indians," which focuses on the boy's discovery of adolescent sexual infidelity; "Now I Lay Me," the concluding story in the volume, which takes up a neurotic, war-wounded Nick terrified that if he goes to sleep at night his soul will disappear from his body never to return; and "In Another Country" (1927), a first-person narrative in which the narrator goes unnamed. This last story presents us with another of Hemingway's professionals—this time an Italian army officer, formerly a fencer, who now comes for machine-rehabilitation of his wounded hand. He does not believe that the machine will have any efficacy. Yet, despite his belief that the only thing a man can do for himself is to keep from putting himself in a position to lose what he values, and despite the bitter, unexpected death of his young wife, he continues to come for the treatments that he knows cannot help him.

In what has proven to be, especially in recent years, the most topically interesting story in the collection, however, Nick Adams is absent. "Hills

Like White Elephants" (1927), in some ways, takes up the theme of heterosexual conflict and complexity of earlier stories, such as "Up in Michigan," "Out of Season," and "Cat in the Rain." In a tightly controlled story in which setting and image brim with potentially symbolic meaning, especially for the woman, whose frustration and anger motivate the dramatic focus, two persons sit at a table in a railroad station bar. The story is told mainly through conversation between two troubled and discomfited people. There is talk but no agreement. The young man, identified as an American, is agitated; the woman is nervous, out of sorts. They argue at some length, as they await their train, but avoid naming the thing that plagues them. The reader begins to sense what the unnamable thing is when the conversation suddenly turns away from open bickering and bitchy talk:

> "Should we have another drink?"
> "All right."
> The warm wind blew the bead curtain against the table.
> "The beer's nice and cool," the man said.
> "It's lovely," the girl said.

The man continues, hoping to persuade her.

> "It's really an awfully simple operation, Jig," the man said. "It's not really an operation at all."
> The girl looked at the ground the table legs rested on.
> "I know you wouldn't mind it, Jig. It's really not anything. It's just to let the air in."
> The girl did not say anything.

He persists:

> "I'll go with you and I'll stay with you all the time. They just let the air in and then it's all perfectly natural" [212].

The man is technically right, of course; it's not really an operation. The current synonym—procedure—is meant to allay fears, reduce trepidation. But the increasingly disturbing note in the scene lies not only in what the man proposes for the woman, but in the irony emanating from his presentation of the procedure as "perfectly natural." There's a subtle transvaluation going on here that goes beyond the ethics or morality of what the girl has agreed to undergo. It is the human potential for so considering, for whatever human reason, valid or not, what is, neutrally speaking, an unnatural act and so domesticating it that it can appear to be entirely natural. It may well be, as has been argued, that the girl fears her own death. But the story seems to resonate beyond that possibility to the recognition of a greater death, that of personal sympathy and the humanistic spirit. The horror lies almost as much in how they talk about what is to be done as in any contemplation of the consequences of the proposed operation itself.

In the fall of 1929 Hemingway published his second major novel, *A Farewell to Arms*, followed three years later by *Death in the Afternoon*, a hefty volume telling the historical and contemporary story of the Spanish bullfight, along with what amounted to his ars poetica. In 1933 appeared *Winner Take Nothing*, a third collection of short fiction, which would prove to be the last such volume of uncollected and new stories to appear during Hemingway's lifetime. Hemingway's title (playing on the phrase "winner take all") echoes the epigraph for the book, lines that he wrote himself in pseudo-Elizabethan speech: "Unlike all other forms of lutte or combat the conditions are that the winner shall take nothing; neither his ease, nor his pleasure, nor any notions of glory; nor, if he win far enough, shall there be any reward within himself."[4] He had never been interested in pyrrhic victories, and too often, he felt, unalloyed victories were impossible (the young Pedro Romero's heroics in and out of the arena in *The Sun Also Rises* constituting an exception), but personal achievement in the face of defeat was a matter he had already treated and would do so again. But in *Winner Take Nothing* Hemingway's overarching theme seems to be that there really are no winners for there is nothing to win. The book opens with "After the Storm" (1932), a story that deals with a sunken ship and its salvageable contents. It is told from the first-person point of view of a Key West tough whose language and outlook make him a forerunner of Harry Morgan, the outlaw hero of "One Trip Across," "The Tradesman's Return," and *To Have and Have Not*. Although the narrator's failure to profit from his discovery of the submerged ship at least superficially embodies Hemingway's overall theme for the volume, it was not the story he wanted to place as his lead. His choice for that spot was "The Light of the World," a story he later insisted was "a very fine story about whores—as good or better a story about whores than Maison Tellier" by Maupassant (*Letters* 393), but his editor, arguing that placing it first "would play into the hands of his critics, who would again accuse him of using a 'small-boy wickedness of vocabulary' simply for its shock effect," talked him into leading with "After the Storm."[5] What he did not argue is that "The Light of the World" was a Nick Adams story, and that taken with "Fathers and Sons," another Nick Adams story, which he insisted from the start must close the volume, they would have given the collection a frame similar to the one organizing *In Our Time*. The third Nick Adams story in *Winner Take Nothing*, "A Way You'll Never Be," again deals with a soldier, still psychologically jittery and jumpy, though he has largely recovered from his physical wounds.

The collection is filled out with a mixture of stories on familiar Hemingway themes and stories that constitute new departures, "The Mother of a Queen" (bullfighting), for example, but "Homage to Switzerland" (1933)

(Americans in Europe as targets for satire, recalling, in its ambience, the earlier story, "A Canary for One" [1927]), "One Reader Writes" (a lonely-hearts letter), and "Wine of Wyoming" (1930) (reminiscent of Turgenev's *A Sportsman's Sketches*, a Hemingway favorite). "A Natural History of the Dead" was an anecdote he culled from *Death in the Afternoon*. This story is in two parts: an essay on dying, the combat dead, and the absurdities of the self-proclaimed humanists of the day, followed by a dramatized incident exemplifying the moral complexities of triage at a battlefield-dressing station. This interest in the professionalism of physicians (and its limitation and breakdown under duress), seen as early as "Indian Camp" and *A Farewell to Arms*, re-surfaces in "God Rest You Merry, Gentlemen" (1933). Set in Kansas City, this story centers on the reactions of two ambulance surgeons to the situation of a boy who, out of a deep Pauline sense of sinning against purity, mutilates himself. The story draws complexly on Christian materials, as does "The Light of the World," in which Hemingway tests the Christian notion of charity, as expressed in Jesus's imprecation to those who would honor him that they do so by extending charity "unto the least" of humankind. Do the obligations of charity extend to the whore, large as "a hay mow"? Does it apply to the "sisters," exemplified in men who put lemon juice on their hands to keep them white and soft?

Filial and parental relationships, a staple in Hemingway's work from "Indian Camp" to the posthumously published novel *Islands in the Stream* (1970), inform two stories in *Winner Take Nothing*: "A Day's Wait" and "Fathers and Sons." "A Day's Wait," which Hemingway insisted was transcribed directly from experience, is structured around a surprising revelation. A sick child has confused a Fahrenheit temperature reading for Centigrade and consequently thinks he is at death's door. This tightly controlled story presents an indelible image of the child as "a little man" whose tight-lipped bravery as he faces death gives way, after the mistake over temperatures is discovered and cleared away, to crying "very easily at little things that were of no importance." In "Fathers and Sons" Nick Adams, aged 38, has a son of his own. The roles of son to father in "Indian Camp" and "The Doctor and the Doctor's Wife" are repeated, but now it is Nick who would coach and teach the child who wants to know about his grandfather. If we go by age, this is the oldest Nick we meet in Hemingway's fiction.

The theme of heterosexual conflict and complexity is again taken up in "The Sea Change" (1931), but with a twist that is particularly interesting for Hemingway. As in "Hills Like White Elephants," the story takes place in a bar. The woman is about to leave the man for someone else. They argue until the man says angrily, "'I'll kill her'" (302). After more arguing, the woman walks away. The man's reaction to what is happening is the focal point of the story. It ends with a note on his behavior after the woman has left. He talks to the barman and then, insisting that he is "a different man," stares at himself in the mirror. Even the potential for irony in the barman's closing observation, "You must have had a very good summer," does not detract from the story's shift away from the woman's sexual choice to the man's narcissism (305).

Published in *Scribner's Magazine* as "Give Us a Prescription, Doctor" (1933), "The Gambler, the Nun, and the Radio" is a Depression story about the illusions and delusions that are humankind's opiates. The neurotic, jumpy hospital patient whose central consciousness structures the narrative lists them: religion, music, economics, patriotism, sexual intercourse, drink ("an excellent opium"), the radio ("a cheap one"), gambling, ambition, new forms of government, and bread ("the real, the actual, opium of the people") (367). The opiate he, a writer, does not mention, is writing. There is much in this significant story that recalls the Hemingway most familiar to readers—the hospital setting; the frazzled, neurotic center of consciousness; the expressions of anxiety and despair. Never a favorite with critics, it continues to suffer from critical and interpretive neglect.

Hemingway's most memorable story of despair, however, is the widely-anthologized "A Clean, Well-Lighted Place" (1933). Told in the third person, the story is set in Spain, first in a cafe and then, briefly, in a bar. Its principal is a so-called "older waiter" who first converses with a younger colleague and then has a brief exchange with a barman. What is revealed is that the two cafe waiters see life differently. The younger one has what he calls "confidence"; the older one does not (290). They talk about an old man who drinks at the cafe, revealing that he has tried to commit suicide but was saved by a niece who feared for his soul. The reader gradually discovers that it is the "older waiter" the author would have us attend to. He questions himself: "What did he fear? It was not fear or dread. It was a nothing that he knew too well. It was all a nothing and a man was nothing too. It was only that and light was all it needed and a certain cleanness and order. Some lived in it and never felt it but he knew it all was *nada y pues nada y nada y pues nada*" (291). Then, in one of the most famous passages in all of Hemingway's writings, he breaks into a nihilistic parody of the Christian prayer: "Our *nada* who art in *nada*, *nada* be thy name thy kingdom *nada* thy will be *nada* in *nada* as it is in *nada*. Give us this *nada* our daily *nada* and nada us our *nada* as we *nada* our *nadas* and *nada* us not into *nada* but deliver us from *nada*; *pues nada*" (291). The waiter has replaced with "nada" nouns and verbs that suggest things and attributes—father, heaven, hallowed, come, done, earth, heaven, day, bread, forgive, trespasses, enemies, lead, temptation, evil, and amen (so be it). From the waiter's point of view, alone or collectively they add up to nothing. Belief in the existence of such entities, like belief in the efficacy of prayers to the Lord or the Virgin, are—to borrow terms from "The Gambler, the Nun, and the Radio"—opiates of the people. The story ends with a characteristic irony as the waiter wryly dismisses his despairing thoughts: "After all, he said to himself, it is probably only insomnia. Many must have it" (291).

In 1935 Hemingway published *Green Hills of Africa*, an account of his experiences on a big-game hunting trip he had taken with his second wife, Pauline. He explained that the book was an experiment in writing intended to bridge the worlds of factual experience and fictional creation; that is, he had invented neither characters nor incidents, but had selected his material and so shaped it to see if a work of fact could compete with a work of fiction on the latter's own grounds. Out of that African safari also came the germ for two stories that would become virtually synonymous with the name of Hemingway: "The Short Happy Life of Francis Macomber" (*Cosmopolitan*, 1934) and "The Snows of Kilimanjaro" (*Esquire*, 1936). No other work of fiction by Hemingway has been more critically controversial than "The Short Happy Life of Francis Macomber." That it is a tightly controlled narrative of the title character's coming of age—a psychological baptism in which he behaves courageously in the face of potential violent death—has seldom been questioned (although one critic was disturbed that Hemingway had chosen, at certain moments, to write from the point of view of the lion). Rather the controversy has waxed, at times hotly, over the precise nature of Mrs. Macomber's character and whether or not, when she kills her husband, she has committed murder. The narrative overall seems to indicate that Margot Macomber, who uses infidelity and a sharp tongue to humiliate her diffident and at times cowardly husband into subservience in what has obviously been a disastrous marriage, might very well murder a husband whose conquest of his fear of the animals he hunts is emblematic of his acquisition of control over the way he will live his life. But in one sentence describing what Wilson, the white hunter, calls, sardonically, "the manner of the accident" (28), Hemingway set interpretive hares that are still running. "Macomber had stood solid and shot for the nose, shooting a touch high each time and hitting the heavy horns, splintering and chipping them like hitting a slate roof, and Mrs. Macomber, in the car, had shot at the buffalo with the 6.5 Mannlicher as it seemed about to gore Macomber and hit her husband about two inches up and a little to one side of the base of his skull" (28). The immediate aftermath of this "accident" is that the guide bullies and taunts the woman who is "crying hysterically." In an exchange replete with irony, he tells her, "Of course it's an accident," but then asks her accusingly, "Why didn't you poison him?" (28) When the author was asked about the matter, he said that he simply did not know, that he could have found out but did not want to probe deeper into the case. As the guide says, there will be an inquest (and indeed in *The Macomber Affair*, a 1947 film based on the story, the entire narrative is presented within the framing situation of an inquest) that will, through legal procedure, decide whether Macomber's death was accidental or homicidal. But Hemingway chose to stop short of such an inquest, because the legal determination, whatever the verdict, would be beside the point.

Hemingway ends his story with mystery, not the detective's, but the psychological moralist's. When this hard woman unexpectedly collapses into hysteria and falls into subservience before the white hunter, the reader witnesses the uncovering of a depth in Mrs. Macomber's character that even she had not expected or feared. Can she, let alone the reader (or the author), ever know whether in her heart of hearts she had not only been capable of murdering her husband but, in the only way that morally and personally counts, had actually done so?

"The Snows of Kilimanjaro," Hemingway's most complexly arranged narrative and his most consciously symbolic story up to that time, dramatizes the final hours in the life of a failed writer who finds himself dying from infection as he futilely awaits the plane that would fly him out of this hunting encampment to the medical treatment that could save his gangrenous leg and his life. Except for the exchanges between the writer and his attending wife, the narrative consists of a long self-examination on the part of the writer in which he mixes memories of incidents and personages with judgments of his past. Printed in italics, these memories, the reader soon discovers, are biographical, constituting materials that the backslider writer, having betrayed his talent, has hitherto failed to turn into art. Recognizing and facing up to his self-deluding rationalization for marrying into the tribe of "the very rich" and living among them, namely that he would study them so that he could write about them, the writer *in extremis* confesses to himself.

To get at the matter, Hemingway employs a double-ending, first, an apocalypse in which the writer experiences the arrival of the salvific airplane and which ends with his perception that he is going directly to the square top of Kilimanjaro, and secondly, closing out the narrative, a bit of symbolic naturalism, in which his wife could see the writer's "bulk under the mosquito bar but somehow he had gotten his leg out and it hung down alongside the cot. The dressings had all come down and she could not look at it" (56). At the last, the act of writing gets the moral right. Notation no longer even matters. At his death the author is once again a writer—a minimalist "telescoping" his "stories" into a paragraph or two.⁶ The mystery of the leopard whose carcass, dried and frozen, was found close to the western summit of Kilimanjaro (as indicated in the epigraph) lends itself to unresolved interpretations, both naturalistic and apocalyptic. About the nature of the writer's final, if implicit, judgment of himself, however, there is no doubt; he has become the writer he should have been all along, once again composing his stories.

Hemingway's African stories were not collected in book form until 1938, when Scribner's published *The Fifth Column and the First Forty-Nine Stories* (1938). The "first forty-nine stories" included, besides "Macomber" and "Snows," and the stories from the three collections, *In Our Time, Men Without Women*, and *Winner Take Nothing*, as well as "Up in Michigan" (1923) and two stories set in Spain: "Old Man at the Bridge" and "The Capital of the World," the latter telling the story of a mock bullfight, held in a restaurant, in which a young boy, "full of illusions," is accidentally killed. Nearly all the short stories Hemingway had published to date were included in this volume. In hand, however, he had another four stories of the Spanish Civil War—"The Denunciation" (1938), "The Butterfly and Tank" (1938), "Night Before Battle" (1939), and "Under the Ridge" (1939)—which were collected only after Hemingway's death. In 1969 Scribner's issued them, along with Hemingway's play, as *The Fifth Column and Four Unpublished Stories of the Spanish Civil War*, a title that contradicts the fact that these stores had all appeared in journals in the 1930s.

The 1938 preface that Hemingway wrote for *The First Forty-Nine Stories* concludes with the statement that the author "would like to live long enough to write three more novels and twenty-five more stories. I know some pretty good ones" (4). He did produce and publish the three novels—if included among them is *The Old Man and the Sea*, the novella for which he received the Pulitzer Prize, along with *For Whom the Bell Tolls* (1940) and *Across the River and Into the Trees* (1950), the story of a U.S. Army colonel's last days in Venice. The posthumous publication of his works includes the novels *Islands in the Stream* (1970), the account of a painter's domestic relationships and wartime exploits, and *The Garden of Eden* (1986), a story of psychological disintegration culled from manuscripts relating to Americans living in France in the 1920s, as well *True at First Light* (1999), African materials put together by his son, Patrick Hemingway. But "twenty- five" was a number he did not begin to approach. Towards that number he left two fables, "The Good Lion" (1951, *Hemingway Reader*), in which a lion drinks martinis at Harry's Bar in Venice, and "The Faithful Bull" (*Fortune*, 1951), several uncollected stories, such as "Nobody Ever Dies!" (*Cosmopolitan*, 1939), and two stories that appeared in the November 1957 *Atlantic Monthly* under the heading "Two Titles of Darkness," "A Man of the World" and "Get a Seeing-Eyed Dog," and a few other unpublished stories. Although there were indications, especially after Hemingway was awarded the Nobel Prize for Literature in 1954, that there would be a new edition of his collected stories (Hemingway even went so far as to write an introductory piece, "The Art of the Short Story," which remained unpublished until it appeared in the *Paris Review* in 1981), no such collection materialized in Hemingway's lifetime.

Only in 1987, in fact, did Scribner's issue an enlarged edition of Hemingway's short fiction. As the publisher's preface acknowledges, there had "long been a need for a complete and up-to-date edition of the short stories of Ernest Hemingway." Unfortunately, this publication was not that long-needed edition. *The Complete Short Stories of Ernest Hemingway* was misnamed, for not all of Hemingway's stories were included, while excerpts from unpublished manuscripts of unfinished novels were. The stories from *The Fifth Column and the First Forty-Nine Stories* volume were included, along with "The Denunciation," "The Butterfly and the Tank," "Night Before Battle," "Under the Ridge," "Nobody Ever Dies!," "Get a Seeing-Eyed Dog" (a sequel to "The Sea Change"), "A Man of the World," "Summer People," and "The Last Good Country," the final two first published in *The Nick Adams Stories*. From the novel *The Garden of Eden*, itself an editorial arrangement of extracts from an unpublished manuscript, the editors culled "An African Story." The two fables "The Good Lion" and "The Faithful Bull" were included, as well as "One Trip Across" and "The Tradesman's Return," both published in magazines as short stories but later incorporated into the novel *To Have and Have Not*. To these were added new stories edited from manuscript. Some, "Landscape with Figures," "I Guess Everything Reminds You of Something" (about a father and son), "Great News from the Mainland" (another father and son story), and "Black Ass at the Cross Roads," were identified as short stories. Others, such as "A Train Trip," "The Porter," and "The Strange Country" were identified as excerpts (of several chapters, in some instances) from unfinished novels. But some published work is excluded—"The Mercenaries," "Crossroads," and "The Ash Heel's Tendon" (early stories included in Peter Griffin's 1990 biography, *Along with Youth*), two anecdotes told to the "Old Lady" in *Death in the Afternoon*, and high-school juvenilia.[7]

In his last years Hemingway prepared a book-length manuscript of reminiscences of his Parisian years in the 1920s. Published posthumously, *A Moveable Feast* was edited, in part, by his widow, Mary Welsh Hemingway, whom he had married in 1946, shortly after divorcing his third wife, Martha Gellhorn. Included is a preface by Hemingway, dated "San Francisco de Paula, Cuba 1960," in which he writes: "For reasons sufficient to the writer, many places, people, observations and impressions have been left out of this book. Some were secrets and some were known by everyone and everyone has written about them and will doubtless write more." (In mode the work is memorial.) But that it is entirely a record of what actually happened, however selective, is called into question by the sentences which conclude this short preface. "If the reader prefers, this book may be regarded as fiction," offers the author, who continues, slyly cautioning, "but there is always the chance that such a book of fiction may throw some light on what has been written as fact."[8] Only the names of persons and places are real, he might have said, the incidents making up the narrative are imaginary—perhaps. If one chooses not to disregard the implications of Hemingway's prefatory statements, one is then confronted with the interesting possibilities in how to regard, describe, and assess the work. It can, of course, be regarded as a book of sketches and portraits deriving from remembered facts, described as a memoir, and evaluated for its fidelity to observation and its reliability as record. It is replete with acidic and not so acidic pictures of by-now historical personages such as Gertrude Stein, Ford Madox Ford, Zelda and Scott Fitzgerald, Ezra Pound, and Hadley Richardson Hemingway. But consider for a moment this possibility: suppose Hemingway had substituted fictitious names for the real ones, as he had in the final version of *The Sun Also Rises*, that earlier account of Paris (and Spain) in the 1920s, would there be any point in denying that in *A Moveable Feast* he had written his final collection of short stories? Once again (as always, but particularly in the case of *In Our Time*) he has combined fully developed stories ("A Matter of Measurements"), paired stories ("Miss Stein Instructs" and "*'Une Génération Perdue'*") and sketches ("Shakespeare and Company") within a structure that successfully conveys an archetypal story of the loss of a golden age, of a young artist's fall from a second innocence. It is less an account of a young man's adventures than a portrait of the man as young artist. Much of what Hemingway is up to in *A Moveable Feast* he reveals in the opening story, "A Good Café on the Place St.-Michel." This simple, direct "story" moves from an account of "bad weather," "a sad, evilly run café" (3), and the dirty and sour smells of certain parts of Paris to a dramatized episode in "a pleasant café, warm and clean and friendly" (5), where the author takes a notebook out of his pocket and a pencil and writes a story. It turns out that the story he writes is one his readers will recognize as "The Three Day Blow." He tells us that since, on the day he writes, "it was a wild, cold, blowing day it was that sort of day in the story" (5). Moreover, the boys in the story were drinking and this made the author so thirsty he ordered "a rum St. James." "This tasted wonderful on the cold day," he writes, "and I kept on writing, feeling very well and feeling the good Martinique rum warm me all through my body and my spirit" (5). When he looks up from his notebook, he watches a very pretty girl with hair as "black as a crow's wing and cut sharply and diagonally across her cheek" (5). He wishes that he could put her into the story he is writing, but he cannot. She must wait her turn until, thirty-five years later, she surfaces in the story we are now reading.

If "A Good Cafe on the Place St.-Michel" does not reveal the mysteries of good writing, Hemingway does tell the reader that the facts of memory are only one ingredient, sensitivity to immediate experience and present ambience being equally important. This "story," leading off the collection, serves to caution the reader of *A Moveable Feast* not to take incidents, events and characters therein displayed as strictly adhering to what actually happened at the time, but as instances, it may be, of a higher, fictional truth. It is an artist's tenet, one that Hemingway would have his readers apply to all the writing he cared about. He was always pleased, as he said elsewhere, that critics, when trying to distinguish those stories he invented from those he had transcribed from actuality and memory, seldom did so accurately. His stories were of both kinds. He wrote some stories "absolutely as they happen," he claimed—"Wine of Wyoming," "One Reader Writes," "A Day's Wait," "The Mother of a Queen," "The Gambler, the Nun, and the Radio," and "After the Storm"—while others he invented—"The Killers," "Hills Like White Elephants," "The Undefeated," "Fifty Grand," "The Sea Change" and "A Simple Enquiry." "*Nobody* can tell," he boasted, "which ones I make up completely" (*Letters* 400).

Hemingway's purpose, in any and every instance, was to create his narrative such that the places and personages he rendered would be truer to his readers than their own actuality. The problem though, as the author saw it, was that critics were invariably too ready to read the author's biography directly out of his fiction. In *A Moveable Feast* he turns their question around: he challenges them not to look for the actuality behind the stories but, if they will look for such things, the invention that went into them. If Hemingway wanted all the stories of *In Our Time*, for instance, "to sound as though they really happened" (400) can it not be said of the stories of actuality in *A Moveable Feast* that he wanted them all to sound as though they were really invented? This melding of fact and fiction in Hemingway's best writing has always interested his readers. In the end it did not much matter to him or, for the most part, to his readers. After all, dissolving the boundaries between imagined reality and recorded imagination enabled him to write *A Moveable Feast*.

Hemingway's work remains vital. He was the innovator of an unmatched style, a shrewd chronicler of his times, a close observer of child and adolescent life, an anatomist of pain, courage, and cowardice, and a poet of aging and death. He liberated the American short story from the constrictions imposed by the plot-driven formula culminating in a final wry twist that marked so many American stories in the early decades of the twentieth century. Rather than playing up to the smaller ironies in single incidents (the so-called O. Henry ending), Hemingway's stories delineate a world in which the fact of human existence is itself discovered to be inherently ironic.

Of the short stories Hemingway most cared about, which included both the recalled and invented sort, we have his own list. In his preface to the *First Forty-Nine Stories*, excluding those stories he considered even then to have been overly anthologized ("The Undefeated," "Fifty Grand," "The Killers" among them, one surmises), he names seven: "The Short Happy Life of Francis Macomber," "In Another Country," "Hills Like White Elephants," "A Way You'll Never Be," "The Snows of Kilimanjaro," "A Clean Well-Lighted Place," and "The Light of the World." His readers would undoubtedly add other titles to this list ("Indian Camp" and "Soldier's Home," for example), but none, one surmises, would omit any of those named by Hemingway, a clutch of stories that rank undeniably among the finest and most influential in the English language. Writers such as J. D. Salinger, Norman Mailer, John Updike, Oscar Hijuelos, Raymond Carver, Antonio Lobo Antunes, and Joyce Carol Oates, to name only a few that come readily to mind, have acknowledged their indebtedness to Hemingway. But let the last word go to a contemporary writer in Brazil. In an interview published in 2002, over forty years after Hemingway's death, Ana Maria Machado was asked to name those writers "from other countries" who had influenced her. "At age nineteen, I discovered John Dos Passos, Steinbeck, Fitzgerald, Faulkner, and Hemingway," she answered. "From these last two I've read all they have written many times over. It was pure passion, especially Hemingway, whom I consider one of that very select group of writers who have thoroughly mastered their craft. He is a writer I would like to emulate someday; his ability to give voice to the land, whether in Pamplona, the Gulf of Mexico or Africa, is truly astonishing. He is so humble amid nature, and his quietness allows nature to speak for itself in his works."[9]

1

Home Delivery

Surely no one hopes to return to the nineteenth-century's ready assumption that literature was to be understood, as Taine saw it, as a function solely of race, milieu, and historical moment. But in the necessity to correct the distortions resulting from the assumptions of that tradition, Taine's kind of criticism fell into quasi-universal disrepute. It is true that occasionally a sociologist has turned to literature for insights and for one form of the social data which will confirm his own observations and buttress the more conventional data of his discipline. Occasionally we have had a student of the sociology of literature, usually when sociology is the discipline and literature the subject matter under scrutiny. But I can think of no important critic of literature who could be called a sociological critic. For obvious reasons the Marxist critics, whose commitment to a set of overriding political and economic ideas makes them a case apart, can be largely ruled out. In any case, theirs is not the sociology that is of interest here.

In short, the very idea of using twentieth-century sociology, in all its various developments, as a tool for the interpretation of literary texts has seldom been broached. Undoubtedly, one reason for this neglect is that much of sociology has moved toward research of an objective, semi-scientific, quantitative nature, with its emphasis on the testing and refining of existing concepts. But another reason is the quick assumption by students of literature that, while the nineteenth-century too often found the key to literature in sociology, twentieth-century sociology by its very nature can offer the reader of literature nothing at all.

Some of the few exceptions to these generalizations are instructive. Edmund Wilson, for one, has always dabbled in the sociological criticism of literature, but only in the way and to the extent that he has dabbled in several other disciplines. Social studies have been more helpful to him in discussing the problems of the Iroquois in New York and in writing sweepingly about Canadian literature and culture than they have in his dealing with modern poetry and fiction.[1] The work of Lionel Trilling, on the other hand, constitutes a more significant exception. Trilling is always keenly aware of relationships between a given literary text and its social-historical context. One need only examine his early books on Matthew Arnold and E. M. Forster to see that Trilling's sociological-historical interests date from his beginnings as a critic.[2]

The distinguishing thing about Trilling's sociology, however, is that it has its roots in the classical nineteenth-century tradition. He, too, has made virtually no use of modern sociology as a discipline pertinent to the study of literature; but he has not denied its relevance. On the contrary. At the time of its publication in the 1950s few sociologists were as favorably impressed with David Reisman's *The Lonely Crowd* as was the literary critic Trilling. Faced with Reisman's appealing examination of the three-fold historical changes in the American character, Trilling was ready to admit that times had indeed changed. The traditional pattern had been for students of society to turn occasionally to the novelist for data and for confirmation of concepts, but for mid-century America there were signs that the pattern had changed. Studies of the nature and quality of *The Lonely Crowd*, predicted Trilling, would seduce the serious student of society away from the novel and toward the fruits of disciplined sociological investigation.[3]

The task before me is to apply one set of sociological concepts on the modern practice of medicine in the United States (at least until recently)—those of Talcott Parsons—to several pieces of modern American fiction. I do so, not to corroborate those sociological theories, but, rather, to enhance our understanding of those fictions. In fact, my critical assumption is that those sociological concepts can help us to understand the themes of those works as well as, and this is, in my view, more important, the very structure of the works themselves.

According to Parsons, affective neutrality is one of the major dimensions of the physician's role. This quality, he affirms, is consciously inculcated from the very first day of medical training and reinforced every day of a physician's active professional life, for without its constant reinforcement the practitioner could not long survive as a doctor.

What is affective neutrality? To simplify—perhaps overly so—one can say that it is the neutralization of the affections—that is, the deadening or the setting-aside of normal human emotions—for the purposes of enabling one's medical training and objectively learned technique to control one's behavior. The practice of medicine, an art in the service of humanity, paradoxically calls for putting aside, indeed the suppression, of personal emotion vis-à-vis individual patients. To foster this objectivity in the first days of medical school, for example, the fledgling physician is given a cadaver. Here is Parsons:

It is interesting to note that the dissection of a cadaver is included in the very first stage of formal medical training, and that it tends to be made both something of a solemn ritual, especially the first day, on the part of the medical school authorities, and medical students often have quite violent emotional reactions to the experience. It may hence be concluded that dissection is not only an instrumental means to the learning of anatomy, but is a symbolic act, highly charged with affective significance. It is in a sense the initiatory rite of the physician-to-be into his intimate association with death and the dead.[4]

Surely everyone has heard stories about these first encounters with the dead. We have heard how the squeamishness of most initiates is soon overcome to the point where in a few weeks they will readily (if perhaps only proverbially) eat their lunches as they cut away. Whether or not we believe that such incidents take place, we can accept their import: that the human being, the human body, is to be handled objectively and clinically, and never subjectively or personally.

All this of course—from the medical student's first day of medical school to the day of the physician's retirement—can create a tension within the physician that must be accommodated if the physician is to continue to practice medicine with emotional honesty and human responsibility. The constant balance between human affections and professional practice is a subtle thing. Move too far in the suppression of the human affections and you move toward monstrosity. Move too far away from objective professional practice and toward human affections and you are rendered unfit for the practice of your humanitarian profession.

This subtle tension has played its role in the work of several American writers in the twentieth-century. It joins, I would suggest, such otherwise diverse works as William Faulkner's story on the theme of all-for-love, "Wild Palms," with its complementary narrative "Old Man." It links *The Wild Palms* to F. Scott Fitzgerald's study of the ruined psychiatrist-"priest," *Tender Is the Night*. It is a bond, which joins several of Ernest Hemingway's short stories. In each case, in one way or another, an individual fails, and in each case the failure is one of professional objectivity—a failure of affective neutrality. I shall try to suggest how this idea might be traced in these literary works.

Let us begin with *Tender Is the Night*. It took Zelda Fitzgerald's grievous mental illness to seduce Fitzgerald into seeing himself as a psychiatrist and into seeing his personal plight as that of a "physician-priest" in love with his patients. In a strikingly emblematic scene Fitzgerald dramatizes Dick Diver's involvement with his "most interesting case," that of a woman of thirty. It is the account of Dr. Diver's "affair" with his scabrous patient.

> "We would like to go into the true reasons that brought you here—," he began but she interrupted.

"I am here as a symbol of something. I thought perhaps you would know what it was."
"You are sick," he said mechanically.
"Then what was it I had almost found?"
"A greater sickness."
"That's all?"

He answers her:

> "That's all." With disgust he heard himself lying, but here and now the vastness of the subject could only be compressed into a lie. "Outside of that there's only confusion and chaos. I won't lecture to you—we have too acute a realization of your physical suffering. But it's only by meeting the problems of every day, no matter how trifling and boring they seem, that you can make things drop back into place again. After that—perhaps you'll be able again to examine—"

But he has qualms about what he is about to say.

> He had slowed up to avoid the inevitable end of his thought: "—the frontiers of consciousness." The frontiers that artists must explore were not for her, ever. She was fine-spun, inbred—eventually she might find rest in some quiet mysticism. Exploration was for those with a measure of peasant blood, those with big thighs and thick ankles who could take punishment as they took bread and salt, on every inch of flesh and spirit.

He would say something more honest and perhaps palliative, but doesn't: "—Not for you, he almost said. It's too tough a game for you."

> Yet in the awful majesty of her pain he went out to her unreservedly, almost sexually. He wanted to gather her up in his arms, as he so often had Nicole, and cherish even her mistakes, so deeply were they part of her. The orange light through the drawn blind, the sarcophagus of her figure on the bed, the spot of face, the voice searching the vacuity of her illness and finding only remote abstractions.

Dr. Diver has failed her at that moment and ends with a bromide:

> As he arose the tears fled lava-like into her bandages.
> "That is for something," she whispered. "Something must come out of it."
> He stooped and kissed her forehead.
> "We must all try to be good," he said.[5]

This is a remarkably dramatic account of one stage in Dr. Dick Diver's professional slippage. He squanders his emotions even as his clinical objectivity runs down and he moves toward entropy. It is startling to recall that Dr. Diver had done much the same thing with another patient. To cure Nicole, Fitzgerald seems to say, Dr. Diver had to marry her; but the price he paid was professionally and personally exorbitant. With his "most interesting case," however, the doctor is neither free to "marry" her or able to cure her. But the tension created by conflicts among affective neutrality, professional objectivity, and emotional commitment ruins him for both patient and wife. For once he realizes that Nicole no longer needs him, that he has in effect fully cured his patient, Dick has seemingly little difficulty in letting her go. By that time both doctor and man have been warped beyond rehabilitation.

Take a second example, this time from William Faulkner: the seemingly idiosyncratic form of *The Wild Palms*, alternating chapters of two separate narratives, called, respectively, "Wild Palms" and "Old Man." There has been considerable to-do and wide critical disagreement over the "unity" of this book, the perversity and genius of Faulkner's form, and so on. But the concept of affective neutrality can help to show the thematic unity of Faulkner's conception of the novel. Harry Wilbourne, weeks away from completing his internship, throws his medical career over, along with everything else, for the love of a woman married to another man. Just as that woman, Charlotte, leaves her husband and children, Harry gives up his occupation and abandons his former life. But we learn that Harry's former life has itself been a retreat into unfeeling. For him the practice of medicine has been an escape from thought and feeling. When Harry melodramatically finds a leather wallet with the twelve hundred and seventy-eight dollars which would enable him to go away with Charlotte, he is torn by confusion and anxiety. Here is how Faulkner presents him:

> He discovered the exact amount only after he reached the hospital however, his first thought was merely, I ought to keep out a dollar for the reward as he walked on toward the branch post office, then (the post office was not only six blocks away, it was in the opposite direction from the hospital) I could even keep out taxi-fare and he should not mind. Not that I want to ride but that I've got to make it last, make everything last so there wont be any gaps between now and six oclock when I can hide behind my white jacket again, draw the old routine up over my head and face like niggers do the quilt when they go to bed.

Then fate helps him out.

> He stood before the locked Saturday afternoon doors of the branch station and he had forgotten that too, thinking, as he buttoned the wallet into his hip pocket, how when he waked the name of today had been in fire letters and no word out of a nursery jingle or off a calendar, walking on, carrying the light bag, walking the now twelve useless blocks out of his way, thinking, Only I have beat that too; I have saved myself at least forty-five minutes of time that otherwise would have been filled with leisure.[6]

Harry Wilbourne's dilemma here anticipates his situation when, much later, the pregnant Charlotte compels him to return to the "practice" of medicine. She insists that for the sake of their love he perform an abortion. Emotionally unfit to perform the surgery, Harry becomes the unwitting agent of Charlotte's death. The poetic logic behind his bungling of the simple operation is that love, an excess of love combined, perhaps, with professional anxiety has rendered Harry unfit for the simple "operations" of a neutralized society. Harry ends up in prison under a life-sentence.

Notice, also, in "Old Man" that the convict-hero can achieve no comfort, no peace of mind or body, until he returns to prison, a place, as Faulkner describes it, characterized by the deadening of normal human emotions of love and affection. The convict nearly perishes from his exposure to the human feelings of affection and love that he experiences during his period of freedom outside the walls of his comfortable prison. Faulkner's narratives of surgeon and convict are complementary in theme and social meaning.

My comments on Fitzgerald and Faulkner are perforce limited, and there is no doubt that the argument in each case could be, and should be, spelled out at length. But I would like to do somewhat better by Ernest Hemingway, much of whose work can be approached directly in terms of Parsons' concepts of affective neutrality and of the sick role. In this regard there are three key stories: "God Rest You Merry, Gentlemen," "A Natural History of the Dead," and "Indian Camp." At this time I shall limit myself to a detailed interpretation of the last story.

Decades ago Philip Young taught us to read "Indian Camp" as the young Nick Adams' story, pointing out that it records the manner of the boy's initiation into a world of pain and destruction.[7] The durability of Young's pioneer reading is affirmed by the fact that in the years since it was first presented, his reading has not been successfully challenged—except by Young himself, and then only implicitly.

When, for the purposes of writing an introduction to the second edition of his book on Hemingway, Young took a retrospective look at the book he had written in the late 1940s but not published until 1952, he also took a hard look at some of the things he would do differently were he first writing about Hemingway in the mid–1960s. As the single most important matter, he pointed to the significance of Hemingway's relationship to his parents, particularly Hemingway's relationship to his father. Subsequent scholarship has made much of this, but one can still go further. Beyond the son's relationship to his father, there is the most important relationship of the author to his father as physician. There is no question in my mind that Dr. Clarence Hemingway's profession colored and steeped his son's personal, spiritual, and even aesthetic outlook. Moreover, the personal and social nature of his father's profession affected Hemingway markedly. Nowhere else in Hemingway's fiction is this influence more clearly strikingly expressed than in "Indian Camp."

To read "Indian Camp" in terms of the doctor—patient relationship as well as the father—son relationship will lead us to a more comprehensive interpretation of the story but one which naturally extends Young's basic interpretation.

Although Dr. Adams' original reason (if he had a conscious reason) for taking his young son along on his early morning emergency visit to the Indian woman who "had been trying to have a baby for two days" is never stated, what he tries to do with the child Nick after they arrive at the camp is clear enough, however. He determines that Nick's education might well profit from the new experience. Putting the matter playfully, though truthfully, he asks Nick how he likes being "an interne." The doctor then proceeds with some "clinical" teaching:

> "This lady is going to have a baby, Nick," he said.
> "I know," said Nick.
> "You don't know," said his father. "Listen to me. What she is going through is called being in labor. The baby wants to be born and she wants it to be born. All her muscles are trying to get the baby born. That is what is happening when she screams."

His father carefully and scrupulously explains all that takes place before Nick's eyes. But nevertheless the Indian woman's cries continue to upset the boy. When he asks his father to give the woman "something to make her stop screaming," the father's answer is objective and professional: "No. I haven't any anaesthetic.... But her screams are not important. I don't hear them because they are not important" (68). Nick's father's attitude is a classical display of affective neutrality. Technique triumphs over emotion that, unchecked, would disable him as a practitioner. The successful delivery of the child is, as it should be, primary. But it is at the moment that the Doctor has made his pronouncement that "the husband in the upper bunk rolled over against the wall" (68). This is the last time we hear of the baby's father until Dr. Adams, self-satisfied and jubilant with the successful delivery of the child under primitive conditions, reaches into the upper bunk ready to congratulate the baby's father only to discover that he has cut his throat with a razor.

> [Nick's father] pulled back the blanket from the Indian's head. His hand came away wet. He mounted on the edge of the lower bunk with the lamp in one hand and he looked in. The Indian lay with his face toward the wall. His throat had been cut from ear to ear. The blood had flowed down into a pool where his body sagged the bunk. His head rested on his left arm. The open razor lay, edge up, in the blankets [69].

Dr. Adams immediately directs Uncle George to take Nick out of the shanty, but it is too late to keep him from seeing what has happened. "Nick, standing in the door of the kitchen, had a good view of the upper bunk when his father, the lamp in one hand, tipped the Indian's head back" (69).

Nick had been instructed that the woman's screams were not important, but he is now faced with an example of ultimate action taken by one who, as Nick's father later explains, was too sensitive to "stand things" (69). The Indian's suicide offers bitter, if mute, comment on Dr. Adams' affective neutrality. In the face of quietly violent death the Doctor's "postoperative exhilaration" ("That's one for the medical journal," (69) he had said. "Doing a Caesarian with a jackknife and sewing it up with nine-foot, tapered gut leaders.") (69) has dropped away.

Seemingly, the Doctor had so skillfully organized things that every individual present had a function. Uncle George and the two Indians must work together to hold the mother down, while young Nick becomes his father's helper and "interne." But the baby's father is an exception. Disabled by a foot-injury, he lies helplessly in his upper bunk. Still, to say that he has no immediate function is not to say that he has no social role.

The point is that the husband (and "father") is cast in the sick role with its socially recognized disabilities. But despite this clearly established role he is not at this time at the center of what ensues. He is disabled, true enough, but the distinguishing fact is that on this particular occasion it is his wife who occupies the primary sick role (the one demanding all immediate attention), and he consequently has neither a role to sustain him (e.g. a central sick role or a professional role), nor, because he is injured, any kind of life-sustaining function. It is the combination of his debilitating (even embarrassing) injury and the susceptibility (both physical and psychological) which always accompanies the sick role, I would submit, that "causes" his suicide (if we can say that "anything" does). With no function to perform the father is at the mercy of his naked affections and the betrayal of his own body. Even Nick is able "to stand things" without breaking down or running away, probably because he is "doing" and "helping." The father's injury, combined with his helplessness in the given situation, makes him acutely vulnerable to the pain and horror, which ensue. He alone of all those at the scene becomes pure victim. Hemingway chose to organize "Indian Camp" around the central consciousness of a child, thereby occasionally limiting and keeping information from the reader when the child Nick averts his eyes to avoid seeing something unpleasant. For him experience is not fated or predetermined. Open to experience in a way that his father is not, he has no clear-cut function to perform, unlike his father, who knows he is there to function as "doctor," and who consequently has a technique and a skill to put between himself and any affective demands growing out of the situation. So Nick, the young "interne," internalizes the experience, something which, ironically, interns must not do. (They must "internalize" the lessons of technique and practice, but they must at the same time repress the "internal" emotions of personality and character.) The Doctor has described pregnancy as an illness, significantly not as a condition of health. Life, then, in Dr. Adams' view, emerges out of sickness. Nick Adams' world, like Sir Thomas Browne's and T. S. Eliot's, is indeed a "hospital." Nick is an "interne" in that world (is he "interned" in it as well?), but he has already looked away when his father (who has largely neutralized his own personal feelings) puts "something," undoubtedly the placenta, in the basin Nick holds for him.

Nick has discovered death in the midst of life. If his father pulls away a hand wet with warm blood from the upper bunk where the suicide lies, Nick on the trip across the lake at daybreak senses life sharply in the midst of death and cold. Trailing his hand in the water, he perceives that "it felt warm in the sharp chill of the morning." "In the early morning on the lake sitting in the stern of the boat with his father rowing, he felt quite sure that he would never die" (70). Partly a childish, illusory sense of immortality, this statement is also a resolution, since at that moment Nick knows death only in the guise of a particularly ugly suicide. He resolves that he will not die, because, he is certain, he will never die in the way the despondent father had died. And for the young boy that death is the only human death he so far knows.

"Indian Camp" questions the idea that affective neutrality can provide the individual with an effective stance against "things." Broadening it into his own ethic of professionalism, Hemingway would wrestle with the idea for a lifetime. Despite the fiestas, the trout streams, the Venetian hotels, the Parisian racetracks, and the wines of Wyoming—all the places and things he threw up against it—the image of the world as a sickroom continued to pursue him. The very parade of bizarre accidents and serious injuries worked to land him in hospital after hospital. "We must try to examine our world with the impartiality of a physician," he was still saying at the age of forty-seven.[8] But there, in the offing, was the specter of that terminal hospital bed. When Dr. Clarence Hemingway discovered that he himself was now his sickest patient, the physician within him could not live with the hard fact. And when the inevitable day came, the Doctor's famous son broke in the same way.

2

This House Is Not a Home

"The physician is, above all, a physician; second to that he is a family man, and, occasionally, an authentic human being." This statement of unidentified authorship appears on the cover of *The Doctor and the Doctor's Wife*, a small paperback published in Lisbon. It serves as a reminder to Hemingway's readers that a physician, although foremost a physician, owes something as well to his family and—perhaps less frequently—to humankind.

Placed second in the 1925 *In Our Time* following "Indian Camp"—Hemingway's initial father-and-son story—"The Doctor and the Doctor's Wife" centers on Dr. Henry Adams, Nick Adams's father. There are three incidents in the story showing Dr. Adams in domestic roles: (1) as property-owner and fuel-gatherer, (2) as husband, and (3) as father. In each case his role (performed successfully or unsuccessfully) is defined by an encounter: (1) he argues with the man he has hired to cut up logs that have washed up at the edge of his property, (2) he bickers with his wife, and (3) he meets his young son and the two them go off to the woods.

In each of the three incidents Dr. Adams's proprietary sense of himself as provider, husband, and father is put to the question. In each case, ownership is questioned, in a way, though the very notion of "ownership" becomes more and more attenuated as the incidents give way to one another. In the fight with Dick Boulton, the question becomes: who does own the logs that have been lost (at least temporarily) from the big log booms? In the contra-temps with his wife, it becomes: who has primacy in the practice of medicine, at least insofar as the wife is "sick" and in need of some attention? In the meeting with his son, the unasked question is whom will the son choose, his mother or his father, his choice presenting the chosen parent with what is in effect a kind of temporary "custody"?

When Dick Boulton, his son Eddy, and Billy Tabeshaw come over from the Indian camp to retrieve and cut up logs for Dr. Adams, it is clear that this is not the first time he has asked them to perform this task. For without a word from anyone, Dick's co-workers walk across the doctor's property straight to the lakeshore where the logs are buried in the sand.

The logs had been lost from the big log booms that were towed down the lake to the mill by the steamer Magic. They had drifted up onto the beach and if nothing were done about them sooner or later the crew of the Magic would come along the shore in a rowboat, spot the logs, drive an ironspike with a ring on it into the end of each one and then tow them out into the lake to make a new boom. But the lumbermen might never come for them because a few logs were not worth the price of a crew to gather them. If no one came for them they would be left to waterlog and rot on the beach.

Even under pressure Dr. Adams insists that these logs are "driftwood." He "assumes" that the original owners of the logs will not come back for them and therefore he can appropriate them before they rot. These logs are, to use the terms Melville applies to whales that have been struck but not caught, "loose fish" rather than "fast fish."[1] But Dick Boulton, for whatever reason, raises the question of the ownership of these "loose" logs. He accuses the doctor of stealing them and under the cover provided by the necessity of washing them clean so that the sand will not damage his saw uncovers the name of the lumber company whose men cut the logs and started them downstream to the sawmill. Dick Boulton looks at "the mark of the scaler's hammer in the wood at the end of the log" and says flatly that it belongs to White and McNally. To borrow another term from Melville, there's a "waif" on this log, which makes whatever claim for ownership the company might still possess.[2] Boulton accuses the doctor of theft. When the doctor denies guilt (it is then that he calls the logs "driftwood"), Boulton repeats the charge: "you know they're stolen as well as I do. It don't make any difference to me." But it does make a difference to Dr. Adams. He answers: "All right. If you think the logs are stolen, take your stuff, and get out." Their exchange continues:

> "Now, Doc ___"
> "Take your stuff and get out."
> "Listen, Doc."
> "If you call me Doc once again, I'll knock your eye teeth down your throat."
> "Oh, no, you won't Doc."

Nothing else is said, and their confrontation works itself out this way:

> Dick Boulton looked at the doctor. Dick was a big man. He knew how big a man he was. He liked to get into fights. He was happy. Eddy and Billy Tabeshaw leaned on their cant-hooks and looked at the doctor. The doctor chewed the beard on his lower lip and looked at Dick Boulton. Then he turned away and walked up the hill to the cottage. They could see from his back how angry he was. They all watched him walk up the hill and go inside the cottage.

Dr. Adams's honesty has been questioned and his character impugned. The four big beech logs almost buried in the sand along the doctor's property line may not be, it is arguable, "loose fish," for the doctor knows that they have come from one of the logging companies, and, thanks to Dick Boulton, in the case of one of the logs, at least, he learns the name of the company. On the other hand, because there is no guarantee that the company will even make the attempt to salvage these logs (and even if they did it is doubtful that the workers themselves would be at all scrupulous about salvaging only the logs identified by their company's markings) these logs can hardly be considered to be "fast fish." Ownership is in doubt, and therefore it is not possible for Dr. Adams to feel good, in the face of a challenge, about his decision to have them cut and split for use as firewood. Possession is considered by some to be half the law, as Melville said, "regardless of how the thing came into possession," but for the doctor, faced with Boulton's challenge, possession turns out not to count for much.[3] The doctor walks away from the fight. Chalk one up for Dick Boulton.

The doctor then enters the house where his wife lies in a darkened bedroom. That there is a failure of sympathy between the doctor and his wife is put first in terms of their fundamental, if unstated, disagreement over the practice of medicine itself. Still angry over the recent nastiness with the "half-breed" Indian who implied that he wants to steal the lumber company's stray logs, the doctor sits down on the bed in the room he shares with his wife. He is irritated to see a stack of his medical journals on the floor by the bureau. They lie there in their wrappers, unopened. It is then that the doctor's wife, lying in a room with the blinds drawn, first talks to him. She learns that he is not going back to work. He has had a row with Dick Bolton, but he has not lost his temper, he insists. She quotes Scripture at him—a slightly modified version of Proverbs 16:32:

> "Remember, that he who ruleth his spirit is greater than he that taketh a city," said his wife. She was a Christian Scientist. Her Bible, her copy of *Science and Health* and her *Quarterly* were on a table beside her bed in the darkened room.

Their studied courtesy to one another scarcely masks their marital incompatibility. That he practices traditional medicine (but doesn't read his journals) and that she is a follower of Mary Baker Eddy's Christian Science (and apparently reads *her* books and *her* journals, for they are on a bedside table) suggests how utterly unsuited the doctor and his wife are to each other, at least at this juncture in their lives.[4]

This contra-temp with his wife, following hard upon his nasty argument with Dick Boulton, turns him murderous—or at least that is the way one can interpret his rather intense preoccupation with a shotgun.[5] While sitting on *his* bed, he cleans his gun: "He pushed the magazine full of the heavy yellow shells and pumped them out again. They were scattered on the bed.... The doctor wiped his gun carefully with a rag. He pushed the shells back in against the spring of the magazine. He sat with the gun on his knees. He was very fond of it." The doctor and his wife argue over whether or not Dick Boulton has picked his fight with the doctor because he owes the doctor money for "pulling his squaw through pneumonia" and doesn't want to have "to take it out in work." "Dear," says his wife in a string of first-person singular pronouns, "I don't think, I really don't think that anyone would really do a thing like that.... No. I can't really believe that any one would do a thing of that sort intentionally." She thus distances herself from her husband on this issue, even as she has distanced herself, as a follower of the practices of Christian Science, from the kind of medicine he practices.[6]

It is no wonder that they then turn to a competition for the loyalty of their young son. Here is how the story ends:

> "Are you going out, dear?" his wife said.
> "I think I'll go out for a walk," the doctor said.
> "If you see Nick, dear, will you tell him his mother wants to see him?" his wife said.
> The doctor went out on the porch. The screen door slammed behind him.
> He heard his wife catch her breath when the door slammed.

Dr. Adams apologizes:

> "Sorry," he said, outside her window with the blinds drawn.
> "It's all right, dear," she said.
> He walked in the heat out the gate and along the path into the hemlock woods. It was cool in the woods even on such a hot day. He found Nick sitting with his back against a tree, reading.

Dr. Adams conveys his wife's request:

> "Your mother wants you to come and see her," the doctor said.
> "I want to go with you," Nick said.
> His father looked down at him.
> "All right. Come on, then," his father said. "Give me the book, I'll put it in my pocket."
> "I know where there's black squirrels, Daddy," Nick said.
> "All right," said his father, "Let's go there."

It is noteworthy that it is against a background of possessive pronouns ("his" mother, "his" wife, "her" window, "your" mother) that the young son decides in favor of the doctor and "against" the doctor's wife. It is, at last, a small victory for the doctor who was first faced down by the man who gives him a difficult time over the stray logs and then quietly but decisively talked down by his wife. Nick's decision gives him his only vindication, but this victory is real.

Hemingway claimed that the biographical incident on which he based "The Doctor and the Doctor's Wife" showed him for the first time that his father was a coward.[7] In fact, Carlos Baker tells us that the story is "virtually a playback of an actual quarrel between Dr. Clarence Hemingway and a half-breed Indian sawyer on the shores of Walloon Lake in the summer of 1912, with the youthful Ernest Hemingway as an interested onlooker." His proof is "a letter from his father to Ernest, written some 13 years after the event."[8] Dr. Clarence Hemingway's letter evoked the following response from his son: "I'm so glad you liked the Doctor story. I put in Dick Boulton and Billy Tabeshaw as real people with their real names because it was pretty sure they would never read the Transatlantic Review [which published "The Doctor and the Doctor's Wife" in December 1924]."[9] If the story is at least in part about Dr. Adams's backing-down, it appears unlikely that Clarence Hemingway viewed it that way. Otherwise, it is doubtful that he could have "liked" the story, especially since he did recognize that it was based on an identifiable incident that involved him. There is considerable evidence to indicate, moreover, that he would never have, out of mere politeness, pretended to like any of his son's stories, let alone one centering on the backing-down of a fictional personage based closely on the doctor himself. Still, in 1925 the author-son could not be entirely sure about such matters. So, in the letter just quoted, he finished his reference to the "Doctor story" with comforting information: "I've written a number of stories about the Michigan country—the country is always true—what happens in the stories is fiction."

Yet it must not be left at that. Because we have Ernest Hemingway's letter to his father, we are tempted to speculate on the personal and familial uses to which the author put his own story, first in the writing of it, then in its publication, and finally in the letter itself. Not surprisingly, in this story about the struggles for power dramatized in the three incidents of the story, ranging from direct confrontation, through more or less covert antagonism, to understated persuasion, the matter is somewhat complex. As we have seen, Dr. Adams "loses out" to Dick Boulton and to his own wife but seems to "win" in the exchange with his young son. For a long time many of the story's readers assumed that Nick Adams was present at the nasty encounter between Dr. Adams and the half-breed Boulton. A more careful reading of the story, insisted upon by several critics, has disabused most readers of this notion. Not only is Nick not present in the historical time in which the first two incidents of the story occur, he apparently knows nothing, when we encounter him at the end of the story, about what has transpired. Had he known about either or both of this father's "defeats," it is likely that the final scene between Nick and his father would have been worked out differently and, perhaps, less pleasantly.

Now we shift to the author's biography and the way in which it informs what we know of Nick's. The boy grew up, and he learned (we don't know how) about his father's encounters with both Boulton and his own wife. He quite probably wrote a story, as Hemingway did, about those encounters in which his father is the central figure. At least he is the only one present in more than one scene and he is in all three scenes. In the story we have, the boy is the only one who does not "defeat" the father. On the contrary, by choosing his father over his mother, the child seems to acknowledge the father's worth. So much for the narrative per se. But the actual writing of the story delivers a different message: the father's power extends unchallenged only (at least in this instance) to his child-son; in the adult world he is seen as a "failure." The adult-author who was the child now puts into perspective his child's adulation and the episodes (now understood from the adult perspective) of this defeat. And further. In reminding Dr. Clarence Hemingway that the story is based on well-remembered episodes of their joint past, he now has extended his authorial power over the meaning of those events. Oddly, even as he affirms his son's loyalty to his father, he informs his father as well that he knows what was really going on in those other encounters. His decision to zero in on these three scenes gives him the opportunity, from one point of view, to cut his father down to size. Looked at from a slightly different vantage point, however, the story presents itself suggestively as a tender reaffirmation of filial love—one that says, perhaps, something like this: "I know what it was all about, though I didn't know then, and it is all right. I feel the same affection for you now that I did then, though I am more knowing now about such things." When Ernest wrote to his father about the story, he was not being apologetic or hostile, I think. As I see it, he was making a deeply meaningful gesture, one that said he knew all and still cared.

3

The Jungle Out There

Before Jack Kerouac's *On the Road* substituted the pleasures and ecstasies of driving hell-bent to Denver for the heartaches and disasters of the long car journey suffered by the Joad family in *The Grapes of Wrath*, there were the accounts of taking to the road by riding the freights. In the last decades of the 19th century and the first of the 20th, thousands upon thousands of tramps and hobos (mostly men, but some women also) rode the freight trains in Canada and the United States. Prefacing Towne Nylander's "Tramps and Hoboes," an article in the August 1925 *Forum*, a journal that Hemingway satirizes in "Banal Story," is an editorial note: "Living and moving among us, in this settled and civilized era, is a nomadic population of over a hundred thousand men and boys,—our tramps and hoboes. Their faults and their virtues,—for they have virtues, even if their behavior is essentially anti-social,—and their picturesque language and habits are depicted in this article by a sympathetic observer."[1]

Such beings journeyed east and west, north and south in close conformity with the changing seasons.

Occasionally, writers experienced in the ways of hobos and tramps provided informative, explanatory, even, at times, romantically apologetic accounts of their wanderlust. Sometimes these books were put forth in an effort to reform the stereotype of tramps as criminals. Such, to varying degrees, were the accounts, all written during the years at the turn of the 20th century, of W. H. Davies, Josiah Flynt, and Jack London, and, a couple of decades later, Glenn H. Mullin, to name just a few of the many authors on the subject of tramping in English. To that list of writers we can add Ernest Hemingway and to the overall company of literary tramps, such as those in Robert Frost's poems, the fictional figure of Nick Adams, Hemingway's first hero.[2] For Hemingway, as he wrote about a young man's initiation into the ways of the world, the literature of tramping would provide a harsh corrective to the prep school and Ivy League educations of Owen Johnson's or F. Scott Fitzgerald's adolescent protagonists.

"The Battler" and "The Light of the World"—stories first published in, respectively, *In Our Time* (1925) and *Winner Take Nothing* (1933)—dramatize the "tramping" adventures of the young Nick Adams. Both stories owe less to young Hemingway's personal, direct experience of life, than to his interest in "tramp and hobo" literature—fiction, journalism, poetry, and autobiography written by the likes of London, Davies, and Flynt. Despite the familiar photograph of the young Hemingway hanging between stationary freight cars, or what he have learned about tramp life when he ventured into the rail yards as a curious cub reporter for the *Kansas City Star* in 1917–18, there is no evidence that he ever rode the rails or assumed, even for a moment, the life of the tramp. And while he was familiar with the territory—Kalkaska to Mancelona—in which he set "The Battler" and "The Light of the World," when Hemingway traveled that route by train he did so legally, his ticket costing him twenty-seven cents.[3] As Philip Young reminded us long ago, not "everything that happens to Nick has happened" to his author.[4] Hemingway's "road" stories, rooted in the tramp conventions of the late 19th and early 20th centuries, are best read in the context of tramp literature rather than biography.[5]

Jack London's essays, first published in *Cosmopolitan* in 1907–08 and collected as *The Road* in 1908,[6] William H. Davies's *The Autobiography of a Super-Tramp*, first published in 1907 and reissued in 1917, and Josiah Flynt's *Tramping with Tramps*, published in 1900, are notable among texts that may have influenced Hemingway either directly or indirectly.[7] Flynt's account, for example, offered him an explanation for "the temptation which the railroads have for a romantic and adventuresome boy. A child possessed of Wanderlust generally wanders for a while, anyhow," he wrote, "but the chance he now has to jump on a freight-train and 'get into the world quick,' as I have heard lads of this temperament remark, has a great deal to do in tempting him to run away from home."[8] Hemingway set the young Nick Adams on this path, sending him into the "jungle out there" inhabited by tramps and hoboes who crossed and re-crossed the country by riding the freights.

In the Nick Adams stories, that "jungle" is hardly the romantic world painted by the panegyrists who celebrated the excitements of mounting a passing freight and riding long stretches through a myriad of small towns separated by stretches of woods and green meadow and pastures.[9] Instead, consider the information offered in the following passage from Davies's *Autobiography*, which would have given Hemingway all he needed for the opening scene of "The Battler," particularly Nick's treatment at the hands of a duplicitous brakeman.

> I was soon initiated into the mysteries of beating my way by train, which is so necessary in parts of that country [USA], seeing the great distances between towns.

> Sometimes we were fortunate enough to get an empty car; sometimes we had to ride the bumpers; and often, when travelling through a hostile country, we rode on the roof of a car, so as not to give the brakesman an opportunity of striking us off the bumpers unawares. It is nothing unusual in some parts to find a man, always a stranger, lying dead on the track, often cut in many pieces. At the inquest they invariably bring in a verdict of accidental death, but we know different. Therefore we rode the car's top, so as to be at no disadvantage in a struggle.

But, no matter, it was always a good policy to be wary of "the brakesman," for "knowing well that our fall would be his own, would not be too eager to commence hostilities." Davies concludes his narration;

> Sometimes we were desperate enough to ride the narrow iron rods, which were under the car, and only a few feet from the track. This required some nerve, for it was not only uncomfortable, but the train, being so near the line, seemed to be running at a reckless and uncontrollable speed, whereas, when riding on the car's top, a much faster train seems to be running much slower and far more smooth [sic] and safe. Sometimes we were forced to jump off a moving train at the point of a revolver. At other times the brakesmen were friendly, and even offered assistance in the way of food, drink or tobacco. Again, when no firearm was in evidence, we had to threaten the brakesman with death if he interfered with us.[10]

In *Tramping with Tramps*, Flynt writes of similar difficulties in the hobo's "railroad life": "When he [the hobo] rides a 'passenger,' for instance, either on top or between the wheels, he encounters numerous dangers and hardships.... Even on freight trains his task is not so easy as some people think.... The main difficulty in riding freight-trains is with the brakeman. No matter where the hobo goes, he runs the risk of meeting this ubiquitous official. If he is on the 'bumpers,' the brakeman is usually 'guying' him from the top of a car; and if he goes 'inside,' so too does the brakeman. Even at night the 'brakey' and his free passenger are continually running up against each other. Sometimes they become fast friends."[11]

The main action of "The Battler" takes place not on the train but around a camp fire in a clearing where Nick meets the beat-up white prize-fighter, Ad Francis, and his black man companion, Bugs, who presumably have also been riding the freights. Nick accepts an invitation to share their food, but when the punch-drunk Ad becomes violent, Bugs knocks him out with a blackjack and advises Nick to leave before his companion regains consciousness. The story is true to lore suggesting that "the jungle was the melting pot of trampdom. In the West no color line was drawn and a crude democracy reigned."[12] Strangers would be welcomed to share a fire and food. In *Adventures of a Scholar Tramp*, Mullin describes his own arrival at someone else's campfire. After having come to a "desolate spot" where "the ground everywhere was covered with the black ash of burned grass"[13] (compare Nick's arrival at Seney in "Big, Two-Hearted River"), Mullin sees "two negroes beside a little fire." He accepts their invitation "to partake of some porridge made of bread and warmed evaporated milk."[14]

However, "The Battler" is unfaithful to custom in that tramps and hoboes rarely paired up, or, if they did, stayed together for short periods only. Atypical too is the idea that tramps on the road would really use or be known by their given names, as are Ad Francis and Mr. Adams in Hemingway's story. Nicknames, if the books by and about tramps are to be trusted, were the principal forms of greeting or reference.

"The Light of the World" tells the story of two teenage boys who have just tramped into an unnamed town. The story begins when the two boys walk into a bar and the bartender, after a cursory look at them, covers the free-lunch bowls. To the vigilant bartender, the boys are untrustworthy outsiders who bear close watching. Beers cost a nickel each and even when drawn, are not handed over until the bartender sees the customer's money. The free-lunch bowls exist for those able to pay for their drinks, and only the narrator's display of a fifty-cent piece triggers the uncovering of the bowl full of pickled pig's feet. This is the rule of the road. Even if a tramp "sponges only one drink," writes Mullin, it "means that he may sink a fork into the sour viands of the free-lunch counter without being molested by the bartender"—in fact, anyone is free "to buy a glass of beer and eat a quarter's worth of free lunch."[15]

Although Hemingway handles it quite differently, the "free lunch" motif in "The Light of World" recalls Davies (though Hemingway handles it quite differently): "Now, once upon a time, there lived a man known by the name of Joe Beef, who kept a saloon in Montreal, supplying his customers with a good free lunch all day, and a hot beef stew being the midday dish. There was not a tramp throughout the length and breadth of the North American Continent, who had not heard of this and a goodly number had at one time or another patronised his establishment."[16] It was characteristic of tramps, as Flynt writes, to "beg just enough to keep them in 'booze,' their food being found mainly at 'free lunches.'"[17]

Hemingway's "free lunch" in "The Light of the World" may also have other identifiable sources, for example, Jack London's memorable encounter with a keenly suspicious barkeeper in a strange town:

> Alas, I had misunderstood the town boys. Beer was five cents in one saloon only in the whole burg, and we didn't strike that saloon. But the one we entered was all right. A blessed stove was roaring white-hot; there were cosey, cane-bottomed arm-chairs, and a none-too-pleasant-looking barkeeper who glared suspiciously at us as we came in. A man cannot spend continuous days and nights in his clothes, beating trains, fighting soot and cinders, and sleeping anywhere, and maintain a

good "front." Our fronts were decidedly against us; but what did we care? I had the price in my jeans.

London continues:

> "Two beers," said I nonchalantly to the barkeeper, and while he drew them, the Swede and I leaned against the bar and yearned secretly for the arm-chairs by the stove. The barkeeper set the two foaming glasses before us, and with pride I deposited the ten cents. Now I was dead game. As soon as I learned my error in the price I'd have dug up another ten cents. Never mind if it did leave me only a nickel to my name, a stranger in a strange land. I'd have paid it all right. But that barkeeper never gave me a chance. As soon as his eyes spotted the dime I had laid down, he seized the two glasses, one in each hand, and dumped the beer into the sink behind the bar.
> "At the same time, glaring at us malevolently," the barkeep said:
> "You've got scabs on your nose. You've got scabs on your nose. You've got scabs on your nose. See!"
> I hadn't either, and neither had the Swede. Our noses were all right. The direct bearing of his words was beyond our comprehension, but the indirect bearing was clear as print: he didn't like our looks, and beer was evidently ten cents a glass.
> I dug down and laid another dime on the bar, remarking carelessly, "Oh, I thought this was a five-cent joint."
> But this does not appease the barkeep.
> "Your money's no good here," he answered, shoving the two dimes across the bar to me.
> Sadly I dropped them back into my pocket, sadly we yearned toward the blessed stove and the arm-chairs, and sadly we went out the door into the frosty night.
> But as we went out the door, the barkeeper, still glaring, called after us, "You've got scabs on your nose, see!"[18]

In "The Light of the World," Hemingway's bartender apparently views the boys, who are obviously bumming around, as a threat to decorum in his bar. The customer who walks in after them orders rye, drinks it down quickly, pays for his drink and leaves. When Tom spits out a portion of the pickled pig's feet he has taken from the free lunch bowl and complains about it to the bartender—"Your goddam pig's feet stink"—there is a moment when it looks as if there will be a fight in the bar. The bartender calls them "punks" and Tom is ready to fight him, but his companion (presumably Nick) gets him out of the bar in and persuades him to walk over to the station.

The bartender's insult is particularly nasty—"punks" are young, inexperienced hobos—and particularly insulting: they are not the young male companions of older tramps who use them for begging[19] or as sodomites.[20] "Within days of hitting the road," writes a student of London's *The Road*, "a rail-riding teenager could expect to be besieged by wolves [older, predatory hobos], promising money, protection, and instruction in the art of 'getting by' in exchange for a sexual relationship."²¹ In fact, the "sardonic tale of a punk's disenchantment with a wolf's promises" was the story told in "the road's most famous folk song, 'The Big Rock Candy Mountain,'" before "it was bowdlerized in the 1920s": "I've hiked and hiked till my feet are sore / And I'll be damned if I hike any more / To be buggered sore like a hobo's whore / In the Big Rock Candy Mountains."²² The word "buggered" looks forward to the name of Ad Francis's keeper, "Bugs," in "The Battler," of course, and to the effeminate cook in "The Light of the World."

The boys leave the bar and walk through the cold night to a nearby train station, where they mix with passengers in the waiting area. Davies's *Autobiography* offers a generalized account of tramps marking time at a railway station, pretending to be paying passengers.

> We loafed all day in the different railway stations, in each of which was kept a warm comfortable room for the convenience of passengers. Although we were passengers of another sort, and stole rides on the trains without a fraction of payment to the company, we boldly made ourselves at home in these places, being mistaken for respectable travellers, who were enjoying the comforts for which we paid. Sometimes a station master would look hard on us, suspecting us for what we were, but he was very diffident about risking a question, however much he was displeased at seeing us in comfortable possession of the seats nearest to the stoves.²³

At the station, the boys find a full complement of men and women, including "six white men," "four Indians," and "five whores." Two of the prostitutes weigh some two hundred and fifty pounds each, and a third tips in at three hundred and fifty. The largest one says that her name is Alice. Three others bear the names Frances (a homonym of Ad's surname in "The Battler"), Hazel, and Ethel, while the fifth is identified only as "the blonde" or "Peroxide."

The boys witness an argument between Peroxide and Alice, who both claim to have known the famous prizefighter Steve Ketchel—to have known him in both senses of the word. In an account intended to reflect glory on herself, peroxide waxes poetic and sentimental about Ketchel's beautiful body and godlike bearing. Alice, the largest of the prostitutes, contradicts Peroxide's claim to have been Ketchel's lover. Alice expresses her own claim in more believable terms: Ketchel, she says, called her "a lovely piece." Although Alice's honesty is never firmly established, the narrator finds her the most attractive of all the women present, a fact that lends some psychological credence to her emotional revelation even if her facts and dates are shaky.²⁴

The passengers at the railway station also include a male cook who is an "outsider" both spiritually and socially. Almost everyone in the station—from the lumberjacks and the prostitutes to Tom—targets him with malicious jokes. The cook is a scapegoat and victim because of his manner (too obviously friendly), appearance (his hands are preternaturally white), and presumed homosexuality (based on their perception of his effeminacy). When he asks the boys their ages, Tom answers with a crude joke—"ninety six" and "sixty-nine"—joining the men in the station who have been baiting the book about being the type who wants to be "interfered with." And, at the end of the story, when the cook, who asks the boys where they will go now, Tom answers, "other way from you."

In "The Battler" and "The Light of the World," Hemingway himself was moving away from a sophomoric vision of youth popularized by writers such as Owen Johnson, founder and editor of the Lawrenceville School's first literary magazine. Johnson made Lawrenceville famous through three novels, *The Prodigious Hickey* (1908), *The Varmint* (1910) and *The Tennessee Shad* (1911), stories about teenage boys that also found, an adult audience. "Just as in *Stover at Yale* [1911], in which Mr. Johnson wrote not only the classic story of the collegian but also the classic satire of the Secret Societies," notes Cleveland Amory, "so in these Lawrenceville stories he wrote not only the classic story of the prep school boy but also the classic satire of prep school life."[25] For decades no literate adolescent growing up in America could have missed knowing about the adventures and pranks of the prodigious Hickey and the Tennessee Shad at the Lawrenceville School. Johnson's tales offered high school kids, including those of middle-class Oak Park, Illinois, long looks into the doings of prep school boys. In Johnson's stories boys wage war, with their jokes and pranks, against the adult figures of authority, the teachers and headmaster. The prep school is a world of men without women, or, more accurately, boys without girls, where setting the record for eating the most pancakes at one sitting marks a boy for everlasting distinction and where bringing chaos to a student election is considered a great triumph against a politically callow young instructor.

The free lunch scene in "The Light of the World" is not only reminiscent of London and Davies, but contrasts with a similar scene in Owen Johnson's *The Varmint*: "Al, without turning his back, carefully moved over to the glass counter that sheltered appetizing trays of éclairs, plum cakes and cream puffs and, whistling a melancholy note, locked the door, scanned the counter, and placed a foot on the cover of the jigger tub."[26] Johnson liked the scene well enough to re-use it in *The Prodigious Hickey*. Knowing "the exact financial status of each of the four hundred odd boys" at Lawrenceville, Al "welcomed" Hickey "with a grunt, carefully closing the little glass doors that protected the tray of éclairs and fruit cake."[27] Of course there are great differences of tone and situation between the incidents in Johnson's books and Hemingway's story.[28] Johnson's Al merely makes a protective gesture against theft by the Varmint or the infamous Hickey. Hemingway's bartender, by contrast, exhibits real hostility towards boys who are undesirable simply because they are strangers, and there is nothing humorous in his actions.

Both Johnson's Lawrenceville stories and his *Stover at Yale* (1911) were important precursors of another literary vision of adolescence that Hemingway may have hoped to challenge with his road stories: F. Scott Fitzgerald's first novel, *This Side of Paradise* (1920).[29] In a 1950 letter to Fitzgerald's biographer, Arthur Mizener, Hemingway claims that he thought the novel was "comic" when he read it after returning from the war.[30] It's easy to imagine how the young Hemingway, just back from the war in Europe, must have chortled when he read in *This Side of Paradise* that "for the next four years the best of Amory's intellect was concentrated on matters of popularity, the intricacies of a university social system and American Society as represented by Biltmore Teas and Hot Springs golf links."[31] The sterling example of what John Updike calls Fitzgerald's "collegiate romanticism,"[32] *This Side of Paradise* prompted at least one reviewer to observe: "Mr. F. Scott Fitzgerald gave us our first glimpse behind the scenes on the modern campus, and he must have resolved many a stern parent to start Freddie right in at the factory the minute he finished high school."[33]

Hemingway's achievement in "The Light of the World" and "The Battler" is more fully appreciated when compared with the artificially colorful world of pranks and shenanigans detailed in Johnson's Lawrenceville stories or in the slightly less ludicrous world of Amory Blaine's collegiate years. Against dormitories and soda shops, Hemingway set his woods, swamps, and rivers, camps by railroad tracks, and bars in small rural towns that were dangerous for strangers. His world turned out to be one where boys drink their fathers' whiskey, a girlfriend is sent packing while the boy's male friend lurks in the nearby woods, and the same boy, riding the freights, comes upon a mysterious and sinister relationship between a punch-drunk fighter and his seemingly companionable handler. The deceptively pastoral world of Nick Adams, Hemingway's first nostalgic self, stands as a "corrective" to both Fitzgerald's Princeton world and the Lawrenceville fantasy concocted by Johnson.

Only at first glance does it seem strange to think of Johnson's prep school tales swapping around in Hemingway's head with the autobiographical hobo stories of London and Davies. Yet from that surprising mix of ingredients emerged "The Battler" and "The Light of the World," two entirely imagined Nick Adams stories that take place in the "out there" Hemingway would always chose over Oak Park for the settings of his fiction.[34] What was said of another writer could also be said of Hemingway: "He never quite lost his sense of scrapping to keep his place on a moving freight train"[35]—even if Hemingway rode the rails only in his imagination.

4

An Angler's Art

> Angling doth bodyes exercise.
> And maketh soules holy and wise:
> By blessed thoughts and meditation:
> This, this is Anglers recreation!
> —Nagrom Notpoh (1659)[1]

> The lore of fishing is, of course, part of American tradition, from Huck Finn to Ernest Hemingway's Nick Adams.—Ronald Reagan (1988)[2]

Izaak Walton's intention for *The Compleat Angler* was to make it a "recreation, of a recreation."[3] This re-creation in words will offer the writer a second form of recreation, following the recreation offered him by the fishing itself. Indeed, as Walton implies, fishing and writing about fishing constitute intimately related ways of re-creating body and spirit. Such notions linking recreation with re-creation put Ernest Hemingway in camp with Walton, aligning *The Compleat Angler* with seemingly disparate works such as *Death in the Afternoon* (bullfighting and writing), *Green Hills of Africa* (hunting and writing), *The Old Man and the Sea*, "Big Two-Hearted River," *Across the River and Into the Trees* (duck-hunting and war memories), *Islands in the Stream* (sub-chasing, fishing, and painting), *The Sun Also Rises* (fishing and bullfighting), *To Have and Have Not* (fishing and smuggling) and *A Moveable Feast* (writing and more writing). The anglers are called Nick Adams, Jake Barnes, Santiago, and Harry Morgan; the hunters (and artists), Harry, Thomas Hudson, and Ernest Hemingway; the warrior, Richard Cantwell. The wedding of contemplation and instruction with the re-creation of a more or less formalized recreational activity describes Walton's work as well as much of Hemingway's.[4] The case in point is the northern Michigan story "Big Two-Hearted River."

Malcolm Cowley, drawing upon Edmund Wilson's insight in a 1940 essay, offered the first major interpretation of Hemingway's fishing story as a post-war parable of trauma. Cowley was followed by Philip Young, who applied his notion that deep-seated memories of a "wound" lay at the heart of Hemingway's truest fiction.[5] From the start Hemingway opposed Young's thesis, and therefore it seems hardly coincidental that shortly after the appearance of Young's study, Hemingway should have authorized the re-publication of "Big Two-Hearted River" in *Field & Stream*, "America's Number One Sportsman's Magazine," as it advertised itself. The cover of its May 1954 issue announced publication of "Hemingway's Greatest Trout Fishing Story," and its contents page described it generically as "Fact Fiction."[6] Here was a way, Hemingway might have thought, to counter those critics looking for deep-seated psychological or even pathological meaning in his fishing story. In *Field & Stream* there was no wild or feverish talk about traumatic war-wounds. Readers of the magazine could read the story simply as the straight-forward account of a fishing trip lasting a couple of days and judge it accordingly,

The Wilson—Cowley—Young reading of Hemingway's story never did achieve the full acceptance of Hemingway's readers, but it did finally make one highly influential convert. After opposing the "wound-reading" for years, Hemingway himself came around to accepting it. In "The Art of the Short Story" (intended for a new edition of his stories) he said as much, as he did in *A Moveable Feast*.[7] Yet even Hemingway's word cannot always carry the day. In the classroom there is always that ingenuous undergraduate who balks at the wound explanation, objecting that the war cannot have anything to do with Nick Adams' state of mind when he is out fishing because nowhere is the war mentioned in the text. Even that other undergraduate who readily admits that there must be something on Nick's mind ("that's why you go fishing, to work out things," he says with certainty) stops short of accepting the notion that Nick's concerns must emanate from his war experience.[8]

It was not until 1980 that Kenneth Lynn published his first full-blown attack on the Wilson—Cowley—Young reading.[9] Denying that there is any evidence—explicit or inferential—to indicate that Nick's dis-ease stems from his memories of the war, Lynn reveals that Nick's inner tension emanates from his situation at home. As he sees it, Nick's main quarrel is with his family, especially his mother. In short, he is still something of an adolescent, vexed by problems he is unable to solve or set aside. Lynn, it seemed, had refuted the old thesis only to replace it with own version of it, trading the war wound for a family wound.[10]

Hemingway wrote "Big Two-Hearted River" in the summer of 1924. To Gertrude Stein and Alice B. Toklas, Hemingway boasted in August of that year that he had written a story "about 100 pages long" in which "nothing happens."[11] A year later, after they had read the story in the magazine

This Quarter, Scott Fitzgerald and Christian Gauss accused Hemingway—"half in fun, half in seriousness"—of "'having written a story in which nothing happened,' with the result that it was 'lacking in human interest.'"[12] Later, less in fun and more seriously, Fitzgerald described the story as "a picture—sharp, nostalgic, tense" that "develops before your eyes." "When the picture is complete a light seems to snap out, the story is over," he continues. There is no tail, no sudden change of page at the end to throw into relief what has gone before."[13] Allen Tate struck much the same note. "Most typical of Mr. Hemingway's precise economical method is the story Big Two-Hearted River," writes Tate, "where the time is one evening to the next afternoon and the single character a trout fisherman who makes his camp-fire, sleeps all night, gets up and catches a few trout, then starts home; that is all … in the most completely realized naturalistic fiction of the age."[14]

Such straightforward readings are not contradicted by what is known of the origins of the story. At the beginning Hemingway hoped to make his fishing story nothing more than the lightly fictionalized account of a trip he had taken with two companions on the Fox river. But this idea did not work out—perhaps, as Michael Reynolds suggests, because it was "too much the straight story about fishing the Fox." He started over. "This time," continues Reynolds, "he took what he knew about the Fox to a river he had not fished. He did not need the other two men, only the river and his invention, Nick Adams."[15] What remained as well, however, was the experience he had mined once before, in a handful of journal pieces on fishing (and, in one case, camping) that he had published in the *Toronto Star* in 1920. In one of those instructional pieces he had written about fishing in the rapids of the Canadian Soo. These rainbow trout "will take a fly but it is rough handling them in that tremendous volume of water on the light tackle a fly fisherman loves. It is dangerous wading in the spots that can be waded too, for a misstep will take the angler over his head in the rapids. A canoe is a necessity to fish the very best water." Here the writer breaks for a new paragraph, to begin again: "Altogether it [such fishing] is a rough, tough, mauling game, lacking in the meditative qualities of the Izaak Walton school of angling. What would make a fitting Valhalla for the good fisherman when he dies would be a regular trout river with plenty of rainbow trout in it jumping crazy for the fly."[16] In the story he would call "Big Two-Hearted River," written in a city thousands of miles away from the Upper Peninsula of Michigan, it is not the rapids-fishing of the Soo that he invokes but the "regular trout river" he knew as the Fox and which he renamed so as to give it a more romantic meaning or, as he said later, "because Big Two-Hearted River is poetry."[17] If not Valhalla, Nick's good place for fishing is idyll enough for this earth.

Izaak Walton, writing in the seventeen century, fishes in the same "regular trout river," whatever name it bears in his narrative. *The Compleat Angler* is seldom featured in Hemingway studies. Yet Walton's popular book, which by 1983 had achieved nearly four hundred editions, reprints, and translations, is an important source for the two-part story with which Hemingway chose to conclude *In Our Time*.[18]

Consideration of just how Walton's book impinged on Hemingway's imagination when writing "Big Two-Hearted River" begins with questions of genre. Praised for its informality, geniality, ingenuousness, *The Compleat Angler* is truly a generic hybrid. Its focus on the sylvan qualities of unspoiled nature has led some readers to call it a pastoral. Its presentation of fishing lore and its description of technique has encouraged others to call it a handbook or guide. On the other hand, its employment of two characters (Walton later added a third) has alerted readers to the dramatic quality emanating from extensive dialogue. Interestingly, "Big Two-Hearted River" started out as an account of a fishing trip taken by Hemingway and two of his friends complete with appropriate dialogue, but in the rewriting Hemingway removed those friends and by doing so eliminated the possibility for dialogue so as to enhance his solitary fisherman's contemplative monologues. But as Hemingway must have noticed, Walton's book carried a significant subtitle: "or, the Contemplative Man's Recreation."[19] And indeed, Walton's book is replete with expressed thoughts, sometimes stated in the voice of his principal character Piscator (his companion is first called Viator and then, in later editions, Venator) sometimes stated directly in the narrative voice, which is indistinguishable from the author's.[20] "To the Reader of this Discourse: But especially, To the honest Angler," Walton says right off that he "did not undertake to write, or to publish this discourse of *fish* and *fishing*, to please" himself or to "displease others." He could not doubt, moreover, that "some readers may receive so much *profit* or *pleasure*, as if they be not very busie men, may make it not unworthy the time of their perusall."[21] For "the whole discourse is, or rather was, a picture of my own disposition, especially," he acknowledges disarmingly, "in such days and times as I have laid aside business, and gone a fishing."[22] In fact, Walton creates, according to John Cooper in his excellent book *The Art of The Compleat Angler*, "a world whose very point is the absence of conflict."[23] So, too, would Hemingway's Nick Adams welcome an adventure—a contest—without inner conflict (though it is arguable that he isn't always successful). In the world of *The Compleat Angler* it is this absence of conflict that provides the key to its generic lineage. Making perfect sense of the generic hybridization of Walton's book, Cooper locates it in the tradition of the georgic.

A "georgic" is "a transplanted Greek term for 'the facts of farming.'"[24] Down through the centuries the term's definition has become generalized enough to refer to "a didactic poem primarily intended to give directions concerning some skill, art, or science."[25] Or, as Joseph Addison put it in the eighteenth century, "some part of the science of husbandry put into a pleasing dress, and set off with all the beauties and embellishments of poetry."[26] "The central theme of the georgic is the glorification of labor and praise of simple country life," expatiates J. E. Congleton, but "though this didactic intention is primary, the georgic is often filled with descriptions of the phenomena of nature and likely to contain digressions concerning myths, lore, philosophical reflections, etc., which are somehow suggested by the subject matter."[27] Virgil's *Georgics* stands forth as the primary model for myriad imitations in English literature beginning with the Renaissance, and peaking, in England in the seventeenth and eighteenth centuries, with "scores of poems" imitating the Roman's poem "in form and content—poems on the art of hunting, fishing, dancing, laughing, preserving health, raising hops, shearing sheep. etc."[28]

In England there were as well various piscatorial georgics. Cooper notes that these fishing georgics have a second predecessor among the ancients in "the fragmentary *Halieuticon* usually ascribed to Ovid [which] may be called a piscatorial georgic, since it is a didactic poem on fish and fishing, with a description, or rather characterization, of various species of fish and, implicitly, a comparison of hunting and fishing."[29] Walton, according to Cooper, worked directly from the georgic tradition, giving it "a form closer to prose fiction than to the traditional georgic poem."[30] In fact, "*The Compleat Angler* is probably the only work in English," he ventures, "that is still read and that teaches a particular skill while associating that skill with a whole cluster of values and emotions."[31]

Decades ago Cooper suggested in passing that "Big Two-Hearted River" be considered within the tradition of the piscatorial georgic. Obviously familiar with the Wilson—Cowley—Young theory of the war wound, Cooper writes:

> In Hemingway's "Big Two-Hearted River," a major georgic theme is presented against a background of war and disillusion. The narrative seems at first to be merely an objective and detailed account of a man on a fishing trip, with the same close attention to the use of bait and rod and even the same concern with food that are found in the *Angler*. A more profound resemblance is revealed, however, by a fuller understanding of Hemingway's story.

Hemingway's hero, Nick Adams, "has been wounded physically and spiritually by war and is attempting to find value and stability by means of the careful, almost ritualistic practice of angling."

As in Walton, the contrast is made between rural simplicity and honesty and urban decadence, here by Nick Adams' thoughts of his friend and former fishing companion Hopkins who has, in effect, sold himself in a materially advantageous marriage.[32]

Cooper's work overall provides useful clues to any study of the influence of *The Compleat Angler* on Hemingway's work, as does a fugitive review of Hemingway's novel *To Have and Have Not* published in an obscure radical journal of the 1930s. The work of James Burnham, this review appeared in the March 1938 issue of *New International*, a journal that described itself as "The Monthly Organ of Revolutionary Marxism."[33] Entitled "Incompleat Angler," echoing Izaak Walton's title but never naming it or its author, this 1200-word review makes a valid and—at the time, surely—original point.[34] Burnham affirms that contrary to the "critical commonplace" which has called Hemingway's work "'purely negative,'" none of his work has been devoid of ideals or values. He finds the chief of those ideals to be two in number: "to fight, in strict accordance with the rules, alone; and to be able to take it." Apparent in the very earliest of his short stories, these ideals are "summed up in the figure of the fisherman, who appears and reappears throughout his writing. The fisherman fights the trout alone," continues Burnham, ending the first paragraph of his review, "with the lightest possible rod and the lightest possible line (what heresy it would be to imagine a Hemingway fisherman using a heavy rod and a worm!); and he shows not the smallest trace of emotion at the heavy disappointment which come to all fishermen." He explains further:

> It sounds rather silly, particularly when the figure of the fisherman is lifted out the admirable prose which describes the stream and the cast and the strike and the sunlight and shadows. But the fisherman is no accident. He undergoes constant metamorphosis. Here he is again as the bullfighter, alone with the bull, executing the delicate steps as prescribed by the immemorial rules, never giving way, allowing the horns just to brush across his belly. Or he searches for big game in Africa—and eternal woe to the Philistine who would shoot from the auto (even his wife, as in one story, will have to shoot *him*).

Burnham concludes; "Sometimes he simply gets beaten unconscious, or shot, or dies, without a murmur. Or he is in a hospital, in terrible and silent pain, recovering from an immeasurably cruel wound or operation. Or he is perhaps a gangster—a movie gangster, really, as the movies have bodied him forth. And like all fishermen, he talks little, and he often kills."[35] What is incomplete about this Hemingway angler, avers Burnham, is that his ideals, in themselves "not necessarily either despicable or absurd"—"To fight alone, and in strict accordance with the rules: this is not so distant from the conscious adherence to principle, which is at the root of moral integrity. To be able to take it: this is at least the negative half of heroism"—had been divorced from "an adequate context, from a completing set of values."[36]

The importance of Burnham's review is that in the 1930s he has already discerned that the figure of the fisherman, in all its avatars, stands at the center of Hemingway's essential work. It is there not only in the early story "Big Two-Hearted River," and in the middle-period novel *To Have and Have Not* (the book under review), but it will be in present in any future work. To measure this implied prediction, one need only name *The Old Man and the Sea*, *Islands in the Stream*, and *The Garden of Eden*.

If Hemingway's anglers owe a general debt to Walton's angler, there is also evidence to indicate that "Big Two-Hearted River" is directly indebted to *The Compleat Angler* for some of its detail. Such indebtedness is always hard to pin down, and in the case of Walton's book of directions and information and Hemingway's story fraught with matters of technique and instruction persuasive evidence of influence is at best elusive. But the details of Hemingway's story need to be compared to similar details in Walton's book. On baiting a hook, Walton writes:

> Suppose it be a big Lob-worm, put your hook into him somewhat above the middle, and out again a little below the middle: having so done, draw your worm above the arming of your hook, but note that at the entering of your hook it must not be at the head-end of the worm, but at the tail-end of him (that the point of your hook may come out toward the head-end) and having drawn him above the arming of your hook, then put the point of your hook into the very head of the worm, till it come near to the place where the point of the hook first came out; and then draw back that part of the worm that was above the shank or arming of your hook, and so fish with it."[37]

When you use a frog for bait, he advises: "Put your hook into his mouth, which you may easily do from the middle of April till August, and then the frogs mouth grows up, and he continues so for at least six months without eating, but is sustained, none but he whose name is Wonderful, knows how; I say, put your hook, I mean the arming wire through his mouth, and out at his gills, and then with a fine needle and silk sow the upper part of his leg with only one stitch to the arming wire of your hook, or tie the frogs leg above the upper joynt to the armed wire; and in so doing, use him as though you loved him, that, harm him as little as you may possibly, that he may live the longer."[38] Walton also gives directions for gathering bait (grasshoppers), keeping bait (flies) in jars, searching out fish, hooking, playing, landing, and cleaning them. He talks about taking "good Trout" in holes and the use of "a moveable string"[39]—the word spelled exactly as Hemingway always spelled it, first in letters and in *Across the River and*

Into the Trees, and, at the end, in *A Moveable Feast*.⁴⁰ Walton's aphorism, "'Tis the company and not the charge that makes the feast," would seem nicely *à propos* to Hemingway's memories of good and bad times in Paris in the 1920s.⁴¹

But what was it after all that *The Compleat Angler* provided Hemingway with? Cooper defines Walton's legacy. "Walton's true successors," he suggests, "are not so much the Romantic nature poets as those writers who have affirmed the value of action informed by a piety to and a close knowledge of nature. Angling, said Walton, combines both action and contemplation, and it is this combination that it is the special province of the georgic to celebrate."⁴² In distinguishing the georgic from the pastoral (which, admittedly, also influenced *The Complete Angler*), Cooper notices that while both of these traditions "deal with the country as an ideal that is contrasted with the less attractive actuality of the city," the country in each case is different.⁴³

> Nature for the georgic poet is not to be passively enjoyed and it is not merely the agreeable setting for equally agreeable activities. It achieves its significance through intellectual and physical activity, Walton's "action and contemplation." It is almost an adversary, although the struggle is the good life. A georgic creates an imaginative experience built around instruction in practical activity. It is precisely this core of practical information that is so foreign to the pastoral tradition....⁴⁴

So, while *The Compleat Angler* is a "prose georgic" (as Cooper notes), "Big Two-Hearted River" is, refining further, a fictional georgic—combining, as it does, action with contemplation.⁴⁵ So, too, to some extent is *The Old Man and the Sea*, while *Death in the Afternoon* and *Green Hills of Africa* can be read as "prose georgics." Even Hemingway's essay "The Art of the Short Story" harks back to the georgic tradition, with its employment of a strong "teaching" voice before an audience of imagined pupils. Such heuristic dialogue (between Santiago and the boy Manolo, between the author and the old woman in the book on bullfighting, between Hemingway and various others in the African book) recalls the dialogue carried on by "Piscator" the teacher and "Venator" the pupil in *The Compleat Angler*.⁴⁶ Hemingway was perfectly aware of Walton's book as a teaching text, for he calls his piece "Out in the Stream: A Cuban Letter," published in 1934 in *Esquire*, "one of those contemplative pieces of the sort that Izaak Walton used to write," even taking over the name Walton gave his fisherman:

> Piscator can see ... great blue pectorals widespread like the wings of some huge, underwater bird, and the stripes around him like purple bands around a brown barrel, and then the sudden upthrust waggle of a bill. He can see the marlin's mouth open as the bill comes out of the water and see him slice off to the side and go down with the bait, sometimes to swim deep down with the boat so that

the line seems slack and Piscator cannot come up against him solidly to hook him.⁴⁷

In this piece, as well as the 1920 piece on fishing for rainbow trout, Hemingway deprecates—but only tongue-in-cheek—"the meditative qualities of the Izaak Walton school of angling." It will be recalled that the first manuscript of "Big Two-Hearted River" contained a nine-page coda on writers, writing, and friends that Hemingway finally excised. Gertrude Stein's observation that remarks were not literature would have been enough to get those pages scrapped, but there is little doubt that he was willing to remove those pages from the story because Stein's reading of the story basically corroborated his own.⁴⁸

Yet from that rejected fragment, published posthumously as "On Writing" in the volume entitled *The Nick Adams Stories*, there are things to retrieve. These pages, which would not have been at all out of place in work truly in the georgic tradition, contain some inferential links to Walton's work. Nick talks about "the books" he read in "the old days" that said that the "only way" to fish for trout was upstream, although if you fished upstream "in a stream like the Black or this [Big Two-Hearted River] you had to wallow against the current and in a deep place the water piled up on you." It was "no fun." Oddly enough, although Walton has been dismissed as no true trout fisherman for doing so, he does suggest (following the lead of Thomas Barker's *Barker's Delight*, one of his sources) that the angler fish downstream.⁴⁹

> Now you must be sure not to cumber your self with too long a Line, as most do: and before you begin to Angle, cast to have the wind on your back, and the Sun (if it shines) to be before you, and to fish down the stream; and carry the point or top of your Rod downward; by which means the shadow of your self, and Rod too will be the least offensive to the Fish, for the sight of any shade amazes the fish, and spoils your sport, of which you must take a great care.⁵⁰

This "advice to fish downstream"—Cooper calls "notorious"—runs counter, according to that modern complete angler Nicholas Adams, to both ease and comfort.⁵¹

One important anecdote survived Stein's advice. Nick recalls his old companion Hopkins, whose dedication to fishing was immediately compromised when he learned that his first well had come in. He might have kept it in, however, as anecdotal support for one of Walton's strongly expressed principles.

> You know Gentlemen, 'tis an easie thing to scoff at any Art or Recreation; a little *wit* mixt with ill nature, confidence and *malice* will do it.... And for you that have heard many grave serious men pity Anglers; let me tell you Sir, there be many men that are by others taken to be serious and grave men, which we contemn and pity. Men that are taken to be grave, because Nature hath made them of a sowre com-

plexion, money-getting men, men that spend all their time first in getting, and next in anxious care to keep it; men that are condemned to be rich, and then always busie or discontented: for these poor-rich-men, we Anglers pity them perfectly, and stand in no need to borrow their thoughts to think our selves so happy. No, no, Sir, we enjoy a contentedness above the reach of such dispositions...."[52]

Hopkins did not come back, Nick says, even though he had promised to return the next summer, to fish, buy a yacht, and take them all sailing along the north shore of Lake Superior. "They never saw Hopkins again."

In the passage from *The Compleat Angler*, Walton refers to "Art or Recreation." This recalls the notion he opened his book with, that in writing his book, he "made a recreation, of a recreation." So, too, in "Big Two-Hearted River," has Hemingway made a "recreation, of a recreation." The story re-creates, in narrative form, the enacted fishing trip in which Nick Adams obviously intends to "re-create" himself. If Nick does not directly reveal why he needs to "re-create" himself (and the narrator does not tell why either), the reader is still left with the recreation of a camping and fishing trip, one in which Nick searches for and regains "all the old feeling"— "Nick's heart tightened as the trout moved." This is the ideal manifestation of all the kinetic pressures that striate the narrative beginning with the first sighting of a trout, in which the "shadow seemed to float down the stream with the current, unresisting, to his post under the bridge where he tightened facing up into the current." These are the tensions and pressures that serve to quicken Nick's spirit.

But "Big Two-Hearted River" is also a teaching text. Replicating *The Compleat Angler*, it offers instruction all the way from securing bait and baiting a hook to eviscerating the catch. In this story "there are in effect two parallel processes of education occurring" in the story, as Walton's critic writes of *The Compleat Angler*, "the dramatically presented pastoral experience and the instruction in georgic skills and georgic values."[53] Nick Adams is Hemingway's modern version of a georgic poet discoursing to himself about the knowledge and practice of fishing and the values of pastoralism, even as, in the *Angler*, Walton's Piscator is "a georgic poet discoursing in a pastoral setting," laying out a "long and careful exposition of practical knowledge and the related georgic themes."[54] It may even be, as Cooper suggests, that "the real source of dramatic interest in *The Compleat Angler* is the process or experience of conversion and education that Venator undergoes through his conversation with Piscator. Walton's *Angler* is more than a handbook of fishing largely because it conveys not simply a certain amount of information on the subject but also the experience of acquiring the information and the whole moral vision that accompanies it."[55] Not a bad description, all in all, of "Big Two-Hearted River."

5

Italian Grammar

The First World War saw the emergence of "curative workshops" devoted to rehabilitation of the wounded. Intensive orthopedic work converted periods of quiescent "convalescence" into programs of "rehabilitation."[1] Responsible for this change was the orthopedic surgeon, who only recently (1912) had gained recognition by the American Medical Association. Nevertheless, within the profession, the orthopedic surgeon's "distinctive feature" was to incorporate "simple mechanical devices into his procedures." Indeed, at the inception of the War, this group had not yet "overcome a reputation as being merely a 'society of buckle-and-strap men' whose claim to unique expertise was based on a manual dexterity with tools."[2]

During the War, however, rehabilitative therapy expanded well beyond the individual efforts of the orthopedic surgeon working alone. The "buckle-and strap" was still the distinguishing element of the therapy he administered, but the orthopedist had now begun to avail himself of the varied skills of the other professionals working in the "curative workshop." He had discovered that patients requiring intensive rehabilitation "need admission to a centre which is structurally and functionally orientated towards recovery; where a purposive atmosphere instills confidence; and where the individual skills of a rehabilitation team are integrated and co-ordinated to assist each patient to achieve maximal functional efficiency."[3]

How much of this medical history-in-the-making the young volunteer, Ernest Hemingway, actually discerned (or later figured out) one can only guess. In any case, that history does provide useful background for his writing about rehabilitative therapy a decade after his own wounding, convalescence and recovery. In the novel *A Farewell to Arms*, for instance, Lieutenant Frederic Henry describes dispassionately his season of convalescence:

> The summer went that way. I do not remember much about the days, except that they were hot and that there were many victories in the papers. I was very healthy and my legs healed quickly so that it was not very long after I was first on crutches

before I was through with them and walking with a cane. Then I started treatments at the Ospedale Maggiore for bending the knees, mechanical treatments, baking in a box of mirrors with violet rays, massage, and baths.[4]

Hemingway does not choose to detail the story of Lieutenant Henry's rehabilitative therapy (which was based on his own experience). Nor, for that matter, did he choose to detail the therapy undergone by Jake Barnes of *The Sun Also Rises* in the same hospital. "[I]t was a rotten way to be wounded and flying on a joke front like the Italian. In the Italian hospital we were going to form a society. It had a funny name in Italian. I wonder what became of the others, the Italians. That was in the Ospedale Maggiore in Milano...."[5]

If he did not write about Frederic Henry's or Jake Barnes's therapy at the Ospedale Maggiore (the same hospital where Jake was cared for, presumably, by Brett Ashley, the V.A.D.), his decision not to do so was undoubtedly the result of his choosing to tell a version of it elsewhere. "In Another Country," a short story, achieved print two years before the publication of *A Farewell to Arms* in 1929.[6]

"In Another Country" opens with this sentence: "In the fall the war was always there, but we did not go to it any more."[7] The narrator soon tells us that he belongs to a small group of wounded soldiers in need of therapy. Instead of being at the front, they walk each afternoon to the hospital. Each one takes one of three possible routes across town to get to an old and beautiful place: "Always, though," the narrator tells us, "you crossed a bridge across a canal to enter the hospital." Crossing over this water, "you entered through a gate and walked across a courtyard and out a gate on the other side." In this stygian crossing in reverse, "there were usually funerals starting from the courtyard"—a routine reminder, it would appear, to these men that the deaths they have avoided continue memorialized in their disabling wounds. "Beyond the old hospital were the new brick pavilions, and there we met every afternoon and were all very polite and interested in what was the matter, and sat in the machines that were to make so much difference." The implication runs—through the narrator's selection of detail—that while the old hospital buildings "breed" death, the new buildings, everyone expects, will foster hope (symbolized by "new" machines), the hope necessary to the therapy which will enable wounded men to return to their more "normal" lives as soldiers or civilians.

> The doctor came up to the machine where I was sitting and said: "What did you like best to do before the war? Did you practice a sport?"
> I said: "Yes, football."
> "Good," he said. "You will be able to play football again better than ever."

But the major is not convinced. He knows better.

> "My knee did not bend," he thinks, and the leg dropped straight from the knee to the ankle without a calf, and the machine was to bend the knee and make it move as in riding a tricycle. But it did not bend yet, and instead the machine lurched when it came to the bending part. The doctor said: "That will all pass. You are a fortunate young man. You will play football again like a champion."

The doctor and the soldier, who is an American (like Frederic Henry and Ernest Hemingway), speak in Italian. But the "football" the doctor refers to differs from the "football" the soldier would talk about. The soldier's willful misunderstanding matters little, of course, since in either sport—football or soccer—no player can be effective without the ability to flex and bend his knees. But this discrepancy in communication is harbinger of additional misunderstandings and misrepresentations. It prepares the way for the doctor's encounter with the next patient.

> In the next machine was a major who had a little hand like a baby's. He winked at me when the doctor examined his hand, which was between two leather straps that bounced up and down and flapped the stiff fingers, and said: "And will I too play football, captain-doctor?" He had been a very great fencer, and before the war the greatest fencer in Italy.

We are not told that the doctor has a reply for this, only that he "went to his office in a back room and brought a photograph which showed a hand that had been withered almost as small as the major's, before it had taken a machine course, and after was a little larger." With his "good hand," the major held the photograph and looked at it carefully.

> "A wound?" he asked.
> "An industrial accident," the doctor said.
> "Very interesting, very interesting," the major said, and handed it back to the doctor.
> "You have confidence?"
> "No," said the major.

The terms of the conflict are set. The doctor has faith in his machines, while the wounded American remains neutral on the matter (at least he is saying nothing), and the Italian major lacks "confidence." Yet every day all three meet at the hospital for the "mechano-therapy treatments."

Of the other soldiers who come for treatment, the narrator singles out three. Like the narrator, they are all officers who have been decorated. But when they read the American's citations, the three of them decide that his medals are worthless. The government has awarded them to him merely because he is an American. After that discovery they can no longer feel any camaraderie for him. Those whose medals count for something come to be known as the "hunting-hawks"; but the American (like his friend, a young man wounded on his first day at the front) is not a hawk. Yet all of them—the three hawks, the American, and his friend—seem still to value courage and bravery. The Italian major does not. Sitting daily at adjoining machines, the Italian major and the American occasionally converse. When the American remarks rather innocently that the Italian language comes easily to him, the major suggests that he learn the grammar. "So we took up the use of grammar," the American says, "and soon Italian was such a difficult language that I was afraid to talk to him until I had the grammar straight in my mind."

The major comes to the hospital regularly. In fact, he never misses a treatment, although, the narrator certifies, he has no faith in the machines. "There was a time when none of us believed in the machines, and one day the major said it was all nonsense. The machines were new then and it was we who were to prove them. It was an idiotic idea, he said, 'a theory, like another.'" The major's outburst precedes his argument with the American. "I had not learned my grammar, and he said I was a stupid impossible disgrace, and he was a fool to have bothered with me." Then, before reporting any more of the major's seemingly ill-tempered complaint, the narrator describes him as he is at the moment: "He was a small man and he sat straight up in his chair with his right hand thrust into the machine and looked straight ahead at the wall while the straps thumped up and down with his fingers in them."

The major again turns to bullying the young American. He asks him what he intends to do when the war ends and insists that, in his reply, the American speak his Italian "grammatically!" But when the latter says that he will go back to the "States" and hopes to marry, his answer meets with the quick reply, "'The more of a fool you are…. A man must not marry,'" the major exclaims. "'He cannot marry. He cannot marry…. If he is to lose everything, he should not place himself in a position to lose that. He should not place himself in a position to lose. He should find things he cannot lose.'"

Given the American's understanding of the situation, it is not surprising that the major's anger strikes us as excessive.

> "He'll lose it," the major said. He was looking at the wall. Then he looked down at the machine and jerked his little hand out from between the straps and slapped it hard against his thigh. "He'll lose it," he almost shouted. "Don't argue with me!"
> Then he called to the attendant who ran the machines. "Come and turn this damned thing off."

Then, again anticipating the language Hemingway would use to describe Lieutenant Frederic Henry's therapy, we learn that the major "went back into the other room for the light treatment and the massage." He leaves the room to use the telephone. When he returns, he wears a cape and a cap. He walks directly to the American at his machine and puts his arm on his shoulder.

"I am so sorry," he said, and patted me on the shoulder with his good hand. "I would not be rude. My wife has just died. You must forgive me."

"Oh—" the American said, feeling sick for him. "'I am so sorry.'"

He stood there biting his lower lip. "It is very difficult," he said. "I cannot resign myself."

After the major leaves, the doctor explains to the American that the major had taken a young woman in marriage, only when "he was definitely invalidated out of the war." He had acted, it seems, on the theory that marriage was not fair to his bride-to-be so long as there were any possibility he would die at the front. But she contracts pneumonia and, a few days later, she dies. As it happens, the major is himself a victim of his theory about war and marriage. It turns out to be nothing more than just another theory, like that of therapy by machines. For the next three days the major stays away from the hospital. When he reappears he arrives at the usual hour, "wearing a black band on the sleeve of his uniform." In his absence, the narrator tells us, the doctor had placed "large framed photographs around the wall, of all sorts of wounds before and after they had been cured by the machines." In front of the major's machine he has placed "three photographs of hands like his that were completely restored." The major does not acknowledge them, but the narrator questions their authenticity: "I do not know where the doctor got them. I always understood we were the first to use the machines." To the major, however, the photographs, like the machines, "did not make much difference ... because he only looked out of the window."

There is an analogy to be made between the "framed" photographs the doctor hangs on the wall by the therapy machines and the atrocity photographs disseminated among the troops and the civilian populace to foment anger and promote feelings of support for the war against the enemy. In each case, the intention is to foster belief, either in the righteousness of the Allied cause or the efficacy of the machine therapy carried out in the new brick pavilions of the old hospital. The problem with the machines is not that they are bogus (they are not); it is that the doctor who claims so much for them—so much so that, in a case of ends justifying means, he is willing to deceive his patients—seems to insist on therapeutic privilege. Such insistence obviates their conflicting need to adhere to the truth. (Of course, it would be anachronistic even to think that either the doctor or the patient would consider anything resembling informed consent.) The major, who used to look straight at the wall, now stares out the window. He does not look at the photographs, which show, perhaps fraudulently, "hands like his that were completely restored." As he had insisted when he learned of his young wife's death, the major cannot "resign" himself to anything—not to his wife's death, not to his disabling injury, not to the doctor's encouraging mendacity. Yet, like the others, he sits strapped to a machine he knows will do him no good.

Something besides its tableau quality connects this scene of the war-wounded imprisoned to their machines and the spectacle of death vouchsafed to us at the outset, beginning with the second sentence of the story:

> It was cold in the fall in Milan and the dark came very early. Then the electric lights came on, and it was pleasant along the streets looking in the windows. There was much game hanging outside the shops, and the snow powdered in the fur of the foxes and the wind blew their tails. The deer hung stiff and heavy and empty, and small birds blew in the wind and the wind turned their feathers.

Retrospectively, the reader sees that the narrator would have us consider this stark display of death, eerily beautiful, as a commentary on the photographs the doctor hangs on the hospital walls—photographs that themselves recall, ironically, the votive tablets that in ancient Greece were placed near the temples erected to honor the healer Aesculapius. Such tablets, marking the fact that the god had prescribed remedies and effected cures, recorded the names of those cured, their illnesses and injuries, and the manner of their healing. This practice, as the young Hemingway must have noted in European countries such as France, Spain, and Italy, was continued into our own day in the form of *ex-votos*, those folk objects in the shape of diseased organs and injured limbs, as well as primitive paintings depicting such scenes as sickrooms and operating rooms, hanging in churches where miracle cures had reputedly been effected.

Read this way, "In Another Country" tells a story about two kinds of therapy: physical therapy, which characterizes the domain of the doctor who has faith in his machines; and a second kind of therapy, one which not only goes unnamed in the story but which seems not even to exist in this Milan hospital during World War I. The doctor's therapy, from which he expects so much (unless he lies to himself), will undoubtedly fail to meet expectations. The major will probably never again fence, let alone regain the form that made him "the greatest fencer in Italy," and the American soldier will surely never again play football. The second kind of therapy, however, comes about not through the doctor's rather buoyant claims for the treatment he prescribes for his wounded patients, but, in the case of the American and the major, through the example of the latter. By precept and example, the major teaches the American that something important inheres in the effort to learn to speak grammatically. There exist many uninformed ways to speak Italian but only one informed way. Only the latter is worth doing. The major shows the American the inadequacy of theories and the dangers inherent in one's placing too much faith in them. The major's theory that it was safe to take a wife after his wounding had precluded his being returned to the front comes crashing down on him when death comes, not to him, as he had originally feared, but to his bride. His own sanity (and somehow the young American soldier's as well) requires that he break down, first in quarrelsome anger and then, after he has apologized for his unseemly behavior, in tears. But "break down" does not really describe what the major has done. His bitter grief may manifest itself in angry tears, but his sense of dignity and dedication to doing things in the right way carry him through: "straight and soldierly, with tears on both his cheeks and biting his lips, he walked past the machines and out the door." That this is not done in bravado we learn (as does the American) from what the major does subsequently. After mourning for three days, he resumes the machine-therapy in which he has no confidence. And when he returns, this champion of Italian grammar arrives at "the usual hour" to sit at the same machine he had always used. "We are not rid of God," wrote Nietzsche, "because we still have faith in grammar."[8] But now even on the subject of grammar, not to say God, the major has at the last fallen silent.

Among the things the American soldier has learned from the major, it can be inferred, is an ethic of personal behavior when one is faced with shock and loss. A second lesson inheres in the major's advice to "find things he cannot lose," the truth of which he comes to embody when, unexpectedly, he survives his young wife. This reversal of the major's expectations opens him to nihilism. This recognition of the dark reaches of the human condition recalls another Hemingway story, "A Clean, Well-Lighted Place," which shares with it images and language. It will be recalled that the wounded soldiers in "In Another Country" frequent the Café Cova (a *cova* is a nesting-place or lair) and that our sense of the place—more like the not-so-clean bar the older waiter visits than the "clean, well-lighted" cafe in which he is employed—emerges from this suggestive description: "We ourselves all understood the Cova, where it was rich and warm and not too brightly lighted, and noisy and smoky at certain hours, and there were always girls at the tables and the illustrated papers on a rack on the wall." Here lounge the wenches who do not die (unlike the major's young wife) and who—habitués of the Cova—re-image the metamorphosed bodies of those animals and birds described earlier. Here, too, hang the illustrated papers (perhaps announcing war victories), something of an out-of-hospital analogue for propagandistic pictures of soldiers rehabilitated by use of the machines. Here, too, sit the soldiers who live in that other country of the maimed and disabled whose boundaries are so clearly demarcated by the "new brick pavilions" that stand behind the old hospital.[9] As Hemingway's story implies, there are countries behind countries, even beyond those countries of the mind and spirit where the hebetude of the neutralized affections has itself become alien. The only "therapy" possible in this world of wounds and ineffectual machines, it would seem, derives from the young soldier's implied awe before the major's exemplary behavior.

6

The Wages of Love

In *Death in the Afternoon* (1932) Ernest Hemingway defined a theory that had guided his practice as a writer: "If a writer of prose knows enough about what he is writing about he may omit things that he knows and the reader, if the writer is writing truly enough, will have a feeling of those things as strongly as though the writer had stated them."[1] This had been his theory as early as the mid–1920s, he would recall in *A Moveable Feast* (1964).[2]

Throughout his career Hemingway would apply his theory of omission in various ways, depending on the specific nature of the tale involved. He might omit an element of plot, as he did in the early story, "Out of Season," leaving out the information that the drunkard-guide would hang himself shortly after the events depicted in the story.[3] Following the same theory, Hemingway could leave out of "Big Two-Hearted River" the thematic information that even though there was no mention of it the story was "about coming back from the war."[4] In "The Short Happy Life of Francis Macomber," to take a third example, he would omit a key reference point in the psychological motivation of one of its principals. Did Margot Macomber intend to murder her husband or was she merely one party to a shooting accident? Indeed, in this story, which once carried the working title of "The Manner of the Accident," it is doubtful that Hemingway himself could answer this question.[5]

Functional omissions in a Hemingway story took still other forms. In "Hills Like White Elephants," first published in *transition* in August 1927, shortly after Hemingway's first divorce and his second marriage, the first omission takes the form of a single key word. Notably, however, that omission serves not to create a puzzle calling for concentration and solution—for the word itself occurs immediately to even the most casual reader—but as a way to enhance the reader's felt experience of the dramatized episode.

Surely some of the power of "Hills Like White Elephants" derives from Hemingway's decision not to employ the obvious term for the operation that the young man wants the young woman to undergo. To this young couple, drinking beer and Anis del Toro in a station by the Ebro River as they await the express from Barcelona to Madrid, the operation is socially, and personally, it turns out, a taboo. The operation can be characterized, as the man characterizes it: "'It's really not anything. It's just to let the air in,'" but it must not be named—not by either party to the decision to have the woman submit to this illegal procedure. Hemingway's point, of course, is to make the reader state the term for himself. This device serves another principal exchange in the story. The man, having just described the operation, insists that "it's all perfectly natural." Its naturalness, of course, makes it all "awfully simple" and "perfectly simple," which the man echoes three times and the woman, sardonically, once.

The phrases "perfectly natural," "awfully simple," and "perfectly simple" do their appointed work. How "simple," really, and how "natural" is this clandestine operation? The author's point is that there is of course nothing "simple" or "natural" about what the woman is about to submit to, just as in no way will the operation make it possible, we suspect, for the couple to become as they were before the woman's pregnancy. The man asserts that "'We'll be fine afterward. Just like we were before.'" But the woman thinks differently. "'And once they take it away,' she insists, 'you never get it back.'"

Induced abortion, under the circumstances, is in no way "natural." Apart from its physical consequences, complicated as they are, the personal consequences, Hemingway's story tells us, are totally determinant. It is the woman, however, who affirms Hemingway's own characteristic values in all matters: simplicity and naturalness. And, despite the denotations of the words he uses, it is the man who stands for what is artificial and unnatural, and therefore, to the author, disturbing. In its sympathetic treatment of the woman in a deteriorating relationship with a man, "Hills Like White Elephants" suggests that we modify our customary view that in his treatment of the sexes under marital and extramarital stress Hemingway always favors the man.

Underlying the entire incident, however, is still another unstated truth: that above all the young woman fears death. Fear emerges in the dialogue only as her concern for what she sees as the inevitable consequences that an abortion will have for their relationship, but the forceful reality of that fear cannot be denied. It is our perception that she is, throughout all, terrified which makes the story, as H. E. Bates calls it, "one of the most terrible Hemingway or anyone else ever wrote."[6] It is, moreover, the theme of death that "Hills Like White Elephants" shares with most of Hemingway's finest stories. As Hemingway remarked in *Death in the Afternoon*, "all stories, if continued far enough, end in death, and he is no true-story teller who would keep that from you."[7]

"Hills Like White Elephants," as we know it in its final form, tells us nothing regarding the woman's ultimate fate. Was that fate the part of his materials that the author knew well enough to omit it from his story? One possible answer might emerge from a consideration of the source of the story. The difficulty in taking that route, however, lies in the fact that there is no single agreed-upon source for it. In 1958, for example, Hemingway described the "incident" behind his story: "I met a girl in Prunier where I'd gone to eat oysters before lunch. I knew she'd had an abortion. I went over and we talked, not about that, but on the way home I thought of the story, skipped lunch, and spent that afternoon writing it."[8]

Without denying that Hemingway had his oysters and a conversation with an unidentified woman who had had an abortion, however, it should be noted that Robert McAlmon, Hemingway's friend of the 1920s, saw himself as the source of the story:

> One night in Rapallo [in February 1923] the lot of us were talking of birth control, and spoke of the cruelty of the law which did not allow young unmarried women to avoid having an unwanted child. Recalling an incident of college days I told a story of a girl who had managed to have herself taken care of. Her attitude was very casual. "Oh, it was nothing. The doctor just let the air in and a few hours later it was over." ... Later Hemingway informed me that my remark suggested the story.[9]

Before choosing between McAlmon's account and Hemingway's, however, we should consider some other factors. Why, for instance, did Hemingway note at the bottom of the final page of the extant manuscript of "Hills Like White Elephants. A Story" the cryptic information: "Mss. for Pauline—well, well, well"?[10] It should be noted, moreover, that the story, started as early as March 1927—shortly after Hemingway's divorce from Hadley Richardson, as we have already noted, and two months before his marriage to Pauline—began originally with this sentence not in the third person as we now have it but in the first person: "We sat at a table in the shade of the station."[11] It may be, of course, that after this start in the first person Hemingway changed his mind for purely aesthetic reasons. Given his customary mode of composition, however, that is, to employ in the first drafts of his stories and novels the names of actual people and places (*The Sun Also Rises* provides the best known example of this), it is rather likely that the "we" of the original draft for "Hills Like White Elephants" referred to Hemingway himself and an unidentified "other." That the "other" might have been Hadley is suggested by an incident during the summer of 1924. The report is Robert McAlmon's. "Walking one night in Roncevalles, the scene of medieval romance and legend," he begins,

> Chanson de Roland Hemingway was most unhappy because he feared he was again to become a father. He told Hadley it would be no fun at all any more if they had

too many children at his age. She wouldn't be a good playmate any more either. He was tragic about it, and Hadley, too, became upset. Finally Sally Bird, who was walking ahead with Bill [Bird] and me, turned back and said to Hemingway, "Stop acting like a damn fool and a crybaby. You're responsible too. Either you do something about not having it, or you have it."[12]

In no way do I wish to imply that Hadley actually underwent an abortion or even that she considered doing so. Nor do I wish to imply anything along those lines about Pauline Pfeiffer, who by 1925 was already displacing Hadley in Hemingway's sphere, and who at the time of the writing of "Hills Like White Elephants" was engaged to Hemingway. What is apparent is that, as McAlmon has informed us, Hemingway had behaved childishly when confronted with the possibility that Hadley was again pregnant. Such an occurrence, diminishing Hadley's value to him as a "playmate," would border on the tragic for the "young" Hemingway. If it cannot be said that abortion was on the young husband's mind, there can be no doubt that the personal consequences of an unwanted pregnancy were very much so. Be that as it may, it would be no more than a matter of months before his marriage to Hadley would begin to collapse. In the midst of such marital difficulties Hemingway set down "Hills Like White Elephants."

The possibility remains that Hemingway drew upon personal experience but extended those details imaginatively to a conclusion that had no basis in the actualities of autobiography beyond Hemingway's fear at what could have happened. Indeed, what might have been a considered solution—a possible decision—was made literal in the "action" of the story. Such a procedure, common enough in writers of all stripe and in all times, was particularly characteristic of Hemingway. To see it as a mark of the way Hemingway's imagination normally worked we need only consider how the autobiographical hints of marital conflict in the later work *Green Hills of Africa* (1935)—this time involving his hunter's apprehension and real fear at P. O. M.'s (Pauline's) following him on the hunt armed with a loaded gun—were imagined into the nightmarish drama we know as "The Short Happy Life of Francis Macomber."

Conclusion. Given the autobiographical matrix of "Hills Like White Elephants" and the thrust of the tale itself—authorial tenderness toward the despondent young woman—the reader of Hemingway's work and life might well be justified in entertaining the possibility that this story, from one significant point of view at least, was Hemingway's attempt to "explain" away his own apparent callousness to that unidentified "other."

7

The Hit in Summit

After an earlier unsuccessful attempt to write the story, Hemingway was finally able to set down "The Killers" on a day in which he was confined to his Madrid hotel room because the San Isidro bullfights were snowed out.[1] He originally entitled the story "The Matadors."[2] In some ways, it is a pity that he dropped this title, for this is a story about a killing that does not take place only because the human being marked for death does not play his part that day. If one considers it as a planned, if not quite ritualized, killing in which the "animal's" own habitual behavior (each day he comes to Henry's lunchroom at the same hour) will bring him to his death at the hands of "professional" killers whose duty is to perform this task for hire, we have license to draw certain analogies between bullfighting and the events in Summit.

The bullring has become Henry's lunchroom, the matador(s), "the killers," Max and Al. Replacing the bull is "the Swede"—the prizefighter Andreson, whose first name is, suggestively, Ole.[3] The matador's sword mantled in cloth and banderillas served up from a case have their analogues in the killers' sawed-off shotguns covered up by their tight-fitting overcoats. To say this much stretches the analogies as far as it is useful to take them. What is more interesting, however, once these broad analogies are suggested, is to see how what takes place in Henry's lunch room differs from what takes place in an arena in Madrid. It is by indirection that "The Killers" parodies the bullfight itself. Because Ole Andreson is not killed "around 6 p.m." on this particular day in Henry's lunchroom, and because Nick Adams discovers that Ole Andreson has no fight left in him (he knows his fate and is resigned to being killed if not now, then later, if not in that place, then elsewhere), the horror of his predetermined fate (even though the killing is itself deferred) gradually suffuses the story. Even if the planned hit has turned out "sloppy" (Al's word) in its execution and the "ritual" has been aborted, the ordered killing ("ordered" both because somebody has commanded it or put in an order for it and because it is to be carried out in an "orderly" fashion) reveals that these men have gone beyond the brutes in that, unlike in the bullfight, their passion has been removed from the act of killing.

Their very competence as professionals, moreover, is impugned from the start. Al and Max are "dressed like twins"—derby hats, black overcoats buttoned across the chest, silk mufflers, gloves. The overcoats are "too tight." They eat with their gloves on. In fact, "in their tight overcoats and derby hats they looked like a vaudeville team." To resume the bullfighting analogy for a moment, Al and Max, acting as a team, recall the comic bullfights thrown into an overall program of bullfighting called the "Charlots" or "Charlie Chaplins." The difference, of course, lies in the threat posed by the sawed-off shotguns loaded to kill.

The widespread acceptance of the Brooks and Warren reading of "The Killers" as a story characteristically pointed toward Nick Adams's reactions, has often kept readers from seeing that this story is also about psychological and physical domination and that much of the horror the story evokes comes through the reader's recognition that something even more powerful than fear for his safety or the naked instinct for survival and self-preservation has overtaken and defeated the ex-prizefighter.[4] Ole Andreson lies on his bed as if his affections have been sedated, as if he has been caught in a trap that he no longer tries to escape. His morale crushed, he has turned his face and body to the wall even, as figuratively, he has turned his back on life.

By failing to leave his bed, let alone his room, Andreson has chosen his place to die, whether today or some other day. A bull will often establish a *querencia*, a place in the ring, where he becomes especially dangerous because the matador must go in after the bull rather than getting the bull to charge over terrain chosen by the bullfighter. Yet without their ever laying eyes on him, let alone confronting and shooting him, Al and Max (because they merely represent the notion and idea of "the killers" who have already "killed" his will to live) have already won the contest.

Were it not for what we learn from Nick's visit to Mrs. Hirsch's boardinghouse and his discussion with Andreson, the appearance of Al and Max, professional killers, would have constituted nothing more than an ugly, if threatening, interruption in the daffy doings in Henry's lunchroom. The two hours or so in which Al and Max take over the restaurant, tie-up and gag both Sam the cook and Nick the customer, and keep a gun trained on George, who runs the place, is a monstrous interlude in a day that has, until that moment, promised to be no different from any other day. And after the killers have left, it is back to business as usual. There is no indication that anyone has called the police, and while it is George who suggested that

Nick go to Mrs. Hirsch's boardinghouse to warn Andreson, George seems not to have been much affected by the events in his lunchroom. Even as Nick tells him about how he cannot stand the fact that Andreson will neither fight back, nor run away from his killers, we watch George performing the same old tasks: he "reached down for a towel and wiped the counter." He is not far from the mark, probably, when to Al's question about the townspeople in Summit, "What do you do here nights?" Max answers, "They eat the dinner…. They all come here and eat the big dinner."[5]

Of course, by their presence and the arrangements they make to facilitate their conduct of business, the two killers pervert the lunchroom routine on which the restaurant's customers depend. Yet the success of their plan depends to some extent on their maintaining the semblance of the usual routine in George's responses to customers that come in and to his own movements. George is their front man, whose presence and behavior, even if he cannot deliver the usual dinners at six o'clock (the cook is tied up), give him enough credibility to keep customers from suspecting that on that day something is amiss in Henry's lunchroom. And yet, to maintain the tone of their total domination and to amuse themselves, claims Max) they work from the start to upset the routine. They ask for items from the dinner menu, even after being told that nothing listed on the dinner menu will be ready before six. When the two plates of eggs are served—one with ham, the other with bacon—Al eats Max's order and Max eats Al's. Their running conversation keeps them amused, George under control, and the overall tension from mounting up. They are so successful in this that when Andreson fails to show up, they are able just to walk away. They are, in Max's words, "through with it." They do no further harm. After all, they haven't even done enough damage to be charged with attempted murder, and they are sure enough of themselves to walk away with their shotguns under their coats. As they go out, they direct one last remark at George, hinting that things could have turned out even worse. "You got a lot of luck," they tell him, "you ought to play the races, bright boy."

8

Writer on Vocation

During the winter of 1925, which he spent in Schruns in the Austrian Vorarlberg with his first wife Hadley and his young son, John (known as Bumby), Hemingway wrote "Banal Story." He confirmed as much in a letter to his editor Maxwell Perkins in 1938 when they were deep in the problems surrounding the contents and their arrangement in the book that would soon appear as *The Fifth Column and the First Forty-nine Stories*.[1] Topical references in the story date the writing of at least the first draft of "Banal Story" as no earlier than late January of 1925.[2] Whether or not Hemingway knew it at the start, this experimental narrative was destined for publication in some small magazine. No large-circulation journal of the day would have tolerated the seemingly cavalier shift both in thematic viewpoint and in narrative point of view, with no attempt whatsoever at providing the reader with a transition, that Hemingway effects in "Banal Story." As it turned out, Hemingway's story appeared in the Spring/Summer 1926 issue of the *Little Review*. The next year Hemingway included it in *Men Without Women*, his second collection of short stories and one in which, as he described it, in all the stories, "almost, the softening feminine influence through training, discipline, death or other causes," was "absent."[3] "Banal Story" melds two contrasting parts, unequal in length, linked by the voice of an implied narrator. The first part, which runs three times as long as the second part, focuses on a writer (much like Hemingway in his middle twenties) and his reactions to what he is reading at the moment, first, one infers, in an unidentified newspaper, and then, at greater length, in a promotional flier for the well-established American monthly magazine, *The Forum*.[4] Eating an orange and moving around in his cold room—from his chair at his writing table to a seat on the electric stove that seems to give off little or no heat—this writer, who (again like Hemingway) is probably an American living at the moment away from his home in Paris, concludes that "Here, at last, was life." He reads about newsworthy events in distant places. There is fresh snow—21 feet of it—in Mesopotamia and a prizefight in Paris. On the night of January 27, 1925, "far away in Paris," Edouard Mascart, the French featherweight champion of Europe, had knocked out an Englishman, Danny Frush. He knocked him "cuckoo" at one minute and 20 seconds of the second round. The Associated Press reported; "No count by the referee was necessary. Frush was out for several minutes."[5] In Australia the English cricketers are "sharpening up their wickets" and end up losing all three matches to the Aussies, a defeat that upsets "all London."[6] This, Hemingway's young writer decides, is "Romance."

He then turns to the promotional flier for *The Forum*. During 1925 *The Forum* promises to bring its readers "prize short-stories"—"warm, homespun, American tales, bits of real life on the open ranch, in crowded tenement or comfortable home, and all with a healthy undercurrent of humor"—"will their authors write our best-sellers of to-morrow?" Like the Hemingway who was, we now know, on the verge of writing *The Sun Also Rises* but who was then fearful that he might never write a first novel, he must read those stories, the writer promises himself.

The flier has more. Momentous questions will be addressed: the growing world population, the threat scientific knowledge poses for believers, the gum-choppers in the Yucatan jungles. His attitude becomes more and more smart-alecky. It anticipates the pose Hemingway's implied author (with similar hints of self-directed irony) would adopt later in the same year when he turned to the writing of *The Torrents of Spring*. "Do we want big men—or do we want them cultured?" asks *The Forum*. "Take Joyce. Take President Coolidge. What star must our college students aim at? There is Jack Britton" (who had provided Hemingway with a subject for his boxing story "Fifty Grand"). I have not found any such flier promoting *The Forum* for 1925, but an examination of the contents of the magazine for that year shows that Hemingway has real targets in mind. The reference to James Joyce seems to have been his own idea, but on the other matters, see the article on the politics of the presidential election, "Coolidge Versus Davis," and look at the earnest piece written by "an observant student at Yale," "Big Men—or Cultured?" which "voices a protest against the spirit of 'be a big man or bust'" that its author believes works against the university's true purpose, which is to serve as a retreat where the student can acquire culture for its own sake and not for some practical purpose or ulterior reason.[7] The article ends on a note, incidentally, that would have touched Princeton's Scott Fitzgerald more closely than it would Hemingway: "Indeed, no matter what his intended college [the author's example throughout has been Yale University], it can do no harm for a prospective undergraduate to consider whether he would rather be a Big Man at twenty-two, or a well-rounded, possibly a great man at forty."[8] It was Nick Carraway, it will be recalled, who wrote about himself in *The Great Gatsby* (1925): "I was rather literary in college—one year I wrote a series of very solemn and obvious editorials for the Yale News—and now I was going to bring back all such things into my life and become again that most limited of all specialists, the 'well-rounded man.'"9

Hemingway's unnamed reader continues: "And what of our daughters who must make their own Soundings. Nancy Hawthorne is obliged to make her own Soundings in the sea of life. Bravely and sensibly she faces the problems which come to every girl of eighteen." The target here is the motherless English heroine of Arthur Hamilton Gibbs's *Soundings*, a novel serialized in seven installments in *The Forum* beginning in the October 1924 issue and running through April 1925, with a nod in the direction of Hemingway's own young heroine in "Up in Michigan," a story that would have been unwelcome at *The Forum* (or anywhere else for that matter, as Hemingway had discovered). The first installment of Gibbs's now long-forgotten piece of fiction had carried an epigraph: "Life is an unchartered ocean. The cautious mariner must needs take many soundings 'ere he conduct his barque to port in safety."10

"Are modern paintings—and poetry—Art?" asks Hemingway. "Yes and No. Take Picasso." In June 1925 *The Forum* did just that. In a debate on the question "Is Cubism Pure Art?" the two sides are argued: "Picasso's Achievement" and "Picasso's 'Failure.'"11 And how about "civilization"? See the multipart series "What Is Civilization?" beginning in the January 1925 issue and running until October of the same year. Then there are the tramps. "Have tramps codes of conduct? Send your mind adventuring," writes Hemingway, who in "The Battler" examined the conduct of Ad Francis and his companion Bugs on the road. His target here, however, is an article entitled "Tramps and Hoboes," which a preliminary note describes: "Living and moving among us, in this settled and civilized era, is a nomadic population of over a hundred thousand men and boys,—our tramps and hoboes. Their faults and their virtues,—for they have virtues, even if their behavior is essentially anti-social,—and their picturesque language and habits are depicted in this article by a sympathetic observer."12

And in the course of his reading Hemingway's writer refers to pieces on other topics and personalities such as George Bernard Shaw ("Ulysses and Einstein: A Dialogue between George Bernard Shaw and Archibald Henderson"), who seems not to recognize the names of any of the contemporary American writers mentioned to him, boasting "I never read any books,—at least hardly any; but I have no prejudice against American books,"13 and Joan of Arc, who is featured in a full-page advertisement plugging Mark Twain's book on the subject.14 Incidentally, it might be instructive or at least amusing, to tick off the 12 stories, one per issue, that Hemingway's writer would have read in 1925, had he kept his promise to himself: "Interval" by Kate Mullen, "Poor Man's Inn" by Richard Hughes, "Too Good to Be True" by James Aton, "Old Mossy Face" by Anthony Richardson, "Aunt Jane's Sofa" by Francis B. Biddle, "Maternal" by Ethel Cook Eliot, "Will Turner's Wife" by Ursula Trainor Williams, "Crown's Bess" by Du Bose Heyward, "An Apostle of Thunder" by, again, James Aton, "Palmleaf Gambling Hells" by Robert Dean Frisbie, "Mr. Rooster Rebels" by Dorothy Canfield, and, at last, in December, "Justice" by Louis Bromfield.[15] "Forum writers talk to the point, are possessed of humor and wit," promises the flier; but unlike the self-parodying author of the first part of "Banal Story" itself, "they do not try to be smart and are never long-winded."

The second part of "Banal Story" is something else. It appears to differ radically from the first part, both in subject matter and tone. The sarcasm that runs through the first portion of the story disappears, giving way to a pervasive irony. This part is shorter than the account of the writer reading *The Forum* flier, running only to a single paragraph comprised of six sentences of short to moderate length. It is not written in Hemingway's breezy, sniping, *Torrents of Spring* style, but more in the style of the vignettes he published in Paris in the Three Mountains Press edition of *in our time* (1924) and then reprinted, with some changes, in the Boni & Liveright volume, his first collection of stories, *In Our Time* (1925). Rather than exuding sarcasm, this part works through irony. While the unnamed writer reads the booklet advertising *The Forum* and exhorting its potential readers to "Live the full life of the mind, exhilarated by new ideas, intoxicated by the Romance of the Unusual," the great Spanish bullfighter Manuel Garcia Maera lies dying of pneumonia. Here, too, in far-off Spain, is life. Contrast the scene of the American writer collecting heat by seating himself on the electric stove ("How good it felt! Here, at last, was life.") with that of Maera, "a tube in each lung, drowning with the pneumonia."

In the writer's part, the word "life" appears four times; in the bullfighter's, not once. Yet in the time of Maera's death there is the life that infuses Hemingway's sensitively ironic style. No matter that the "men and boys bought full-length colored pictures" of Maera "to remember him by, and lost," sad to say, "the picture they had of him in their memories by looking at the lithographs" and then rolling them up and putting them away in their pockets, thereby burying the reproductions even as they had attended to the burial of the bullfighter himself. Intended to memorialize Maera the bullfighter, whose glory lay in his actions in the bullring, the colored pictures show him at full length, static, inert, impersonating what a photographer would take to be *the bullfighter as celebrated public figure*.

No wonder the "bull fighters were very relieved he was dead, because he did always in the bull-ring the things they could only do sometimes." Yet the fact is that 147 bullfighters showed sufficient respect for Maera to follow him out to the cemetery where he was placed in the tomb next to that of Joselito, universally considered to be the greatest bullfighter modern Spain has known.

Elsewhere Hemingway would insist that only the bullfighter lives his life all the way up. And even the stark naturalism of Maera's death cannot diminish the quality of his life. In *Death in the Afternoon* (1932) Hemingway would pay his final tribute to Maera:

> He was generous, humorous, proud, bitter, foul-mouthed and a great drinker. He neither sucked after intellectuals nor married money. He loved to kill bulls and lived with such passion and enjoyment although the last six months of his life he was very bitter. He knew he had tuberculosis and took absolutely no care of himself; having no fear of death he preferred to burn out, not as an act of bravado, but from choice.[16]

In the final year of his life Maera had "hoped for death in the ring," writes Hemingway admiringly, "but he would not cheat by looking for it."[17] As a matter of fact, Hemingway had himself already given Maera the very death he wanted. In the fourteenth vignette of *in our time*, published in the spring of 1924[18] (and therefore well before Maera's death in Seville in December 1924), Hemingway had imagined the death in the bullring that would elude Maera:

> Maera lay still, his head on his arms, his face in the sand. He felt warm and sticky from the bleeding. Each time he felt the horn coming. Sometimes the bull only bumped him with his head. Once the horn went all the way through him and he felt it go into the sand. Some one had the bull by the tail. They were swearing at him and flopping the cape in his face. Then the bull was gone. Some men picked Maera up and started to run with him toward the barriers through the gate out the passageway around under the grandstand to the infirmary.

Once there, Hemingway continues:

> They laid Maera down on a cot and one of the men went out for the doctor. The others stood around. The doctor came running from the corral where he had been sewing up picador horses. He had to stop and wash his hands. There was a great shouting going on in the grandstand overhead. Maera wanted to say something and found he could not talk. Maera felt everything getting larger and larger and then smaller and smaller. Then it got larger and larger and larger and then smaller and smaller. Then everything commenced to run faster and faster as when they speed up a cinematograph film. Then he was dead.[19]

Surely this was a story that would not have appealed to the editors of *The Forum*. Neither, of course, would "Banal Story," which can hardly be described as "warm" or "homespun" or a bit of "real life on the open ranch." Its theme is banality, the banality of both the kind of story (fictional or otherwise) that *The Forum* promises and delivers to its readers and, in a deeper sense, the kind of smart-alecky narrative told in the first part of Hemingway's "Banal Story." The irony is that the self-parodying writer warming himself from the bottom up, with his pseudo-Mencken facility for rather easy sarcasm, was never completely exorcised by the author who, in a different mood and at the top of his form, could write such deeply sensitive stories as "Indian Camp," "Hills Like White Elephants," and the two vignettes on Maera's death, imagined and actual. Minor though it otherwise may be in the Hemingway canon, "Banal Story" gathers considerable biographical significance when it is seen for the ironic gesture towards its author's own self-conscious need for exorcism that it was at least partly intended to be.

9

Winner Take All

"So far you lost money, on the advance anyway, of two books," wrote Hemingway to Maxwell Perkins, his editor, in 1943. "I will bet you anything you want to bet they will both pay out," he added. "All the others made money."[1] The two books Hemingway had in mind were *Green Hills of Africa* and *Winner Take Nothing*—both of them published in the 1930s, just about the time the Great Depression settled in for the long haul. Hemingway was right, of course. Eventually the two books did pay out. But then everything he wrote seemed to pay out—though usually sooner than later.

Still there are levels of critical and commercial success that neither of these titles has yet achieved, critically or financially. This fact is less surprising for *Green Hills of Africa*, perhaps, than it is for *Winner Take Nothing*. After all, for some of Hemingway's readers, Hemingway's stories alone, if he had not written anything else, would assure him of lasting fame. Lionel Trilling, for example, recognized the "high virtues" of the stories, especially in comparison with Hemingway's other fiction of the 1930s, and forty years later Marvin Mudrick boldly asserted that the publication of a selective volume of Hemingway letters in 1981 was "the biggest American literary event since the publication of *In Our Time*" in 1925.[2] In that first collection of stories, Hemingway had forged a literary style, as the English writer Ford Madox Ford expressed it, in which the "words strike you, each one, as if they were pebbles fetched fresh from a brook."[3]

Hemingway followed *In Our Time* with only two other collections of stories: *Men Without Women* (1927) and *Winner Take Nothing* (1933). Each of the three collections contains stories that have become classics of English-language literature, such as "Indian Camp," "Big, Two-Hearted River," "The Killers," "Hills Like White Elephants," "A Clean, Well-Lighted Place," and "The Light of the World." A handful of other stories—six of them, including two greatly admired African stories, "The Short Happy Life of Francis Macomber" and "The Snows of Kilimanjaro"—and a play were added to the forty-three stories ("Big Two-Hearted River," divided into two parts presented as if they were separate stories) in the three collections to make up the collective edition *The Fifth Column and the First Forty-Nine Stories* in 1938.

Much has been written about Hemingway's short stories. There has been a book-length collection of essays devoted to *In Our Time*, as well as book-length studies of the same work; but there exists nothing comparable for the *Men Without Women* or *Winner Take Nothing*. This alone does not justify an essay of this nature, one devoted to the last of Hemingway's three discrete volumes of stories, but the quality of the stories themselves does.[4]

Composition, Arrangement, Publication, Reception and Reputation

Winner Take Nothing was Hemingway's first book of fiction after the publication of *A Farewell to Arms* in 1929. Charles Scribner's Sons published *Winner Take Nothing* on October 27, 1933, in a printing of 20,300 copies. By the end of the Christmas season 12,500 copies had been sold, but sales slowed down after the holidays and subsequent sales, in the opinion of Hemingway's publisher, did not warrant a second printing for the book.[5] This decision did not sit well with the author. Early on, he complained to his editor at Scribner's, Maxwell Perkins, that the firm had failed to get behind the book, not promoting it at the right time or in the right places. He charged that the advertising department at Scribner's, because of the book's mixed first reviews, had backed off from "a book you have to do a little work to push."[6]

Whether or not Hemingway's charges were warranted, the overall tone and tenor of the reviews did not help matters. The book never really caught on. On November 16, 1933, to Perkins, who had found the reviews to be "absolutely enraging,"[7] Hemingway complained: "Does it seem of any significance to you that they [the reviewers] all say there are 3 really good stories and nearly all pick 3 different ones?"[8]

It is instructive to test Hemingway's complaint against what the reviewers singled out for praise and what they chose to denigrate. Fanny Butcher, in the *Chicago Daily Tribune* (Oct. 28, 1933), found "A Natural History of the Dead" to be "life burned to the quick" and "Homage to Switzerland" evidence that Hemingway was "a humorist of the first water."[9] Clifton Fadiman, in the *New Yorker* (Oct. 28, 1933), found "A Natural History of the Dead" to be nothing more than an exercise in which the author worries "excessively about third-position exercises in the macabre"; while "Homage to Switzerland," "The Mother of a Queen" and "One Reader Writes" left him "a bit cold." "Fathers and Sons" he found to "contain a kind of youthful Red Indian brutality which everyone is happy to admit" only Hemingway could "make interesting." "But at bottom," concludes Fadiman in a review that got well under Hemingway's skin, "it doesn't seem to me very different from the atmosphere surrounding college-boy fraternity initiations." The reviewer for the *Hartford Courant*, unnamed but self-identified as "an elderly woman whose artistic standards do not fit with the modernistic ideal," was satisfied merely to quote Fadiman's hectoring with full approval.

In the *Saturday Review of Literature* (Oct. 28, 1933), Henry Seidel Canby singled out "A Natural History of the Dead" for its "unforgettable incisiveness." Horace Gregory, in the *New York Herald Tribune* (Oct. 29, 1933), found that in "Wine of Wyoming" and "The Gambler, the Nun and the Radio" it was evident that there had been "a sudden expansion of Hemingway's range": both stories were "beautifully simplified and pure." The unnamed reviewer for the *Kansas City Star* (Nov. 4, 1933) warned readers that there was much of "the raw stuff of the world" in the Kansas City tale, "God Rest You Merry, Gentlemen." On the other hand, the review continued, "Hemingway fans will tell you there are some of his finest stories in this collection, particularly 'Wine of Wyoming' and 'The Gambler, the Nun and the Radio.'" The *Cincinnati Enquirer* (Nov. 4, 1933) found that *Winner Take Nothing* marked "no advance in the author's established art" but found "an expression of human sympathy" in "Wine of Wyoming." Strangely, in evidence against Hemingway's own later statement on the matter, the reviewer found "action" in all the stories. Louis Kronenberger, in the *New York Times Book Review* (Nov. 5, 1933), regretted that "in the main such incomparable equipment as Hemingway's goes off so many times with a proud and clean report—and hits nothing." He thought "After the Storm" to be the "finest" piece in the volume. *Time* (Nov. 6, 1933) agreed: "For sinister atmospheres Hemingway has never been better than in 'After the Storm,' an eerie story of a Florida beachcomber's wreck of a liner." In the *New Republic* (Nov. 15, 1933) T. S. Matthews praised "After the Storm" as "an almost magical story, of the kind that will haunt a reader for years" and suggested that all "enthusiasts" for Booth Tarkington's Penrod and Sam be made to read the incisive story "A Day's Wait." In the *English Journal*, a periodical aimed at American teachers, Harvey Curtis Webster expressed his view that "Mr. Hemingway's latest collection of stories is inferior to his earlier *Men without Women* and *In Our Time*. No artistic development is indicated in these tales, which are, for the most part, slight variations upon themes which he had elsewhere treated more successfully. [Still] 'A Way You'll Never Be,' an excellent reproduction of the atmosphere of *Farewell to Arms*; 'Homage to Switzerland,' an amusing skit; and 'The Gambler, the

Nun, and the Radio,' an echo of *The Sun Also Rises*—all are well worth the reading."¹⁰

William Troy, writing in the *Nation* (Nov. 15, 1933), charged that "Mr. Hemingway's latest collection of stories includes what is actually the poorest and least interesting writing he has ever placed on public view." He regrets, for instance, "that a specimen like One Reader Writes should ever have been exposed to that view."

> As for most of the stories in the volume, their dullness may be traced either to a lack of growth or to growth along what is for Hemingway a new and unfortunate direction. There is, first of all, a recurrence of all the old nostalgias—the nostalgia for Europe (Wine of Wyoming), for the church (The Gambler, the Nun, and the Radio), for adolescence (Fathers and Sons), and for death (A Clean, Well-Lighted Place).

Throughout the book, in fact, "There is also the monotonous repetition of the subjects attached to these themes—eating and drinking, travel, sport, coition."

Troy continues in this vein until he reaches the moment to deliver what he seems to consider his coup de grace, lashing out in one sentence: "Ignoring the preoccupation with death, which in the reprinted Natural History of the Dead almost amounts to an enthusiastic delectatio morbosa, there are enough other indications that Hemingway is in danger of becoming as fin de siècle as his contemporary, William Faulkner." His does concede, however, somewhat pro forma, that "The Gambler story is from every point of view the most successful in the book."

John Chamberlain began his review in the New York *Times* with a reference to Frank E. Campbell, a well-known New York City undertaker, for Hemingway is "beginning to make Frank E. Campbell look pretty unenterprising in a mortuary way."

> [His] latest collection ... is one of the grisliest books ever published. Statistical method, applied to the subject matter, would result in a table very like that kept in the recording room of Bellevue Hospital. Death, dishonored old age, fatty degeneration of the personality, disease of the more loathsome variety, injury such as that sustained by the hero of *The Sun Also Rises*, perversion, shell shock, poisonous complacence and vanity, lust, fever, "A Natural History of the Dead," and a common or garden variety of shooting among gamblers—such are the subjects of Mr. Hemingway's undertaker's garland.¹¹

Seldon Rodman decided that Hemingway was squandering his talent as well as wasting his readers' time with stories that were not worth reading, let alone writing. He starts out by admitting that "in sheer ability to tell a story simply and effectively Hemingway has no rival" and that "each of the stories [in *Winner Take Nothing*] is a miniature work of art." Then we have the qualification:

My God, why can't Hemingway find something worth writing about? Is there nothing in this exciting world to engross his attention but the emptiness of it all? Nothing in this fateful year, 1933, but the way a man waiting for a train wastes his time, the provincialism of a French woman in Montana, what a waiter in a café thinks about (or doesn't think about) when he's about to go to sleep. Well, perhaps we are too serious.

Yet, Rodman continues, while "these things deserve some attention,"

hasn't it come to the point where Hemingway is just giving us an exhibition of his skill in making something of nothing or of a very little? Isn't there something a little pretentious in the continuation of this attitude, this manly scorn for the heroic, the ideal? If Hemingway is not actually escaping from the realities and struggles of life, from history and all that it implies in human aspirations, conquests and defeats, isn't he at least treating himself pretty roughly?

Hasn't "the reader who buys his books year after year," Rodman concludes "something more to expect—than a lion playing with a mouse?"[12]

When Hemingway received a batch of reviews from his publisher, he was not pleased. Worried that any review that was not favorable might lessen the desire of those at Scribner's to push the book through advertising, Hemingway fired back with his estimate of the reviewers. Horace Gregory was a "bird," he writes, who "when he labeled me as approaching middle-age was trying to get rid of me that way," John Chamberlain simply did not know what he was talking about when he found the story "After the Storm" to be "more imaginative than the others," Henry Seidel Canby, who calls him "a reporter," does not see that he is "a reporter *and an imaginative writer*," and Clifton Fadiman puzzles him when he asks him to "write better stories than some that I have written."[13] With Fadiman he brings his peroration against the reviewers of *Winner Take Nothing* to an end: "I can't write better stories than some that I have written—What Mr. Fadiman asks for—because you cant write any better stories than those—and nobody else can—But every once in a long while I can write one as good—And *all the time* I can write better stories than anybody else writing. But they want *better* ones and as good as *anyone ever* wrote. God damn it. There cant be better ones."[14]

In mid–July 1933, Hemingway had proposed an order for the stories in his still not definitively named volume:

1. The Light of the World
2. A Clean, Well-Lighted Place
3. After the Storm
4. God Rest You Merry Gentlemen
5. The Sea Change
6. A Way You'll Never Be

7. The Mother of a Queen.
8. A. Day's Wait
9. Homage to Switzerland
10. One Reader Writes
11. A Natural History of the Dead
12. Wine of Wyoming
13. The Gambler The Nun and The Radio

He also mentioned that he was now revising what would be the volume's fourteenth story—"The Tomb of His Grandfather" (ultimately published as "Fathers and Sons")—that would "be either next to last or last in the book."[15]

On Aug. 2nd, Hemingway heard from Max Perkins. Leading off the collection with "The Light of the World" was not, in Perkins' opinion, a good choice. He implied as well that "A Clean, Well-Lighted Place" was also unacceptable for the first spot. "My point about the order of the stories is simply a practical one," he insists.

> The story you have put first is the one to which people will most object. Utterly enrage all those who do get enraged in the most hateful way about those things. Its most conspicuous position would give it a tremendous emphasis, and would greatly damage the book in sales, and I think in other ways too, in reviews or such things. So I hoped you could put it elsewhere.

Then Perkins turns to objections over Hemingway's use of objectionable words.

> I have underlined the words and phrases I think you ought to get around. There is one in "God Rest You" that you did not have in the version I read. I really think that one of the best of all the stories is "A Clean Well-Lighted Place" though it is of that kind, I suppose, which not many people would respond to as much as to others. I think "After the Storm" is probably the most popular sort of story.[16]

Hemingway was persuaded by Perkins' argument. The writer who had so skillfully organized *In Our Time* for his first publisher, Boni & Liveright, in 1925, leading it off with a Nick Adams story, "Indian Camp," now allowed himself to be persuaded away from again leading off this collection with "The Light of the World," another Nick Adams story. To lead off with a story featuring a complement of five prostitutes in a railroad station, the example of Guy de Maupassant's brothel story "La Maison Tellier" notwithstanding, would hurt the financial and critical reception of the book, or so Perkins argued.[17] It was decided to change the order of "After the Storm" and "The Light of the World," with the more impressive of the two stories now relegated, less prominently, to second place.[18]

With the decision to switch the two stories, the book's working title became *After the Storm, and Other Stories*. But this title did not please Hemingway and he kept trying to come up with something, he hoped, that would be "infinitely better"—"a title which describes the whole book."[19] Finally he came up with *Winner Take Nothing*, a phrase seemingly culled from the epigraph he had himself written for the volume. He had composed a single sentence in the "Medieval" manner. On June 11, 1933, from Havana, he wired Max Perkins:

> TITLE IS WINNER TAKE NOTHING STOP WITH THIS QUOTATION QUOTES UNLIKE ALL OTHER FORMS OF LUTTE OR COMBAT THE CONDITIONS ARE THAT THE WINNER SHALL TAKE NOTHING SEMICOLON NEITHER HIS EASE COMMA NOR HIS PLEASURE COMMA NOR ANY NOTIONS OF GLORY SEMICOLON NOR COMMA IF HE WIN FAR ENOUGH COMMA SHALL THERE BE ANY REWARD WITHIN HIMSELF CLOSE QUOTE HOWS THAT TELL YOUR FRIEND EASTMAN WILL BREAK HIS JAW REGARDS—ERNEST[20]

The sentence is to be given within quotation marks, Hemingway advises, implying that it has some attributable, though not-to-be-named, source. Yet the title was "not meant to be tricky," he insisted, "any more than *Men Without Women* was"; and it had "the same sort of application to the contents."[21] Interestingly, the phrase "winner take nothing," a play on the familiar phrase "winner take all," was in use well before Hemingway thought it up. In 1930, for example, John Kieran, a sports columnist for the *New York Times*, wrote a piece entitled "A Wicked Sham Report on Sports," in which he quoted a fictitious "Tammany Young," a member of the equally fictitious "Wicked Sham Committee on Sports," who says, knowing, of course, that he cannot win: "I herewith challenge Jack Sharkey [the heavyweight boxing champion] to fight for a purse of $1,000,000, winner take nothing."[22]

F. Scott Fitzgerald did not like his friend Hemingway's new title and told him so. "While I admire your use of purely abstract titles," he wrote on June 1, 1934, "I do not think that one was a particularly fortunate choice."[23] Unfortunately, he did not explain why. Yet it can be argued, Fitzgerald notwithstanding, that Hemingway's title was a title for the 1930s, just as the phrase for the 1920s, considered by many to be "The Golden Age of Sport," especially in the United States, might well have been "winner take all," suggestive of the purse for a match race among horses or an early prize-fight. In the euphoria of the 1920s everybody was a winner, if not today then tomorrow. But things changed with the onset of the Depression of the 1930s. Everybody became a "loser," it seemed, including the so-called winners. As Michael Reynolds puts it (echoing "My Old Man," the story from *In Our Time*), in Hemingway's *Winner Take Nothing* "the fixed race was his metaphor for life, the outcome of which was always foreknown: you lose."[24] At no time, it seemed, was this more evident than during the Depression. Reynolds, in a late essay, writes that Hemingway's third collection of stories "was even more abrasive" than his previous work to the "prevailing American moral view of itself.

> When two young boys walk into the train station in "Light of the World," they are confronted by five whores and a homosexual cook, with whom anyone can "interfere." In "God Rest You Merry, Gentlemen," we read a Christmas Day story in which a young boy emasculates himself with a razor to avoid sins against purity. Other stories involved homosexuality, insanity, suicide, nihilism, and venereal disease. In the anchor story, "Fathers and Sons," Nick Adams, now a father, finds he is no more capable of speaking truthfully to his son than was his own father a generation earlier.

In short, to readers "mired in the economic woes" of a Depression, these stories "offered no significant hope and no exit."[25]

The Depression, the world's ills, and his own pessimism notwithstanding, Hemingway was disappointed in the reception of *Winner Take Nothing*. Sales had fallen far short of his expectations, as has been noted. Of the fourteen stories in the collection, only the first one, "After the Storm," Hemingway said later, had any appeal for the "so-called plain reader," that is to say, the reader who wants "action" in his stories. His book had failed, he insisted, because there were too many "quiet" stories in *Winner Take Nothing*—thirteen of them, to be "exact."[26]

Fitzgerald compared the new collection as a whole with the first two—*In Our Time* and *Men Without Women*—and found it wanting. "If I'd been in Max's place I'd have urged you to hold the book for more material," he told Hemingway on May 1934; "It had neither the surprise of I.O.T. (nessessesarily) nor its unity, and it did not have as large a proportion for first-flight stories as M.W.W. I think in a 'general presentation' way this could have been atoned for by sheer bulk."[27] Two weeks later Hemingway answered Fitzgerald, even going so far as to misrepresent things a little, by agreeing with him about *Winner Take Nothing*, explaining only that he had "wanted to hold it for more." "The last one I had in *Cosmopolitan* ['One Trip Across'] would have made it."[28] Fitzgerald wrote back in agreement: "just exactly what you suggested, that the addition of that Chinamen-running story in the *Cosmopolitan* would have given *Winner Take Nothing* the weight that it needed, was in my head too."[29] But what Hemingway had not revealed to Fitzgerald was that he had at the time deliberately decided not to include the story in *Winner Take Nothing*. Eleven days before the publication date of his book he was saying: "['One Trip Across'] is almost entirely action and takes place in Cuba and on the sea. Plenty of action. It is exactly the story that this present book needs i.e. *Winner Take Nothing*.

But it will be as well or better in another book. You can't very well put a story that you know will sell like hotcakes in a book called *Winner Take Nothing*." Hemingway continues, apologizing, complaining, and explaining (in a letter to his mother-in-law):

> I don't expect anybody to like the present book of stories and don't think you have to make an effort to—or even be polite about them. I am trying to make, before I get through, a picture of the whole world—or as much of it as I have seen. Boiling it down always, rather than spreading it out thin. These stories are mostly about things and people that people won't care about—or will actively dislike. All right. Sooner or later as the wheel keeps turning I will have ones that they will like.[30]

Yet when the first reviews appeared (as we have seen), Hemingway was not ready for them. He was disappointed that reviewers were not responding to what he considered to be the strongest stories in the collection. Among the stories ignored or only barely mentioned in the contemporary reviews that came to matter most to Hemingway's readers are "A Clean, Well-Lighted Place," "The Light of the World," "A Way You'll Never Be," and "Fathers and Sons." Even when they picked one out as a "classic," such as "Hills Like White Elephants," about which Hemingway complained, "not one damn critic thought anything of when it came out."[31]

Winner Take Nothing was reviewed by Philip Rahv in the first issue of the *Partisan Review*. Rahv mentioned only one story, the title of which he shortened to "Gambler, Nun, and Radio," only to dismiss it by saying that Hemingway unfortunately wrote better about the radio than he did about Mr. Frazer's thoughts about the opium of the people. He took issue, however, with those reviewers who saw a falling off in Hemingway's achievement in these stories, insisting that "these new stories of Hemingway's differ in no way from those in preceding volumes." The problem, as he saw it, was that "In the nineteen-twenties the stimulus to 'second-hand nihilism' offered by the Hemingway mode was necessary to many middle class readers whose own abject ideological poverty mirrored itself in him. Today these readers are beginning to be repelled by what formerly aroused their enthusiasm."

> True, he is still in full control of his formal effects—that dry and racy freshness that is almost unique in modern prose, the wistfulness generated by a method of capricious understatement, and the charm of his success in reducing writing to its state of nature. But these, of course, being in the main an artistic formation subtly reflecting a social formation, are powerless to arrest the withdrawal of interest at a time when the reader no longer stands solidly on the social basis reflected in the author.[32]

The English critic V. S. Pritchett, writing in the *Fortnightly Review* at just about the same time, warned about a decline in Hemingway's abilities as a short story writer as evidenced by *Winner Take Nothing*. Explaining that "the accumulated sound of stories already written" had "clouded" his ears, he complained that Hemingway's "laconic naturalism is disintegrating and petering out into catalogues of perfunctory reporting."

> Mr. Hemingway's book has many excellent passages, though the book as a whole disappoints. It contains nothing as good as "The Killers," for example. "Fathers and Sons" and "A Way You'll Never Be"—a curious study in shell-shock—are good stories; the rest show what a dangerously borderline method Mr. Hemingway's kind of naturalism is. Sometimes it enables him to get close to the skin of sensations; at other times it is little more than a sketchy commentary.

Pritchett turns to the question of Hemingway's way with dialogue, always considered one of the writer's fortes.

> His dialogue depends upon immense eliminations, as well as upon close fidelity to the spoken word. In fact, he relies for his effects more on the suggested and unspoken—or that which cannot be spoken—than is at first apparent. Now this suggestion must be definite and calculated, building up a strong invisible pattern which must increase the potency of the spoken words, otherwise they will be merely realistic, weary, futile, vague. They will drop into perfunctory reporting. The excellence of "The Killers" and of the Indian part of "Fathers and Sons" is in the drilled definiteness of suggestion; the banality of such pieces as "Homage to Switzerland" is due to the fact that it suggests nothing at all. There is a subtle difference between a personal sense of the emptiness of the world, and that sense translated into terms of art. Translation is the difference.[33]

An entirely different view is expressed by the South African poet and novelist William Plomer, who did see enduring merit in *Winner Take Nothing*. Writing in the Spring 1934 issue of *Now and Then*, Plomer moved through his spirited review to this peroration:

> Combined with the motives of protest and escape, and lurking also beneath the manner—the fastidious brutality of this laconic wanderer—there is a genuine nihilism, like that of the waiter in A Clean, Well-Lighted Place who says to himself, "Hail nothing full of nothing, nothing is with thee" and "Our nada who art in nada, nada be thy name." This is partly the nihilism of our time, the time of the War and of our permanent Crisis and of our spiritual dislocation, but it is also the nihilism that so often goes with vitality. Mr. Hemingway's vitality, which has led him into the waiting rooms of Swiss railway stations and the Spanish bullring, to Milan or Kansas City, observing various sorts of people, the French exiles in Wyoming, the bull-fighter who was a "queen," the sick child in bed, or "the biggest whore I ever saw in my life"—this vitality quickens his eye and shapes his style.

In fact, Plomer concludes: "To me he is the most interesting contemporary American short-story writer. Vivid, adroit, and an expert in brevity, he can put more point into an anecdote than many writers can into a novel."[34]

Perhaps the harshest of all commentaries on *Winner Take Nothing* appeared in *Sur*, a journal published in Buenos Aires, in July 1934. In a review of Gertrude Stein's *Autobiography of Alice B. Toklas*, the French translator of *The Sun Also Rises* and *A Farewell to Arms*, Maurice Edgar Coindreau, writes: "One need only open Hemingway's latest volume, *Winner Take Nothing*, to verify" Gertrude Stein's judgments, "which now take on the value of prophecy."

> All those who admired the power, the nervous concision of Ernest Hemingway's first stories cannot but be saddened by the banality of these new tales. Some of them are unforgivable. The only excuse that can be made for their author, as Gertrude Stein puts it, is that he does not know what he is doing. He is unaware that the genre he practices has been cast aside. His boldness does not go beyond words and seems woefully insipid next to the naturalism—violent and sincere—of young writers like Edward Dahlberg, Albert Halper and James T. Farrell. Ernest Hemingway belongs to the past.[35]

No critic since Coindreau has come close to finding the stories in *Winner Take Nothing* to be "irredeemable,"[36] but it cannot be said that subsequent criticism of the collection has done much to overturn Coindreau's judgment entirely. Here are sample views, beginning with Henry Seidel Canby, who was already looking back on Hemingway's achievement in his 1936 book *Seven Years' Harvest: Notes on Contemporary Literature*:

> I find nothing in this volume as poignant as certain sketches of trout fishing (a passionate subject for Hemingway) in earlier writing, or as beautifully organized as the retreat from Caparetto in "A Farewell to Arms," unless it be the dangerously macabre descriptions of horrid death in "A Natural History of Death," [sic] or the hysterical account of fornication in "Fathers and Sons." Yet no one can read of the brute who looks through his water glass at the sunken steamer, with bodies floating inside the port holes, his rudimentary pity only felt, not realized like the frustration of his greed, without hailing one of the most skillful writers of our generation.

"And yet, and yet," Canby admits,

> When you are bored by Hemingway, as I frankly am by a half dozen of these new stories, which are repetitive with the slow pound, pound of a hammer upon a single mood, there is nothing to revive you except flashes of excellent observation.... [Hemingway] is at his best precisely when (if one insists upon regarding him as a novelist) he is at his worst,—when he takes one episode, one phrase of a temperament, one mood, one moment, and eliminating all context, all verbiage, cuts a stencil of it and stamps it on the page with unforgettable incisiveness.[37]

Even more supercilious it the put-down published by *The Saturday Review* (July 1, 1939):

> Set in the low point of the depression, they [these stories] have a curiously remote and irrelevant quality. Indeed, the urgent problems of the depression have made clearer the highly specialized world of Hemingway's hard, tough characters. They seem as much an "escape" from the major issues of the time as the most romantic historical novel, or woman's magazine serial. They are noticed here for the inner emptiness of the characters, the absence of normal human values of the characters.

They fit, as fiction, perfectly into behaviorist psychology; they have action, but no moral absolutes or even moral values that are at all transcendent to immediate conduct.

Hemingway's "much imitated style is an admirable medium for the content. It is a cliché to call it clipped and stripped of verbiage."

> It represents a world clipped and stripped also,—stripped of standard human spiritual equipment. In this sense, they are "grotesques" to the same degree that many of [Erskine] Caldwell's misshapen characters are. That famous style has been described as a combination of "a grunt and a hiatus." There is a notable hiatus where the soul is frequently found. He is an amazingly skilled observer; one has the feeling that if he ever looked at anything really worth describing the result would be great literature. But the game of continually observing and reporting the behavior and speech of a static world of characters much alike, hard, stupid, cruel, greedy and lustful, is not worth the candle of the skill.

The title of the collection, "*Winner Takes Nothing* [sic], strikes the note of futility felt through the stories."

> The central characters do take nothing from life. They are for the most part his favorite primitives, or "simples," hardly distinguishable from morons, some of the inarticulate prizefighters. The opening story, "Fathers and Sons," resolves about a theme of not remarkable freshness, fornication; the hero of "The Mother of a Queen" is a prizefighter [sic] touched with megalomania. The human qualities have been so depleted that a blood transfusion is necessary.
>
> Yet one cannot overlook the fact that in a world in which the reversion to the primitive looms as the most disturbing feature, in which a dehumanized mentality with sadistic gifts runs amuck, the people whom Hemingway records are of real importance. For our present interest, however, the stories give evidence of a fact of first importance about literature and its relation to morals and religion.

For the truth is that "books without any moral standards or any hope of them, especially the ones which pride themselves on such lacks, are beginning to approach the end of a blind street."

> It is hard to keep on making interesting stories out of people who are only game and unafraid and headed for the rocks. The fiction readers have found this out. The writers are finding it out. Alcoholism is all right as a fictional setting for a while, but anyone, even a reader, gets tired of being with people who are tight all the time. He gets tired of being with people who keep on going to bed with each other. It stops being interesting and credible.

This account turns to generalizations about the day's fiction:

> If realistic fiction is to hold its readers today, it must have as much of a moral pattern as has sound contemporary biography. This implies an adherence to no single rule of conduct, nor to a definite set of morals. Fiction is not propaganda. But it does mean that in so far as there is effort in the world toward creation of a better society and the preservation of the spiritual quality in life, fiction must take cognizance of these things or lose its public. All this is a long way around Robin

Hood's barn to say that fiction is no more devoid of moral standards than is life. And at the moment it needs heroes and heroines in the literal sense quite as much as the world does.[38]

In 1941, Oscar Cargill wrote that *Winner Take Nothing* "shows no advance in Hemingway's art nor radical shift in his subject matter. Label the book a grisly calendar of ills or 'typical Hemingway,' and it is sufficiently characterized."[39]

In 1944, Malcolm Cowley wrote that most of the stories in *Winner Take Nothing* are "quieter in tone than the stories in his two earlier collections." Hemingway is now "dealing with the aftermath of tragic events, rather than with the events themselves; and he is writing, often, in a tone of somber resignation."[40] While in a piece for the New York *Times* in 1962, commemorating the first anniversary of Hemingway's death, Maxwell Geismar pointed to the 1930s "as the period of the great dark short-stories of Ernest Hemingway which will remain as his most enduring contribution to world literature." From *Winner Take Nothing* he singled out the high achievement of "The Gambler, the Nun, and Radio" and "A Clean, Well-Lighted Place."[41]

In 1990, Jackson Bryer suggested: "Hemingway's third major collection of short stories, *Winner Take Nothing* (1933), has not attracted as much critical attention as the first two because most of its stories are ignored in favor of a few very popular ones."[42] In the same year, 1990, Brian Harding was a bit more judgmental. "*Winner Take Nothing* has less coherence and is a less consistently powerful volume than either of its predecessors," he wrote, "but its best stories show no slackening in artistic achievement."[43] Harsher in their assessments of the volume are Peter L. Hayes and Matthew J. Bruccoli. Hayes finds "A Clean, Well-Lighted Place" to be a "truly exceptional" story, but finds the rest of the collection "disappointing."[44] Bruccoli agrees that "A Clean, Well-Lighted Place" is a "major story," but this, "the least impressive of Hemingway's three story volumes," is replete with "weak stories," like "The Mother of a Queen," "One Reader Writes," "Homage to Switzerland," and "A Day's Wait."[45] More circumspect is Joseph Flora's observation that *Winner Take Nothing* "reveals Hemingway's continuing wish not to repeat himself and to continue experimenting with form."[46]

The Fourteen Stories

1. *A Mariner's Tale*: "After the Storm"

First published in *Cosmopolitan* (May 1932), "After the Storm" sustains a first-person narrative told in a voice that would reappear (under a different identity) in "One Trip Across," also published in *Cosmopolitan* (Apr. 1934), and "Tradesman's Return," which appeared in *Esquire* (Feb. 1936).

In "After the Storm" the narrator never reveals his name. In the other two stories he is called Harry Morgan and in that identity he (and the two stories that introduced him) found a home in the novel *To Have and Have Not* (1937). It is possible to speculate that Hemingway considered incorporating "After the Storm" into his novel but decided against doing so because he had already used it in a collection of stories. Certainly there is nothing in the characterization or voice of the narrator or in the tale he tells to militate against seeing in him and his tale an early run at the materials he would develop further in *To Have and Have Not*. It is notable, moreover, that the earlier portions of the novel are told as first-person narrations by the tough guy operator of a boat in the Keys, who is much like the narrator of "After the Storm."

Although I would hesitate to argue for a literary connection, namely that Hemingway's story is expressly related to the poem, it is nevertheless instructive to read "After the Storm" against a background provided by Samuel Taylor Coleridge's "The Ancient Mariner."[47] True, there is in Hemingway's story no wedding guest, no wedding feast to be missed, and no truly ancient mariner with glittering eye per se. But there is a mariner with a story to tell about a death ship discovered by emblematic birds first and then by the narrator. It, too, is a story in which the principal can get nothing further out of his experience than the narrative he is now able to tell and, one presumes, retell. And just as there is something of the moral "outlaw" in Coleridge's ancient mariner so, too, is there something of the "outlaw" in Hemingway's narrator. In fact, there is a good deal more of the outlaw in him, for during the period in which he experiences his adventure with the sunken liner he is running from the police.

At this point the differences between the poem and the story become more salient. If Coleridge's narrator tells a deeply mysterious and highly charged tale in a strikingly figurative and symbolic poem, Hemingway's narrator tells his tough-guy's story in a slangy, non-metaphorical, non-poetic, largely unemotional prose that is full of the touches of recreated spontaneous conversation. There are long sentences made up clauses connected by coordinate conjunctions with even less subordination among the thoughts and events narrated than Hemingway taught us to expect in his work. And there are sentences beginning with such flickerings of conversation as "well" and "brother." There is nothing of Coleridge's "high" poetic use of language. Instead there is a highly successful attempt at mimetic speech. Particularly effective, in this regard, is the narrator's thoroughly convincing, if cavalier and slippery, use of such quantitatively imprecise calculations of "all the pelicans in the world" and "all kinds of birds flying," not to mention the unfortunate liner which lies all under water "as big as the whole world." Indeed, in this story, even more so than elsewhere in Hemingway, style is character. It is not only what this would-be scavenger does (and fails to do) that characterizes him but his way of narrating retrospectively—his language, his selectivity, his emphasis: of details, procedure, and feelings. Throughout he tells his listeners how he did things, what worked, what did not work, what he noticed that led him to make accurate inferences about what was hidden under the water and how he might try to get at it. All his feelings, one gathers from his retrospective narration, were tied up in the so-near yet so-finally-impossible quest he undertakes. All his emotions have to do with himself and his craft or trade as a boatman and "treasure" seeker. They are all very human, of course, but they are never humane toward a just-sunk ship with over four hundred bodies on board. To quote the narrator, "There I was looking down through the glass at that liner with everything in her and I was the first one to her and I couldn't get into her. She must have had five million dollars worth in her. It made me shaky to think how much she must have in her." He continues:

> Inside the port hole that was closest I could see something but I couldn't make it out through the water glass. I couldn't do any good with the grains pole and I took off my clothes and stood and took a couple of deep breaths and dove over off the stern with the wrench in my hand and swam down. I could hold on for a second to the edge of the port hole and I could see in and there was a woman inside with her hair floating all out. I could see her floating plain and I hit the glass twice with the wrench hard and I heard the noise clink in my ears but it wouldn't break and I had to come up.

Hemingway focuses on a single body rather than on those of the many who have actually died when the ship went down (he withholds the number of dead until later in the story), not for the pathos surrounding the single death, the single body, that writers, from poets to journalists, can always count upon but to accentuate the disparity between most traditional narratives about such solitary deaths and single bodies and the narrative as this free-lance chooses to tell it. After having had to come up, he hangs onto the dinghy and gets his breath back.

> [T]hen I climbed in and took a couple of breaths and dove again. I swam down and took hold of the edge of the port hole with my fingers and held it and hit the glass as hard as I could with the wrench. I could see the woman floated in the water through the glass. Her hair was tied once close to her head and it floated all out in the water. I could see the rings on one of her hands. She was right up close to the port hole and I hit the glass twice and I didn't even crack it. When I came up I thought I wouldn't make it to the top before I'd have to breathe.

He tries and tries again. In fact, the bulk of the narrative he tells deals in lovingly precise detail of these many attempts and unrelieved failures to get at the unspecified treasure he is sure awaits him. His account is one of technique and procedure. Indeed, in what is almost a parody before the fact of Santiago's defeat by the sharks in Hemingway's 1952 novella *The Old Man and the Sea* Hemingway's narrator concludes his story of failure:

> My head felt cracked open and I lay in the skiff and rested and then I sculled back. It was getting along in the afternoon. I went down once more with the wrench and it didn't do any good. That wrench was too light. It wasn't any good diving unless you had a big hammer or something heavy enough to do good. Then I lashed the wrench to the grains pole again and I watched through the water glass and pounded on the glass and hammered until the wrench came off and I saw it in the glass, clear and sharp, go sliding down along her and then off and down to the quicksand and go in.

He then recognizes that he "couldn't do a thing."

> The wrench was gone and I'd lost the grapple so I sculled back to the boat. I was too tired to get the skiff aboard and the sun was pretty low. The birds were all pulling out and leaving her and I headed for Sou'west Key towing the skiff and the birds going on ahead of me and behind me. I was plenty tired. That night it came on to blow and it blew for a week. You couldn't get out to her.

Not only can he not get out to her but he is arrested for the assault and cutting up of a man that put him on the run in the first place. By the time the weather clears up and he is able to get himself extricated from his troubles with the law, it is too late to get anything out of the sunken liner. The "Greeks" had gotten to her and had "blown her open and cleaned her out. They got the safe out with dynamite. Nobody ever knows how much they got. She carried gold and they got it all. They stripped her clean. I found her and I never got a nickel out of her."

Only then, after he has fully told his own professional story in thoroughly professional terms, does he turn to an account of what he thinks probably happened to the ship when the hurricane struck. He speculates on what probably happened based on where and how the liner has come to rest under water in the quicksand. In the course of such speculation he tells an entirely new, imaginary narrative of what must have happened aboard ship while the captain made his own professional decisions based on what he knew and what he was confronting in the midst of the hurricane.

> Must have been something though when they struck in that rain and wind and he told them to open her tanks. Nobody could have been on deck in that blow and rain. Everybody must have been below. They couldn't have lived on deck. There must have been some scenes inside all right because you know she settled fast. I saw that wrench go into the sand. The captain couldn't have known it was quicksand when she struck unless he knew these waters. He just knew it wasn't rock.

From the bridge "he must have seen it all."

> He must have known what it was about when she settled. I wonder how fast she made it. I wonder if the mate was there with him. Do you think they stayed inside the bridge or do you think they took it outside? They never found any bodies. Not a one. Nobody floating. They float a long way with life belts too. They must have took it inside.

Then, in conclusion, he turns philosophically to a consideration of the spoils he did not get. "Well, the Greeks got it all. Everything. They must have come fast all right. They picked her clean. First there was the birds, then me, then the Greeks, and even the birds got more out of her than I did."

Surely, if the race is not to the swift and the battle to the strong, the spoils in this case have gone to the Greeks, who were swift enough and strong enough to get to the liner third and still they shall be first. Some winners take nothing, some get it all. Others survive, to live in the retelling of the tale of the big one that got away.

2. *In the Shadows*: "A Clean, Well-Lighted Place"

It is no wonder that James Joyce considered "A Clean, Well-Lighted Place" to be "masterly"—"one of the best short stories ever written."[48] Just consider that in this story we not only encounter nihilistic parodies of "The Lord's Prayer" and the beginning of the Catholic prayer to the Virgin recited by the so-called older waiter, but we have, setting up a context for those culminating prayers, a conversation between the two waiters about an old man (a "client") and his unsuccessful attempt at suicide: his failure to commit, in short, the unpardonable sin against the Holy Ghost, an act undertaken in the first place because, as the older waiter explains, the old man was in the state of despair. He was "in despair," the waiter says wryly (in what is, after all, a privately grim joke), about "Nothing." Three times on the opening pages of this dark parable we are told that the old man, in a deliberate echoing of the shadow image of the "Twenty-Third Psalm" ("though I walk through the valley of the shadow of death"), is sitting there in the "shadow" the leaves of the tree made. (But note as well the even closer echo of Luke 1:72 on the purpose of John the Baptist: "To give light to them that sit in darkness and the shadow of death.") The old man, deaf and alone, orders another brandy. The younger waiter pours him one, filling up his glass. But then, in a remarkable literalizing into action of one of the most familiar metaphors employed in the "Twenty-Third Psalm"—"my cup runneth over"—Hemingway writes: "The old man motioned with his finger. 'A little more,' he said. The waiter poured on into the glass so that the brandy slopped over and ran down the stem into the top saucer of the pile."

At one point in "A Clean, Well-Lighted Place," the older waiter tries to spell out just how his situation differs from that of his fellow-waiter. When the latter asserts, "I have confidence. I am all confidence," he replies: "you have youth, confidence, and a job." As for himself, he is no longer young, he acknowledges, and he has never had "confidence." Even as it was for Herman Melville, "confidence" is a key term here. If it can mean something like self-assurance (as it does, undoubtedly, for the younger waiter), it also means "faith"—the Spanish term *confidenza*. Indeed, if the older waiter has never had such *confidenza*, such "faith," then we can feel even more certain, as interpreters of the story's meaning, that his expressions of nihilism are a form of displaying his acedia. The consolations to the believers—to men of faith—that are the "Lord's Prayer" and the prayer to the Virgin Mary are not available to those who lack "confidence," even as the "Twenty-Third Psalm"—labeled in some editions of the Bible as "David's confidence in the Grace of God"—serves only as a repository of sentiments and images that can only be taken ironically by the author who not only constructed parodies of the "Twenty-Third Psalm" but also wrote *A Farewell to Arms* and "A Clean, Well-Lighted Place." To the expansive pastoral consolations of the "Twenty-Third Psalm"—with its "still waters," "paths of righteousness," the "table" prepared "in the presence of … enemies," and the promise of anointment—man can only counter with the narrow virtues of a localized cleanliness and manmade light. For the "house of the Lord" in which the psalmist, confident in the grace of God, shall "dwell … for ever," Hemingway's older waiter offers only the café, "clean, well-lighted," which, though he would "stay late," will perforce close each night while the night is still dark and will remain so long before, ostensibly, the first glimmer of "daylight." "It is probably only insomnia," the waiter says to himself, "many must have it." And indeed they must in Hemingway's peopled world, from the rattled Nick Adams of "Now I Lay Me" (with its ironic titular reference to still another prayer) to the author who himself compulsively parodied the "Twenty-Third Psalm" in the late 1920s, especially in *A Farewell to Arms*, his novel about the loss of confidence in war, love, and self.

Yet the story is not a simpler re-imagining of the implosive matter of the novel. Although the themes of faith and *confidenza* appear and reappear thematically in the novel, the emphasis there is superficially more secular than in the story. In fact, the novel and story differ in this matter nowhere more distinctly than in the way each of the texts handles the shared matter of empty high-mindedness, bankrupt idealism, and the words and beliefs attending both. Although it is not common to relate the two passages, I shall juxtapose here two of the best known excerpts in all of Hemingway. I have in mind the passage from *A Farewell to Arms* in which Lt. Henry identifies the words that embarrass him, along with those that do not, and the sentences from "A Clean, Well-Lighted Place" in which the older waiter utters his prayer to "nada" (echoing the "nothing" in the title *Winner Take Nothing*). The first quotation comes from *A Farewell to Arms*:

> I was always embarrassed by the words sacred, glorious, and sacrifice and the expression in vain. We had heard them sometimes standing in the rain almost out of earshot, so that only the shouted words came through, and had read them, on proclamations, now for a long time, and I had seen nothing sacred, and the things that were glorious had no glory and the sacrifices were like the stockyards at Chicago if nothing was done with the meat except to bury it.

Then he riffs, famously, on the "words" he can no longer stand:

> [There] were many words that you could not stand to hear and finally only the names of places had dignity. Certain numbers were the same way and certain dates and these with the names of the places were all you could say and have them mean anything. Abstract words such as glory, honor, courage, or hallow were obscene beside the concrete names of villages, the numbers of roads, the names of rivers, the numbers of regiments and the dates.[49]

In "A Clean, Well-Lighted Place," it can be noted, there are no words that seem to convey connotations of the idea of "dignity," and when the word "dignity" actually appears, it is used to characterize the erratic gait of the old man, who, as the waiter watched him, "walked unsteadily" down the street "but with dignity." Later the word is used to indicate not its existence but its absence: "Nor can you stand before a bar with dignity." As for the reality behind "words," here is the older waiter's utterance of the "Lord's Prayer":

> Our *nada* who art in *nada*, *nada* be thy name thy kingdom *nada* thy will be *nada* in *nada* as it is in *nada*. Give us this *nada* our daily *nada* and *nada* us our *nada* as we *nada* our *nada*s and *nada* us not into *nada* but deliver us from *nada*; pues *nada*.

To make clear just what is at stake in this prayerful blasphemy of prayer, we need only recall the Catholic prayer itself to see that the older waiter has substituted the word *nada* for, among others, words such as *Father, heaven, hallowed, earth, heaven, day, bread, Forgive, trespasses, temptation, evil* and *Amen*."[50] Denied here—not just their putative value but their very existence—are not the abstract words of *A Farewell to Arms*—like "sacred," "glorious," and "sacrifice," along with the virtues encoded in the expression "in vain"—but all the meaningful words of the "Lord's Prayer," most of which in this context might be considered to be at least as real as those proper names and nominative numbers that still carry meaning for Frederic Henry. If it can be said that the strongest subtext of *A Farewell to Arms* is religious, it is equally clear that in "A Clean, Well-Lighted Place" Hemingway makes that theme fully explicit. In the story he succeeded in again drawing on the same emotional pressure and spiritual capital that energized his novel about a young soldier's memories of his experiences in war and love.

3. *On the Road*: "The Light of the World"

Originally Hemingway wanted to lead off his third collection with "The Light of the World," a favorite story that he had not managed to place in a magazine or journal. The new editor of *Scribner's Magazine*, Alfred Dashiell, found the story too outspoken to print.[51] That the Boston police had pulled the May 1929 issue of the magazine from newsstands because it was serializing *A Farewell to Arms* was still a fresh memory.[52] Hemingway's editor at Scribner's, Maxwell Perkins, who had had problems with what he considered to be obscene language in the original manuscript of *Farewell*,[53] also had qualms over "The Light of the World." If this new story were given first-place prominence in *Winner Take Nothing*, predicted Perkins, its author would once again be accused of deliberately confronting his readers with distasteful language and unacceptable subject matter.[54] Editorial caution prevailed, and it was decided that the story would be placed third, following "After the Storm" and "A Clean, Well-Lighted Place."

But over the years Hemingway continued to hold "The Light of the World" in high esteem. In his preface to *The Fifth Column and the First Forty-nine Stories* (1938), he listed it among the half dozen or so of his stories that he had decided he liked best when he re-read them. In fact, he even found need to complain that "The Light of the World," a story about "whores" that was better, in his estimation, than Guy de Maupassant's "La Maison Tellier," had never been liked by anyone else.[55] Malcolm Cowley went against the grain when he included it in the *Viking Portable Hemingway* in 1944.

"The Light of the World," historically rooted in the tramp and hobo conventions of the 1920s and early 1930s,[56] centers on two teen-aged boys—Nick and Tom—who have taken to the road. In a strange town they walk into a bar, but are treated badly by the bartender. He denies them access to the free lunch bowls until he sees their money. He then uncovers the bowl full of pickled pig's feet. Tom, wanting to pick a fight, complains after one taste: "Your goddam pig's feet stink." But Nick, sensing the danger in the situation, gets him to leave the bar. They then decide to take shelter in the railway station. There they encounter a strangely mixed group, all presumably awaiting the train—"six white men," "four Indians," and "five whores," one of the men, a "cook," asks the boys their ages. Having already picked up on the hints given them by the lumberjacks, who have joked about the cook's being the type who permits being interfered with, the boys answer crudely that they are "ninety-six" and "sixty-nine." At the end of the story, when the cook asks where they are going now, Tom answers, "other way from you."

Of the five women, two of them weigh two hundred fifty pounds each, and a third weighs in at three hundred fifty. The largest one says that her name is Alice. Three others are called Frances, Hazel, and Ethel, respectively, but the fifth one is known only as "the blonde" or "Peroxide." The boys witness an argument between two of the women. They fight over the famous prizefighter Steve Ketchel. Both of them claim to have known him in both senses of the word. Eager to bask in reflected glory, "Peroxide" waxes poetically and sentimentally over Ketchel's body and godlike bearing. But her claim that she was Steve's lover is contradicted by Alice, the largest of the prostitutes, expressing herself wistfully and believably, says conclusively that Ketchel had called her "a lovely piece." Alice's truthfulness is never incontrovertibly established, but that Nick finds her attractive lends psychological credence to her revelation even if her facts and dates are shaky.

"The Light of the World" has evoked considerable critical debate. There has been the attention paid to unraveling the snarl surrounding the confusing names and identities of Steve / Stanley Ketchel. And there have been contradictory views of the way in which the obvious Christian allusion in the story's title contributes to authorial intention. Two principal Scriptural sources for the phrase—statements attributed to Jesus—have been adduced. "I am the light of the world; he that followeth me shall not walk in darkness, but shall have the light of love" (John 8:12) and "Ye are the light of the world" (Matthew 5:14). But according to Carlos Baker, the title of his story probably derives from another source: Holman Hunt's picture, "I am the Light of the World." Hunt "depicts Jesus crowned with thorns, wearing a richly brocaded mantle, holding a starry lantern, and knocking at a cottager's door," writes Carlos Baker. "Copies of this picture were widely distributed in EH's youth. One was Number 93 in a series called Wilde's Bible Pictures. Grace [the author's mother] used a copy as frontispiece to Vol. 4 of her series of scrapbook albums which she kept for EH 1899–1919."[57] Undoubtedly, the young Hemingway saw this illustration and it is entirely likely that Hemingway the writer recalled it when he chose a title for his story. If so, the phrase "Light of the World" seems to refer to Jesus and as such seems naturally to lead the reader to thoughts of the apotheosis of Steve Ketchel by, as it turns out, the somewhat discredited peroxide blonde, whose claims seem to fall before the testimony of Alice (from the Latin *Ali-*

cia, *Alithia*, and the Greek *aletheia*—truth), who cuts down naturalistically the apotheosized Steve Ketchel to the human being he was in his physical beauty and sensual nature.[58] Perhaps, then, the reference to "Light of the World" is sardonic.

That the phrase might well have a different source for Hemingway can be suggested by adducing a third Scriptural authority: Philippians 2:14–15—"Do all things without grumbling ... that you may be blameless and innocent children of God ... among whom you shine as lights in the world, holding fast the word of life...." It is possible, then, if this is the principal source of Hemingway's title, that the author intends to see all the "children" in the story—the lumberjacks, the two boys, the five prostitutes—as not so blameless and innocent children of God, though children of God nevertheless. Ironically, they are the "light(s) of the world," though their shining is dim indeed and surely they do not proceed through this world "without grumbling." For everybody in this story, except those who say nothing and the "shy" man, bicker, argue, and grumble. These, then, are the lights of the world.

One last matter. "The Light of the World" also recalls John Bunyan's *Pilgrim's Progress* (1843) and its satirical sequel Nathaniel Hawthorne's "The Celestial Railroad" (1843), two allegories centering on spiritual traveling, though no one would mistake the travels of Nick and Tom for the spiritual journey of Bunyan's two travelers. "It was laughable," writes Bunyan, "to observe two dusty foot travellers in the old pilgrim guise, with cockle shell and staff, their mystic rolls of parchment in their hands and their intolerable burdens on their backs. The preposterous obstinacy of these honest people in persisting to groan and stumble along the difficult pathway rather than take advantage of modern improvements, excited great mirth among our wiser brotherhood."[59] Closer to Nick and Tom and everyone else in the railroad station are the travelers described by Hawthorne:

> A large number of passengers were already at the station-house awaiting the departure of the cars. By the aspect and demeanor of these persons it was easy to judge that the feelings of the community had undergone a very favorable change in reference to the celestial pilgrimage.... There was much pleasant conversation about the news of the day, topics of business and politics, or the lighter matters of amusement; while religion, though indubitably the main thing at heart, was thrown tastefully into the back-ground.[60]

4. *The Flesh Is Weak*: "God Rest You Merry, Gentlemen"

"God Rest You Merry, Gentlemen" remains an important document for anyone concerned with the paradoxes of Hemingway's personal behavior, the puzzling variety of his literary responses to Christianity, and the implications of his fascination with the professionalism of physicians and surgeons. There is value, therefore, in sorting out the ways in which the structure of the story and its themes both interlock and fail to interlock.

"God Rest You Merry, Gentlemen" has been read in various ways: naturalistically as "a sardonic Christmas tale in which two City Hospital interns argued over the case of a neurotic youth who had emasculated himself from motives of mistaken piety," in psychological terms as the story of a boy's "refusal to accept the stage of puberty at which he has arrived as the extreme of the via negativa," and mythically as an ironic variant of the Fisher King archetype.[61] (It is worth noting, incidentally, that Baker makes two rather significant errors in summarizing the story: (1) the doctors are "ambulance surgeons," not interns, and (2) the boy "mutilates" himself with a razor, but he does not emasculate himself. "Castrated?" asks the narrator. Doc Fischer answers, "No.... He didn't know what castrate meant."[62]) Such readings are not, of course, fully exclusive, although each one of them does depend upon a choice among the perspectives available to the reader. If he assumes one perspective, the story appears to center on the doctors; if he assumes another, it centers on the narrator; when he assumes a third the dying boy is at the center of attention. Without rejecting the particular insights derived from reading the story as exclusively the doctors,' or the boy's, or the narrator's, I would like to present a comprehensive reading of Hemingway's story that calls for a triple focus, and which argues that it is, first, the story—at two removes—of a god-ridden boy in extremis, secondly the story at one remove of two surgeons' personal and professional conflicts, and finally—directly—the narrator's story.

In the dramatic present of the story, "Horace" (we are never certain whether that is his actual name or merely a sardonic nickname) reports on a conversation in a hospital reception room among two ambulance surgeons (Wilcox and Fischer) and himself. He recalls a Christmas day when seemingly casual remarks on the dinner he had just eaten and on Dr. Wilcox's ineffectual medical training (he relies exclusively upon an indexed copy of *The Young Doctor's Friend and Guide*) led to a discussion of the fate of a young boy who, plagued by the fortunes of lust, had tried to castrate himself. The conversation concluded, he tells us, with rather short-tempered bickering over the matters of Christianity, Jesus, and the Jews.

It is important to emphasize that the dying boy's drama is played out retrospectively in the consciousness, first of the two doctors, and then in the narrator's, for the boy himself is never actually present. And even though the boy's drama is in itself important, their dwelling upon it has the indirect effect of revealing the callous ineptitude of the one doctor and the helpless sympathy of the other. Through direct and oblique references Hemingway creates a context for the boy's actions and the relative "Christianity" displayed by the two ambulance surgeons.

Hemingway's title echoes both the Christmas carol from which it derives and the Scriptural source of the carol itself: the physician Luke's account of Satan's power over the flesh and the Savior's role in keeping men safe from that power. There are other suggestions that the boy's story should be read in the context established by echoes of the New Testament. We learn, for instance, that Horace has "partaken" of the free Christmas turkey dinner at the Woolf Brothers' saloon.

> "Well, Horace," Doc Fischer said as I came in the receiving room which smelt of cigarettes, iodoform, carbolic and an over-heated radiator.
> "Gentlemen," I said.
> "What news along the Rialto?" Doc Fischer asked. He affected a certain extravagance of speech which seemed to me to be of the utmost elegance.
> "The free turkey at Woolf's," I answered.
> "You partook?"
> "Copiously."
> "Many of the confrères present?"
> "All of them. The whole staff."
> "Much Yuletide cheer?"
> "Not much."
> "Doctor Wilcox here has partaken slightly," Doc Fischer said. Doctor Wilcox looked up at him, then at me.
> "Want a drink?" he asked.[63]

Few readers will immediately make much of Fischer's extravagant speech, particularly of his seemingly harmless play on the inflated idea of "partaking" by the "confrères." Later, however, after the reader has heard of the boy's losing battle against what he considers to be lust, he will recall that "confrère" refers, ambiguously, to, among other things, a fellow-member of a religious order and a fellow-member of a learned profession or scientific body. Moreover, he will see the exchange over the idea of "partaking" in a new light. The New Testament provides the context for the doctor's use of the term: "our fathers ... did all eat the same spiritual meat; and did all drink the same spiritual drink," insists Paul:

> [T]hese things were our examples, to the intent we should not lust after evil things.... Neither let us commit fornication.... There hath no temptation taken you but such as is common to man; but God is faithful, who will not suffer you to be tempted above that ye are able; but will with the temptation also make a way to escape, that ye may be able to beat it.... The bread which we break, is it not the communion of the body of Christ? ... for we are all partakers of that one bread ... ye cannot be partakers of the Lord's table, and of the table of devils [I Corinthians 10:1–21].

But Horace is not the only one present who has "partaken." Doctor Wilcox, it will be recalled, has also "partaken" (and is indeed still drinking); and his feast, if not the other, is less than spiritual.

Fischer then goes on to introduce the matter of the boy's self-mutilation:

"Good old Horace. We've had an extremely interesting case."
"I'll say," said Doctor Wilcox.
"You know the lad who was in here yesterday?"
"Which one?"
"The lad who sought eunuch-hood."

Here the conversation, equally sardonic, recalls Matthew: "there are some eunuchs ... which have made themselves eunuchs for the kingdom of heaven's sake" (19–12).

The boy in Kansas City has been tempted far beyond, undoubtedly, that which he could bear and withstand. And his attempt at achieving "eunuch-hood" is his attempt at escaping "that awful lust," as he calls it, which is a sin "against our Lord and Saviour." We learn that the boy had refused to listen to Fischer's physiological explanation for his libidinous feelings, and that at one point Wilcox, inadvertently speaking more truth than he understood, called the boy "just a goddamned fool." Fischer then changed his tack with the boy. "You have a fine body," he told him, "and you must not think about that. If you are religious remember that what you complain of is no sinful state but the means of consummating a sacrament." But just as he was not receptive to a clinical explanation, the boy would have nothing of this argument. "'I can't stop it happening,' the boy said. 'I pray all night and I pray in the daytime. It is a sin, a constant sin against purity'" ("all things, whatsoever ye shall ask in prayer, believing, ye shall receive" was Jesus' promise [Matthew 21:22]). Whereupon Doctor Wilcox solemnly advised the boy to "'go and jack-off.'"

Their cross-purposes account of the boy's tragedy at an end, the two doctors fall to sniping at one another over such matters as Christianity and Jesus the Savior. The one, a would-be fisher of men, looks "at his hands that had, with his willingness to oblige and his lack of respect for Federal statutes, made him his trouble," and he refers ironically to the birth of Jesus and to the ambivalence in the "Saviour's" triumphant ride into Jerusalem on Palm Sunday. Fischer is then reminded by Wilcox, the Christian, that Jesus is not the Jew's Saviour.

When we read "God Rest You Merry, Gentlemen" as the boy's history, we find that it centers on one of the most puzzling and excruciating of all Christian antinomies. The human body, according to Paul, is "the temple of God, and the Spirit of God dwelleth" in it (1 Corinthians 3:16). Moreover, he warns, "if any man defile the temple of god, him shall god destroy; for the temple of Gods is holy which temple ye are" (3:17). Can it be said with certainty, then, that in mutilating himself the boy has defiled "the temple of God" that is his body? The world might well decide that he has. But Paul's warning is pointed: "Let no man deceive himself. If any man among you seemeth to be wise in this world, let him become a fool [as Wilcox had called the boy], that he may be wise. For the wisdom of this world is foolishness with God" (3:18–19); and, indeed, in Paul's terms, it is not necessarily mutilation or self-inflicted eunuch-hood that defiles the body, but rather fornication. "Know ye not that your bodies are the members of Christ?" he asks. "Shall I then take the members of Christ, and make them the members of an harlot? ... he that commiteth fornication sinneth against his own body" (6:15–18).

Is the boy's fate an exemplum for those who would follow Pauline dictates on purity of the self by obeying the strictures against lust and sin? Or is he an example to those who would attempt to apply Christian teachings literally in a secular world? Answers to these questions would help us to decide just how ironic or transcendent Hemingway intended his title to be.

Thus far we have been concerned with "God Rest You Merry, Gentlemen" primarily as the boy's story. But if it were only his story, we would be hard pressed to account for the particular narrative structure Hemingway employs. No reading can ignore the fact that at one remove the boy's drama is imbedded in the consciousness of the two doctors and that it is the immediate source of their own conflict. If the boy's religious pre-occupation with purity and lust and the consequences of that obsession form one center of meaning, then the relationship of the two doctors and the drama generated out of their different responses to the "case" form a second center.

What emerges between Dr. Wilcox and Doc Fischer from the latter's account of the boy's experience is a conflict of private emotions thrown up against professional objectivity. It would form an overly neat pattern if one doctor embodied the idea of emotional commitment while the other one embodied that of unalterable professional objectivity. Since the author pursues a theme and not a thesis, however, he complicates the neat conflict of emotional involvement versus professional neutrality. The doctor who bodies forth, unprofessionally, excessive emotional involvement is also, in skills, the better practitioner of medicine. That is to say, he knows more about the science and practice of medicine than does his colleague. The doctor who is objective and unfeeling, on the other hand, is not at all well-versed in medicine. The objectivity he manifests is a direct function of his personal callousness. It is an irony that a modicum of medical knowledge, one surmises, combined with his objectivity, might have made him an effective practitioner. While, on the other hand, it is clear that it is his very human concern, despite his skill and knowledge, which makes the second doctor less effective. For example, there is the broad but clear hint that Doc Fischer's difficulty with Federal statutes which has caused his banishment from coastal hospitals is the result, probably, of his having performed an abortion. (Given the sexual-religious-professional themes of Hemingway's story, it seems far more likely, I think, that Doc Fischer had performed abortions than that his difficulties resulted from, say, his having aided "fugitive criminals without reporting that aid."[64])

Hemingway's sympathies lie with the doctor whose affections have not been neutralized by training to the detriment of his human sympathies. But, as Hemingway senses, these very sympathies feed back on the doctor's effectiveness so as to render him all-too-conscious of his own helplessness. The boy has twice needed his help, and twice he has failed him. Dr. Wilcox would put the entire matter aside. Dr. Fischer broods upon it, trying to overwhelm his pity with irony and anger.

While the nested narrative structure of this story calls for a perspectivist reading, such a reading points, finally, to the story's principal deficiency. As we have seen, perspectivism works reasonably well in directing us to the thematic and dramatic strands which connect the twice-deflected story (the boy's) to the "remembered" story (the doctors'); but it also reveals that there are no solid connections between them and the first-person story (the narrator's). When we focus on the narrator, we soon discover that Hemingway has simply not given us enough information. "Horace" reveals so little of himself (hardly more than that he was once so callow a youth as to think that "Dans Argent" meant "silver dance or the silver dancer") that it seems bootless to try to discover his reason for telling us about what he has heard in the ambulance waiting room.

The narrator has bothered other readers, who have found his character, insofar as its lines can be determined, unnecessary to the tale. Julian Smith, however, proposes a solution to this problem.[65] "God Rest You Merry, Gentlemen" reads best, his argument runs, when it is recognized that it belongs within the context of the characters and action of *The Sun Also Rises*, for the narrator's personal remarks at the beginning of the story take on meaning only when we realize that "Horace" is really the young, still undamaged Jake Barnes. Such a reading sees "Horace" as a witness at second hand to a situation he will understand fully only after he has himself experienced an amputation. The argument appeals, and if one were preparing a psychograph of the author's life and work such an explanation might usefully fit the story into place. But even so, it fails to explain away the aesthetic weakness of the story. To fill in the narrator's biographical void with the whole of *The Sun Also Rises* upsets the nice balance between the other two centers of the story. Curiously, even the proponent of the Jake Barnes—Horace theory seems to recognize this: "To see the story as about anyone but the narrator is to negate all the narrator tells us about himself, to make him superfluous," he writes. "Yet on the evidence within the story, he seems totally unnecessary, and the story seems lacking in focus." Having built his story around perspectives, Hemingway fails to weld the narrator's to the others. The consequence, one concludes, is that the structure of "God Rest You Merry, Gentlemen" sets up expectations that are not satisfactorily fulfilled.

5. *The Other Woman*: "The Sea Change"

When "The Sea Change" appeared in the pages of *This Quarter* in 1931, an anonymous reviewer for the Paris edition of the *Chicago Tribune* predicted that the "theme of his story would cause more editors to think twice, or possibly oftener, before running it, despite the essentially chaste character of Hemingway's writing."[66] If times and mores have changed such that no editor would think twice about advisability or propriety of printing any good or even satisfactory story on the theme of same-sex love or alliance, it is useful to recall that Hemingway had every right to count on the shock that his daring (though not entirely explicit) story would have on the average reader of fiction in his day. What was left out of the story he revealed, years later, in "The Art of the Short Story," a preface for a volume of his collected stories that did not materialize: "In a story called 'A Sea Change' [sic], everything is left out," he wrote. "I had seen the couple in the Bar Basque in St.-Jean-de-Luz and I knew the story too too well, which is the squared root of well, and use any well you like except mine. So I left the story out. But it is all there. It is not visible but it is there."[67] It is possible, I think, to try to get at some of the story (or stories) that Hemingway "left out" of "The Sea Change."

In his own way Tennessee Williams tries to get at the same thing. In *Clothes for a Summer Hotel: A Ghost Play*, a 1980 work about Scott and Zelda Fitzgerald, there is an inaccuracy about Hemingway that should interest students of both authors in general and readers of "The Sea Change" in particular. In the second act the characters Ernest and Scott hold the following puzzling conversation. Scott speaks:

> I'm trying to recall a certain story of yours. The title doesn't come back to me right now but the story does. An Italian officer has been removed from any contact with women for weeks or months in some snowbound Alpine encampment during the war, the First. He has a young orderly waiting on him, a boy with the sort of androgynous appeal that you said I had in wherever after Lyon.—At last he asks

the boy if he's engaged. The boy says he is married. He says it blushing, avoiding the officer's eyes, and goes out quickly. The officer wonders—significantly—if the boy was lying about it.

Hemingway answers:

> I've also written a story called "Sea Change" about a couple, young man and older young man, on a ship sailing to Europe and—at first the younger man is shocked, or pretends to be shocked, by the older one's—attentions at night. However the "sea change" occurs and by the end of the voyage, the protesting one is more reconciled to his patron's attention.[68]

In this exchange Scott is trying to recall the story "A Simple Enquiry" from *Men Without Women* (1927). An Italian military officer—a major—asks his young orderly whether he has ever been in love with a woman, not whether he is engaged, and he answers that he is in love with a girl now. He does not claim to be married. As for the story described by the Hemingway of Williams' "ghost play," it is not entitled "Sea Change." In fact, the "story" carries no title and appears only as part of the otherwise undifferentiated text of *Death in the Afternoon*, Hemingway's big book on Spanish bullfighting and his ars poetica.[69] Unlike the story Hemingway called "The Sea Change," this untitled "story" does tell of two young American men who reach an accommodation after considerable resistance on the part of the younger of the two men, and it takes place in a Paris hotel rather than on a ship. "The Sea Change," of course, is another matter. Rather than a story about two men, it will be recalled, it tells a tale about a man's response to the fact that his lover is leaving him for another woman.

One result of Williams' conflation of story and title is that we can now consider the notion that "The Sea Change" makes as good a title for the untitled story in *Death in the Afternoon* as for the Hemingway story that does carry it. After all, Williams' disremembering was a writer's lapse, which is to say, that there is almost certainly, if perhaps inadvertently, something creative in it.

In the midst of their quarrel the male half of the "handsome young couple" whose sentimental life constitutes the substance of "The Sea Change" quotes some lines from the poetry of Alexander Pope. At least he makes an effort to quote from the "Essay on Man," Epistle II, not quite getting the lines right. He wants this:

> Vice is a monster of so frightful mien,
> As to be hated needs but to be seen;
> Yet seen too oft, familiar with her face,
> We first endure, then pity, then embrace.[70]

What he remembers, however, is this: "Vice is a monster of such fearful mien ... that to be something or other needs but to be seen. Then we something, something, then embrace."

He sets off this quotation, carrying the modernist's authority of the poetic allusion, in an argument with a woman who will in a few minutes leave him for someone else. He intends it, apparently, as a way to stigmatize the new relationship—between two women—that will replace the relationship he has had with this woman. She will have none of this characterization. "'Let's not say vice,' she said. 'That's not very polite.'" He then counters with "perversion."

> "I'd like it better if you didn't use words like that," the girl said. "There's no necessity to use a word like that."
> "What do you want me to call it?"
> "You don't have to call it. You don't have to put any name to it."
> "That's the name for it."
> "No," she said. "We're made up of all sorts of things. You've known that. You've used it well enough."
> "You don't have to say that again."
> "Because that explains it to you."
> "All right," he said. "All right."
> "You mean all wrong. I know. It's all wrong."

What impresses the reader most is that the man and the woman argue about words. What, specifically, or what not to name this thing that has happened between the woman of the "smooth golden brown" skin and "blonde" hair and another woman (who is not described)? Whether it should be called a "vice" or a "perversion" or neither of those terms, it is a thing that, though unnamed, is "all wrong." That they have agreed upon. And they agree further that the woman will return to him.

> "'Yes,' he said. 'That's the hell of it. You probably will.'"
> "'Of course I will,'" she replies.
> "'Go on, then.'"

A moment later she leaves the café, alone. He gets up from the table, picks up the two checks, and walks over to the bar.

The author-narrator then tells us that this man was "not the same-looking man as he had been before he had told her to go." And Phil (as he is called by the woman, whose own name, incidentally, is never given) agrees with the author.

> "I'm a different man, James," he said to the barman. "You see in me quite a different man."
> "Yes, sir?" said James.
> "Vice," said the brown young man, "is a very strange thing, James." He looked out the door. He saw her going down the street. As he looked in the glass, he saw he was really quite a different-looking man.

When next he looks at himself in the mirror behind the bar, he again finds confirmation that he is "a different man." "Looking in to the mirror he saw that this was quite true." It is only with the conclusion of the narrative that we see that there are two possible meanings for the title of the story, a phrase taken from Shakespeare's *The Tempest*. There have been two possible changes wrought by the "sea" of (Phil's) love's experience, both of them modifying the nature of the primary relationship of the couple that is so "tanned" at the end of the summer that they look "out of place in Paris." The woman will leave her male companion for a woman (signifying what looks like an unexpected change, at least temporarily, in her sexual orientation), and the man will himself, as he discovers in the course of their quarrel, acquiesce to the new arrangement. It may even be, as has been argued, that the man is a writer and that it is the writer in him that encourages him to acquiesce in the woman's change of love partner so that when she returns to him she will make him privy to "forbidden" experience he can then transform into the better thing that is his art.[71] Be that as it may, vice is a strange thing, as Pope goes on to explain in the "Essay on Man" just ten lines below those alluded to by the well-tanned young man:

> Virtuous and vicious ev'ry man must be,
> Few in the extreme, but all in the degree;
> The rogue and fool by fits is fair and wise;
> And ev'n the best, by fits, what they despise
> 'Tis but by parts we follow good or ill;
> For, vice or virtue, self directs it still;
> Each individual seeks a several goal;
> But Heaven's great view is one, and that the whole.[72]

The young man, because of the self-knowledge he has gained through this very experience, now reacts less self-righteously to the woman's decision to leave him than he had apparently thought possible. This is the "sea change" Phil (love) has undergone. Just how virtuous he is entitled to feel, however, is a question answered implicitly by his look at himself "in the glass," a narcissistic act he repeats by immediately afterwards seeing himself in the mirror behind the bar. For regardless of the change he sees in himself, others see him differently. And that's a truth, too. After all, the barman tells him, "'You look very well, sir.... You must have had a very good summer.'"

Interestingly enough, "The Sea Change" has a sequel, published a quarter of a century later. "Get a Seeing-Eyed Dog," first published in the *Atlantic Monthly* (December 20, 1957), takes up a much later incident in the lives of the man and the woman in the earlier story. Although the later story reads independently (even as the related stories "The End of Something" and "The Three Day Blow" from *In Our Time* read separately), it takes on an odd significance in the Hemingway canon when the link is made.

In "Get a Seeing-Eyed Dog," Phil and the still unnamed woman, both now middle-aged, are still "together." The man, whom the woman now calls, more distantly, "Philip," has gone blind. The story moves, like the earlier one, on the existing tension between the two of them. The woman insists that she wants to stay with him but he is certain that she must go away. It is evident that he is not handling his blindness well and thinks, as he suggests to her, that she should go to Paris and London. "[You] could have some fun and then you'd come back and it would have to be spring by then," he encourages, "and you could tell me all about everything." She refused to go, of course, and he persists—but to no avail. "I just don't want to be sent away," she implores; to which he answers disingenuously (for he's still silently plotting), "nobody is ever going to send you away."

The two stories revolve around the issue of the woman's going away. In the first one, it is she who wants to leave and the man who wants her to stay. In the second one, she wants to stay and the man wants her to go. At the end of the first story, the man makes much of the fact that he sees himself in a mirror. In the second story the only sight left to him is the possibility of insight (and resulting self-knowledge), and he does not seem to have very much of that.

Curiously, there is also a Fitzgerald-like cast to Hemingway's stories about "Phil." In *A Moveable Feast* he writes: "Scott was very much in love with Zelda and he was very jealous of her. He told me many times on our walks of how she had fallen in love with the French navy pilot. But she never made him really jealous with another man since. This spring she was making him jealous with other women...."[73] The writing of "Get a Seeing-Eyed Dog" seems to have been entwined with Hemingway's memories of Scott and Zelda.

When the *Atlantic Monthly* asked him to write something for their centenary number, he decided that he didn't want "to take a chunk out of a book nor give them stories [he] was doubtful about" or that were not suitable for the *Atlantic*, so he decided to write something "that would be worthwhile and good for them," and he started to write about Fitzgerald and how he first met him. But, as he wrote further in his letter to [Harvey] Breit of 16 June 1957, he had qualms about sending this portrait of Fitzgerald and wrote them a good story about "out west."[74]

What Hemingway finally sent the *Atlantic* was two stories, "A Man of the World" and "Get a Seeing-Eyed Dog," which the *Atlantic* published in November 1957.

Jacqueline Tavernier-Courbin offers a different kind of evidence for the connection between "Get a Seeing-Eyed Dog" and the F. Scott Fitzgeralds. "There are in fact three versions of this story, one of which is quite different from the other two," she tells us.

> The version in File 648b features the same characters as File 529a—James Allen and Dorothy Rogers—and the stories are similar. The version in File 648a, however, differs significantly from the other two, and the name of the male protagonist is Philip Haines. What seems particularly important about the version in File 529a is that starting with page eleven it is written on the same type of rather peculiar paper as the draft of his meeting Fitzgerald (File 486). This suggests that the two sketches were probably written during the same period, although it is not in itself sufficient proof.[75]

Tavernier-Courbin's account also supplies some physical or material evidence: "The stationery used here is an uncommon one for Hemingway to use: long and narrow (8 × 13 inches), heavier than usual, with perpendicular lines in the grain. In his attempts at dating Files 648a and 648b, Donald Junkins points to their geographic and tonal intimacy with *A Moveable Feast*. However, he does not mention File 529a, which establishes a tangible link with the book."[76]

Circumstantial evidence such as this, when combined with a biographically based reading of the text, along with Hemingway's having sent on "Get a Seeing-Eyed Dog" in (part) replacement for the piece on Fitzgerald, links it to the earlier story, "The Sea Change," and strengthens the possibility that both stories are rooted in Hemingway's knowledge of the details of Zelda and Scott's shared life, especially Zelda's ability to make Scott "jealous with other women."[77]

6. Parading the Uniform: "A Way You'll Never Be"

"I thought the war story a very fine story, almost felt as if I were 'that way' myself when I read it, and for sometime after it. It is a curious story, and most effective."[78] This was the immediate response of Max Perkins, Hemingway's editor at Scribner's, to "A Way You'll Never Be." His quiet enthusiasm, however, was not shared by reviewers of *Winner Take Nothing*. In fact, it took a while for the story to catch on with Hemingway's critics, years before Kenneth Lynn, for instance, called it "another eerie Nick Adams masterpiece and the outstanding story" in *Winner Take Nothing*.[79]

At the heart of the literary character and personality of Nick Adams in "A Way You'll Never Be" lies something that is never named. That unspecified thing is a source of fear and considerable apprehension. "He felt it coming on now. He would quiet down." Later there is this exchange:

"All right," said Nick. He felt it coming on again.
"You understand?"
"Of course," said Nick. He was trying to hold it in.
"Anything of that sort should be done at night."
"Naturally," said Nick. He knew he could not stop it now.
"You see, I am commanding the battalion," Para said.
"And why shouldn't you be?" Nick said.
Here it came. "You can read and write, can't you?"
"Yes," said Para gently.

Hemingway never, in so many words, explains what "it" is, but there are enough details given when "it" occurs to reveal that the term stands for a mental episode in which Nick loses control over his thoughts and feelings, over his very words. These are episodes in which he lashes out, sometimes sardonically, at other times illogically, with no respect for immediate relevance. One of the ways Nick knows "it" is upon him is that he finds himself talking too much. He is also conscious of when such episodes have ended. "'You don't need to worry,' Nick said. 'I'm all right now for quite a while. I had one then but it was easy. They're getting much better. I can tell when I'm going to have one because I talk so much.'"

Only toward the end of this story about the wounded Nick Adams's mental condition do we learn that, far from having recovered sufficiently to warrant his return to active service, he has found himself compelled to revisit an old war scene, which has just been the scene of a fresh battle in which the dead have not yet been gathered and buried. Indeed, he finds himself physically within the landscape which so dominates his recurrent nightmares. Indeed, Nick alternates between periods of lucid observation and episodes in which his mind spins off on its own. At the outset he very skillfully determines just how the battle for this piece of terrain was waged by seeing how the corpses are deployed and the debris scattered: "The attack had gone across the field, been held up by machine-gun fire from the sunken road and from the group of farm houses, encountered no resistance in the town, and reached the bank of the river. Coming along the road on a bicycle, getting off to push the machine when the surface of the road became too broken, Nicholas Adams saw what had happened by the position of the dead." The clarity and reasonableness with which he views this scene strewn with bodies, paper, the implements and weapons of war can be compared with the rush of incoherent thought and semi-coherent images when an episode ("it") happens to him while he lies resting on a bunk:

> Keep behind them, sergeant. It's no use to walk ahead and find there's nothing coming behind you. Bail them out as you go. What a bloody balls. All right. That's right. Then, looking at the watch, in that quiet tone, that valuable quiet tone, "Savoia."

9. Winner Take All 115

> Making it cold, no time to get it, he couldn't find his own after the cave-in, one whole end had caved in; it was that started them; making it cold up that slope the only time he hadn't done it stinking. And after they came back the *teleferica* house burned, it seemed, and some of the wounded got down four days later and some did not get down, but we went up and we went back and we came down——we always came down.

Then he thinks of a figure from the past.

> And there was Gaby Delys, oddly enough, with feathers on; you called me baby doll a year ago tadada you said I was rather nice to know tadada with feathers on, with feathers off, the great Gaby, and my name's Harry Pilcer, too, we used to step out of the far side of the taxis when it got steep going up the hill and he could see that hill every night when he dreamed with Sacré Coeur, blown white, like a soap bubble.

At times, in the midst of conversation, he gets locked into the literalness of a simile, having originally intended only to make a figurative comparison. Watch how something snaps in his brain and his mind just takes off in mid-thought:

> "I am demonstrating the American uniform," Nick said. "Don't you think it is very significant? It is a little tight in the collar but soon you will see untold millions wearing this uniform swarming like locusts. The grasshopper, you know, what we call the grasshopper in America, is really a locust. The true grasshopper is small and green and comparatively feeble. You must not, however, make a confusion with the seven-year locust or cicada which emits a peculiar sustained sound which at the moment I cannot recall. I try to recall it but I cannot. I can almost hear it and then it is quite gone. You will pardon me if I break off our conversation?"

What conversation?—it might well be asked. Nor is Nick through with the subject of the American locust, for he returns to it, going on and on about its suitability for fishing, along with offering a disquisition on how to seine for them. The problem, of course, as his friend the captain readily discerns, is that Nick has not recovered from the trauma and shell-shock resulting from his head-wounds.

> What has burrowed into his brain are the vivid scenes of violent death. For this young veteran, who now "can't sleep without a light of some sort," the change within him is one of both perception and memory. Of his cloth-covered helmet, he can say only that it is "a damned nuisance wet or dry." "'You know they're absolutely no damned good,' Nick said. 'I remember when they were a comfort when we first had them, but I've seen them full of brains too many times.'" Of course, given such memories, the helmet is a nuisance. So, too, is it "a hell of a nuisance once they've had you certified as nutty," complains Nick. "No one ever has any confidence in you again."

The captain sees the fragility (and worse) of Nick's psychological state and would send him "back"—away from the front lines with a "runner" to get him there safely. But Nick appeals to his old friend not to do it.

"I'd rather you didn't. I know the way."
"You'll be back soon?"
"Absolutely."
"Let me send ___"
"No," said Nick. "As a mark of confidence."
"Well, *ciaou* then."
"*Ciaou*," said Nick.

Nick wins this small victory, but he is not yet, psychologically, fit for making his way back along the sunken road toward the place where he had left his bicycle, his thoughts and memories begin to get jumbled up again. "It was on that stretch that, marching, they had once passed the Terza Savoia cavalry regiment riding in the snow with their lances. The horses' breath made plumes in the cold air. No, that was somewhere else. Where was that?" It is no wonder that Nick begins to get nervous. "'I'd better get to that damned bicycle,' Nick said to himself. 'I don't want to lose the way to Fornaci.'" It's not much, finding his way to Fornaci, but it is something to hold on to.

7. *Roger's Version*: "The Mother of a Queen"

"The Mother of a Queen" has attracted very little critical attention. The notable exception is Sheldon Grebstein, who was the first critic to question the reliability of the narrator Roger.[80] He tells the story of an erstwhile friend, a bullfighter who has allowed his mother's remains to be removed from the cemetery and thrown on the public bone-heap. The nagging thing about Roger, of course, is that he does not tell us anything about his own motives.

What motives can Roger have for so telling his story about Paco that everything the bullfighter does and says seems to redound to his discredit? Grebstein's answer is that Roger is so envious of the other man that he selects and colors the details of his narrative such that he himself will appear superior to the young man whom he has once served as manager. Hence, he will tell you that he himself is better at driving the bullfighter's car, for example, than is its owner. This boast, whether it has any basis or not, reveals that there is some ulterior motive for the story he tells and the way he tells it.

One key to "The Mother of a Queen" is that it functions like a dramatic monologue. It shows the telltale marks of that literary form, with the major exception that it is written in prose. The first person point of view is maintained faithfully from beginning to end. This narrator directs his story at a listener who, although unnamed and uncharacterized, is present during the telling of the story of the Mexican bullfighter and his behavior over the matter of his mother's remains. "Sure he's a queen, didn't you know that, of course he is," the narrator addresses his implied listener early on. The monologue, while ostensibly revealing to us a great deal about the homosexual bullfighter, generates several interesting questions about the narrator and the nature of his own relationship to the bullfighter.

What do we learn about him? First of all, there are several indications that he is not Mexican or Spanish. We learn, when he quotes the bullfighter, that his name is "Roger." And then there is the otherwise odd way in which he switches, in talking about money, from dollars to pesos and back again to dollars. It cost "only twenty dollars" for perpetual care for the bullfighter's mother's grave, but he won't cover the amount even though he is paid at the rate of "four thousand pesos" for each of the six fights of his contract, which in Madrid alone comes to more than "fifteen thousand pesos." The narrator claims that he is owed some six hundred pesos, a debt the bullfighter tries to pay off for "twenty pesos," even as he gives "fifty pesos" to a "punk" (as Roger calls him) from his hometown. It is as if he is talking with another American.

While the bullfighter is in Madrid, the narrator takes care of matters back in Mexico, paying out over six hundred pesos of his own money to cover the bullfighter's accounts. After Paco returns to Mexico, the narrator keeps his "cash box." This reveals that the narrator has replaced the manager who had originally, when the bullfighter was still a kid, buried his father "perpetually," but who, later, when his mother died, buried her for only five years. The reason for the difference in the manager's behavior, the narrator tells us, is that the manager "thought they might not always be so hot on each other." It is the narrator who reveals that they were "sweethearts," that the bullfighter is a "queen." After they argue, the narrator addresses him as "you motherless bitch." The narrator's eagerness to brand the bullfighter in this way right at the outset and his choice of epithet, along with the fact that he has the use of the bullfighter's car and must get his "things" from Paco's "place," suggest that the exact nature of the narrator's relationship to the "queen" requires specification. That at one time Roger and Paco were lovers seems to be the fact that lies behind the malice with which the narrator disapproves of the bullfighter's every move. When he sneers at the bullfighter's "trying to make himself seem a man and fool people" by "spending all kinds of money around women" and when, meeting Paco, "this year," on the Gran Via in Madrid, Roger tells him what he thinks of him in front of his "three friends," the narrator seems to be behaving rather "bitchy" himself. This is not to say, however, that there is any compelling reason to question the literal truth of the narrator's account of the bullfighter's failure to attend to the matter of his mother's grave or the accuracy of his quotation of Paco's explanation, after his mother's bones have been dumped on the public bone heap, that "Now she is so much dearer to me. Now I don't have to think of her buried in one place and be sad. Now she is all about me in the air, like the birds and the flowers. Now she will always be with me." There is good reason, though, to examine Roger's own undisclosed motives for telling the story he tells and particularly for telling it in the way he chooses to tell it. It reads like a tale told by a lover scorned, and it is told so as to put the worst possible construction on an old friend's character. After all, a "queen" who would do that to his own mother cannot be said to have had a mother. Such a "queen," the narrator implies, is capable of even worse, for "you can't touch them"—"they never pay." Yet isn't there something to be said for Paco's even-tempered reaction to Roger's attacks, a quality that comes through even in Roger's jaundiced narration? After all, it is Roger who goes around saying unpleasant things about his old friend. He himself quotes Paco without denying the truth of his statements: "People say you are talking against me. That you say all sorts of unjust things about me."[81]

There's something suspect is Roger's monologue. Unwittingly, he reveals even more of himself than he does of the friend who never pays. We have only to listen to his talk.[82]

8. *Borrowed and Blue*: "One Reader Writes"

At first glance "One Reader Writes" looks very like a chapter left out of Nathanael West's crisp novella *Miss Lonelyhearts*. The resemblance does not appear to be entirely coincidental, for West's book was published on April 8, 1933,[83] while *Winner Take Nothing* was published almost seven months later, on October 27, 1933.[84] Yet Hemingway always claimed that "One Reader Writes" was one of those stories he wrote directly from life, just as it had happened—to distinguish it from those stories that he had invented in their entirety.[85] His claim that this was so is supported by Carlos Baker, who gives us details about how "One Reader Writes" grew out of Hemingway's friendship with a Kansas City physician:

> Dr. Logan Clendenning ... conducted a syndicated medical column, and his daily mailbag was crammed with instances of human woe. He sent Ernest a sheaf of six letters from his correspondents, including one from a woman in Harrisburg, Pennsylvania, whose husband had contracted syphilis while serving with the United States Marines in Shanghai. She has asked the doctor whether or not it would ever again be safe for her to cohabit with her husband. Ernest edited the letter slightly, changing the date and the place-name, and adding a short introduction and conclusion.[86]

There is no reason to question the facts given by Baker. Yet there is no denying that in West's novel, employing as its protagonist the writer of a sob-sister column and offering examples of the kind of letter that readers of such columns would write to the likes of "Miss Lonelyhearts," lay a repository of literary precedents.

The woman in Hemingway's story addresses her letter to a doctor, whose writings appear regularly enough in the newspaper to have his picture printed in its pages. Ostensibly she writes for advice. Can she ever hope to live again with her serviceman husband, who has returned from China suffering from syphilis? Since his return, after three years, she has not been in "close contact" with him, but now while her father had always said "one could well wish themselves dead if once they became a victim of the malady," her husband tells her that after his doctor finishes with him he will be "OK." Is it really so? What is she to do? She implores the doctor to help her.

She signs the letter (though we do not learn her name), thinking that maybe the doctor will be able to tell her what to do. "He looks smart, all right," she admits. "Every day he tells somebody what to do." She continues her interior monologue: "I want to do whatever is right. It's such a long time though. It's a long time. And it's been a long time. My Christ, it's been a long time." In these sentences the repetition of the phrase "a long time" conveys something of the obsessive nature of her nervous anxiety. In the sentences that follow the reiterated words are "get" and "got," and "it"—especially combined in the phrases, "get it" and "got it." The literary model for this interior monologue is not one of West's letter-writers, as it was for the example of the letter itself, but Gertrude Stein in *Three Lives*.

> It could never come to Melanctha to ask Rose to let her. It never could come to Melanctha to think that Rose would ask her. It would never ever come to Melanctha to want it, if Rose should ask her, but Melanctha would have done it for the safety she always felt when she was near her. Melanctha Herbert wanted badly to be safe now, but this living with her, that Rose would never give her.[87]

There is a difference here from Hemingway's practice in that Stein gives her character's thoughts indirectly, while Hemingway gives his character's thoughts in her own words. Yet the similarity between them is clear, when we look at Hemingway:

> He had to go wherever they sent him, I know, but don't know what he had to get it for. Oh, I wish to Christ he wouldn't have got it. I don't care what he did to get it. But I wish to Christ he hadn't ever got it. It does seem like he didn't have to have got it. I don't know what to do. I wish to Christ he hadn't got any kind of malady. I don't know why he had to get a malady.

If the repetitive and iterative interior monologue in Stein's *Three Lives* (Melanctha's, for instance) is one immediate source for Hemingway's unnamed woman's complaint, it is also likely that both instances—the recreation of Melanctha's thoughts and the recreation of those of the letter-writer in Hemingway's story—anticipate Marie Morgan's interior monologue after her husband's death in the novel *To Have and Have Not* (1937).[88] In each case the author has ventured to create, if not recreate, the thoughts, at least partly sexual, of an otherwise less than fully articulate woman. If there is an important difference between Stein's Melanctha and Hemingway's letter-writer, of course, it lies in the fact that the former thinks about her experience in rather tempered terms, while the latter torturously complains about her fate and laments her situation. Hemingway's Marie, on the other hand, combines an elegiac complaint of loss with a paean to the life and love she had with her husband.

Nathanael West could not have written "One Reader Writes," at least not judging from the writing of the writer we know from his four novels, especially *Miss Lonelyhearts*. The irony in Hemingway's story inheres in the woman's very bad luck; it's in the situation. It is true that she puts her faith in the newspaper doctor, a true indication of the pathos of her dilemma. But there is nothing satirical in the narrative voice, as there is in West's novel; nor is there a choral newspaper editor like Shrike to laugh cynically and pointedly at the letters, their ingenuous authors, and the sympathetic sob-sister himself. In Hemingway's story there is implied authorial sympathy. As Miss Lonelyhearts discovers, satire and sympathy make for a lethal mixture.

9. *Beyond Baedeker*: "Homage to Switzerland"

The Simplon–Orient Express makes its way across Switzerland from east to west but it is an hour late at Saint Maurice. At each of three stops, just up the line—Territet, Montreux and Vevey—in similar if not identical railway stations sits an American. These three settings, with three solitary American males, each one of them having to kill time until his train arrives, enable Hemingway to tell the three narratives that in the aggregate make up "Homage to Switzerland."

Each of the narratives begins with a description of the station café. Every such café on this line replicates every other one. What exists in Territet is duplicated in Montreux as well as in Vevey. This tells us something about Switzerland, Hemingway seems to be saying. Each café is "warm and light" with tables shiny from wiping. On the tables are baskets filled with pretzels in glazed paper sacks. The chairs are carved but the wooden seats are worn and comfortable. There is a carved wooden clock on the wall and a bar at the end of the room. It is snowing outside. At Montreux and at

Vevey, two of the station porters sit drinking wine at the table under the clock; while at Territet it is an old man that sits at a table under the clock and he drinks coffee. In all three instances the "action" begins with the words of a waitress to the American sitting alone, bringing him the news that the Simplon–Orient Express is an hour late. She offers him coffee. In each case there is some banter between them. Each one of them takes the coffee offered by the waitress and asks her the same question, "Do you speak other languages besides English?" In each case he receives the same answer, "Oh, yes, sir. I speak German and French and the dialects." In each case, the waitress is offered a drink and refuses because drinking with a client is not permitted. She is offered a cigar and refuses. The author's drift is clear. Everything is the same in Switzerland, at least at the railway stations. The social homogeneity of this country, judging from these scenes and episodes, is complete.

It is at this point in each of the three narratives that things go differently. Mr. Wheeler, at Montreux, propositions the waitress, who refuses his offers of payment. As it turns out there is a double irony in these proceedings. First, it is only that there exists no place upstairs in which to carry out the deed which keeps the waitress from accepting Mr. Wheeler's offer of three hundred francs "for a thing that is nothing to do." In fact, the waitress thinks, "How many times have I done that for nothing. And no place to go here." But the truth is that Mr. Wheeler has had his perverse way with the maid after all, for he has known all along that there was no "upstairs to go to" and has counted on that fact. "He was very careful about money and did not care for women. He had been in that station before and he knew there was no upstairs to go to. Mr. Wheeler never took chances."

Mr. Johnson, at Vevey, asks the waitress to "play" with him, to "make up a party and see the night life of Vevey." She turns him down, after which he jokes with her about Scott Fitzgerald and the "undergraduates" at the Berlitz school where she has learned her English. He then walks over to the three porters sitting at the table under the clock. He orders two bottles of champagne for them, discusses marriage with them, and reveals that he is about to get divorced. He soon leaves the men, though his train is still three-quarters of an hour away. He goes outside, looks back into the window at the three porters and the waitress, who takes the unopened bottle of champagne back to the bar ("That makes them three francs something apiece," he decides and thinks, "Inside the café he had thought that talking about it [his divorce] would blunt it; but it had not blunted it; it had only made him feel nasty."

Mr. Harris, at Territet, makes small-talk with the waitress, including an American's little joke about David Belasco, after which she excuses herself. The rest of the Harris story runs to a conversation, largely about the National Geographic Society, between him and a Dr. Sigismund Wyer, Ph.D., whose personal card identifies him only as a member of the Society. They talk about past issues of *National Geographic*, T. E. Lawrence, and Harris' father. When Dr. Wyer says that he would like to visit America and attend a meeting of the Society where he would be "very happy" to meet Harris' father, Harris answers sardonically,

> "I'm sure he would have liked to meet you but he died last year. Shot himself, oddly enough."
> "I am very truly sorry. I am sure his loss was a blow to science as well as to his family."
> "Science took it awfully well."

The story ends when the two of them exchange personal cards. The Wheeler and Johnson stories offer a final mention of the train, though not here.

According to Carlos Baker, anyone acquainted with Hemingway's marital history would easily recognize in "Homage to Switzerland" that Messrs Wheeler, Johnson and Harris were Ernest himself, "attempting to recover from the trauma of separation from his first wife, Hadley."[89] Surely the talk about Johnson's impending divorce and Harris' revelation that his father has committed suicide by shooting himself tie in directly with the facts of Hemingway's biography. But when the author tried to sell the story to *Cosmopolitan* magazine, he quite naturally described it as being entirely concerned with the country itself. To W. C. Lengel he wrote:

> This is a damned good story—3 stories in one.... It's a new form for a story. The fact that the three parts all open the same way or practically the same is intentional and is supposed to represent Switzerland metaphysically where it all opens in the same way always and where a young man will not marry a young lady until she has had her original teeth out and her store teeth in since that is an eventual expense that the girl's father, not her husband, should bear. But, possibly, Mr. Lengel, you have been in Switzerland yourself. Anybody will have been there when they read the Homage.[90]

When *Cosmopolitan* rejected the story, it was offered to *Scribner's Magazine*, where it appeared in April 1933, six months before it was collected in *Winner Take Nothing*.

Despite Hemingway's insistence that "Homage to Switzerland" is "a damned good story," it has not proved to be a favorite among readers or critics. One reason for that judgment, surely, is that for all of its structural devices, deliberate (even insistent) narrative repetitions, and very close organization, this three-part story (three stories in one) lacks clear intention. The sociological point the story makes about Switzerland in the late

1920s (and it is a rather obvious one) has very little to do with the three character portraits—whether or not Wheeler, Johnson and Harris are three versions of the somewhat disaffected author. The result is that the attempt at a double focus fails to bring off the kind of thematic resonance that Hemingway's best stories achieve. Even if the three incidents successfully reveal the nuances of at least moderately interesting characters, that they take place in Switzerland seems incidental and hardly necessary.

10. *Death Watch*: "A Day's Wait"

At the 1999 Hemingway meetings in Oak Park, Illinois, two of Hemingway's sons—John and Patrick—answered questions. "What would you have high school students read to keep Hemingway's reputation in the future?" was one of those questions from the audience. "The short stories, any of the major novels," answered the older brother John. "Jack's being modest. I'd say have them read 'A Day's Wait,'" countered Patrick.

Hemingway's first biographer tells us that Hemingway based "A Day's Wait" on an autobiographical incident. The model for Schatz, the sick child, was Hemingway's first-born, John, otherwise known as "Bumby." Baker recreates the incident in which Bumby came down with influenza. "On learning that his temperature was 102," Bumby "turned pale, and could not seem to concentrate even when Ernest read aloud to him from Howard Pyle's *Book of Pirates*."

> Ernest went out quail shooting with a young Irish setter belonging to the Pfeiffers [Hemingway's in-laws at the time]. When he came back, Bumby was still behaving strangely. His schoolmates in France had told him that no one could possibly survive with a temperature of 44. Since his own was more than twice that high, he was sure that he was going to die. He relaxed visibly when Ernest explained the difference between Fahrenheit and Centigrade. Once again, though he did not discover it for some years, Bumby had given his father an idea for a story.[91]

This account of the incident behind the story is instructive. It reads much like a plot summary, so closely does the fiction follow the actual incident. However, if Baker does manage to suggest the extent to which Hemingway's fiction parallels the events of his own life, his summary offers no clue into how those events are transformed into fiction. It offers no indication that the story is structured around a series of contrasting ironies. Through an examination of that structure, in fact, we can see how one of the great modern realists transformed the stuff of personal experience into durable fiction.

In a few hundred words worked around contrasting ironies, Hemingway gives us a direct and deeply felt impression of a father's relationship to his young son in a period of emotional crisis. This set of ironies can be presented schematically.[92]

First, while the boy believes that the doctor has just announced his death sentence, his father tries to divert the boy's attention from the discomfort attendant to a minor illness. He would entertain him by reading from Pyle's *Book of Pirates*, under other, less taut, circumstances a sure-fire favorite. How these adventures of pirates pale in the face of the boy's own much greater and fearsome adventure—the prospect of his own death—is never made explicit.

Second, while indoors the child shivers and burns with fever, his father walks outside in the cold:

> It was a *bright, cold day*, the ground covered with a *sleet that had frozen* so that it seemed as if all the bare trees, the bushes, the cut brush and all the grass and the bare ground had been *varnished with ice*. I took the young Irish setter for a little walk up the road and along a *frozen creek*, but it was difficult to stand or walk on the *glassy surface* and the red dog slipped and slithered and I fell twice, hard, once dropping my gun and having it *slide away over the ice*. [Italics added.]

Sickness opposed to health, fire to ice, immobility to activity—all this is suggested by the interplay of the sequence of the sickroom and outdoor scenes.

Third, as the boy lies within awaiting death, his father is outdoors shooting animals, complaining only that "icy" conditions make difficult the killing of quail. The consequence is that the hunter manages to kill only two quail, missing five others.

Fourth, the father's good intentions lead him into lying to his son about his body temperature—"'Something like a hundred,' I said. It was one hundred and two and four tenths." This lie, told to minimize the boy's sense of danger, is in ironic counterpoint to his son's own information, gathered in France, that a human being "can't live with forty-four degrees." The unexpected result is that to the boy, because of the cues provided by his limited information, "something like a hundred" is as intimidating as 102.4 degrees.

As a narrative twist, the confusion over Centigrade and Fahrenheit registrations rivals O. Henry on his own special ground of the surprise ending. But the last irony which rounds out "A Day's Wait" is mint Hemingway. While convinced that he is dying, the nine-year-old child holds manful reign over his emotions, even to the extent of cautioning his father to risk no further exposure to his disease, but he now breaks down as he learns of his mistake: "his gaze at the foot of the bed relaxed slowly. The hold over himself relaxed too, finally, and the next day it was very slack and he cried very easily at little things that were of no importance." Hemingway's exact psychology fulfills the ironic structures of his story.

11. *Benthamite Ethics*: "A Natural History of the Dead"

> During the trench-warfare slaughters of World War I, a system for separating the wounded into three groups was practiced in Allied medical tents. The groups consisted of those likely to die no matter what was done for them, those who would probably recover even if untreated, and those who could survive only if cared for immediately. With supplies and manpower limited, the third group alone received attention. Such a practice was called triage—from the French verb *trier*, to sort.—Wade Greene, New York *Times*, Jan. 5, 1975

Death in the Afternoon is unique among Hemingway's major works in that it alone is predominantly non-fictional. Even *Green Hills of Africa*, a "true" book in that it is purely autobiographical, was so shaped as to compete with works of fiction on their own terms, and *A Moveable Feast*, presented as a fragmentary memoir of the 1920s, is perhaps better described as a unified collection of fictionalized sketches. Closer to these works than to any other in the canon, *Death in the Afternoon* nevertheless differs from them because it is actually an extended discursive essay. A handbook on the Spanish bullfight, a sermon on the decadence of modern bullfighting, and a detailed ranking of living and dead bullfighters, the book is also Hemingway's *ars poetica* and commonplace book, listing his opinions on subjects such as humanism and warfare. Indeed, Hemingway put so much of himself into this "technical book" (his description) and liked the result so well that for a while he thought he would follow it with a comparable book on revolution, though, regrettably, that second volume never was written.

Even *Death in the Afternoon*, however, is not devoid of "fiction." Adopting the ploy of having a Shandyean interlocutor, an "Old Lady," ask the author for examples of his kind of story, the author occasionally drops into his text self-defined tales, stressing that they are exemplary and heuristic.

The best known of these interpolated stories, and perhaps the most intentionally heuristic, is the section of the book now called "A Natural History of the Dead." It includes references to the writings of such self-proclaimed naturalist-travelers as W. H. Hudson (who was defamed in *The Sun Also Rises*), Gilbert White, and Mungo Park, a harsh attack on all "self-called Humanist[s]," a warning against those writers who would insist that generals do die in bed. Not everyone was of Hemingway's party on this matter. The poet Robert Frost, for one, reacted strongly to Hemingway's attack on humanists. In a letter to Louis Untermeyer, dated Dec. 21, 1933, he wrote, with a swipe at Archibald MacLeish, Hemingway's friend:

> Did you happen to notice the terrible kind of death Hemingway wished the humanist in his "Winner Take Nothing" dedicated to your Archie MacLeish? He

hoped he would die without dignity or decorum. I suppose he must have been after Irving Babbitt for getting under his skin for a humanitarian sentimentalist. Just about the time he wished it, Babbitt was dying as if with humanitarian pens stuck into his wax figurativeness, which was good as far as it went, but unfortunately for Hemingway I'm afraid he died with Graeco-Roman euthanatos.[93]

Yet Hemingway found this section of *Death in the Afternoon* too valuable a piece of fiction to relegate it permanently to a work of non-fiction devoted largely to the highly specialized subject of bull-fighting. Consequently, when in the next year he assembled *Winner Take Nothing*, he included it, after minor excisions, as the eleventh story in the collection.

Surrounded by such closely crafted stories as "A Clean, Well-Lighted Place," "The Light of the World," "The Sea Change," "The Gambler, the Nun, and the Radio," and "A Day's Wait," this story, as it stands, just does not mesh. As it *now* stands, I should say, because although Hemingway did not err in reprinting "A Natural History of the Dead" as a free-standing short story, he did insist on including his treatise—mocking naturalists, travelers, and humanists—as part of the short story.[94] Had he cut away this extraneous material he would have left a more efficient story about a military doctor practicing his craft in the midst of the wounded and dying and an artillery officer who, losing control over himself, threatens to plunge the whole operation into chaos. As such, this story groups naturally with those other Hemingway stories about physicians as professionals, particularly "Indian Camp" from *In Our Time* and "God Rest You Merry, Gentlemen."

The trouble had started, as Hemingway sees it, with the stretcher-bearers' anxiety over a wounded man "whose head was broken as a flower-pot may be broken." Prematurely moved into a cave housing the dead, this man haunts those who must go in and out of the cave precisely because he is *not* dead. In the house of the dead his presence is so overwhelming that they hear only his breathing. After managing to get the doctor to examine him—"once in daylight, once with a flashlight"—as a result of which the doctor decides to do nothing for him or to him, the stretcher-bearers ask the doctor to allow them at least to move him outside among the living wounded. When he refuses their request as a waste of effort, they suggest that the doctor kill the man by administering an overdose of morphine. The doctor, whose "business is to care for the wounded, not to kill them," tells them that he has a better use for morphine. In the exchange that follows the doctor's humanity is called into doubt precisely because he will do nothing to reduce the anxiety of those who must continue to hear the sounds emanating from the soldier lying among the dead.

At the heart of the story is an antinomy. Despite their disagreement, neither the doctor nor the men are wrong. From a broadly humanistic point of view, the doctor and the other soldiers are equally in the right. It is inhuman for the doctor to do nothing for the all-but-dead soldier just as it is inhuman for the others to ask the doctor to do something to him for their sake. The doctor does have better uses for his morphine and, undoubtedly, better uses for his skill than to expend it on a man who, as he predicts accurately, will soon be dead. Why carry the wounded man back out to the surviving wounded if he will soon have to be carried back into the cave of the dead?

If the men seem to express decent human emotions, the doctor stands adamantly for economy—an economy of effort, time, supplies, and emotion. In fact, the doctor's kind of economy has long since acquired, since the Great War, the name of *triage*—the system whereby priorities for medical treatment to casualties are assigned on the basis of urgency, calculated chances for survival, and time and effort required. The successful practice of *triage* promises to maximize results quantitatively by ignoring the needs and claims, entirely legitimate in nearly all other contexts, of individuals. Statistics tell the tale. Society accepts the principle that it is more desirable to save two than one. When that principle applies, *triage* does not—is not meant to—accommodate the individual when it is not cost effect. So much for the rights of one man alone.

That from his own perspective Hemingway's doctor is absolutely right about the wounded man (he will soon die) is merely incidental to his commitment to the higher of two conflicting professional principles. Disastrous to the individual though it might be, fidelity to the *system* of *triage* enables the doctor to establish and to maintain order in his rudimentary camp. And still another "truth" applies. If "a surgeon cannot desist while operating for fear of hurting the patient,"[95] neither can he allow actions emerging out of rising emotions to disrupt the procedures of his station. Yet, once having survived the threat to that order, he can then turn, dispassionately and professionally, as Hemingway's doctor does, to attend to the needs of the very officer he has himself wounded. "Wipe out this officer's eyes with alcohol and water," he directs with calmness and assurance. "He is in much pain. Hold him very tight." The doctor prescribes no anesthetic.

12. *Dinner at Fontan's*: "Wine of Wyoming"

The experimental part of the non-fictional work Hemingway called *Green Hills of Africa* (1935) lay in his attempting to see whether a book based on fact and following actual incidents could be so well written as to compete with a work of fiction on fiction's own terms. It was an experiment that he had undoubtedly conducted in smaller compass and to a lesser extent many times before, it is safe to infer, trying it in his short stories.

Clearly one such experiment was the story "Wine of Wyoming." Based on incidents (they are hardly more than incidental) experienced by the author himself while on a hunting trip to the state of Wyoming and focusing on a French immigrant couple he had become friendly with on that and other such hunting trips, this "Prohibition" fable tells a simple story with no fanfare and little or no drama.

The story is comprised of four parts, each of which involves a time change, though the times, covering a couple of days, are chronological. Let's consider these parts to be four acts of a play. Act one takes place at the home of the Fontans. The time is a hot afternoon. The narrator sits at a table on the back porch drinking beer and talking with Madame Fontan. After a brief interruption caused by the arrival of potential customers for Fontan's beer, who leave when they are told there is no more beer, the narrator and Madame Fontan talk. ("She spoke French, but it was only French occasionally, and there were many English words and some English constructions.") At his departure the narrator agrees to come back that evening for supper.

Act two takes place in the dining-room at the Fontans' the same evening. Present are Fontan, his wife, their sixteen-year-old son André, the narrator and, presumably, his wife. (There is someone with him, and who, although given lines to speak, is never named or in any way identified.) They talk about America, the Fontans' older son, who is married to an overweight American woman who feeds him beans out of a can and spends all her time reading and going to the movies, Al Smith's chances at the presidency, and Catholicism.

Act three takes place the next afternoon, another hot day, again at the Fontans' house. They sit on the back porch, drinking beer. They discuss Fontan (who is absent), particularly his difficulties with the law over his making and selling beer and wine, and the strange drinking habits of some of Fontan's customers. The narrator, who is leaving soon, promises to come back to see the Fontans, to "drink a bottle" of wine "together," before leaving for good.

Act four breaks into four principal scenes with intervening events summarized in the exposition. Scene one, again at the Fontans' place, has the narrator, his wife, and Madame Fontan drinking beer in the dining-room. Madame Fontan extracts from them the promise that they will return for dinner that night. Fontan will have "the wine" for them. Scene two takes place between the narrator and his wife as they lie in bed before going to sleep. Running around attending to pre-departure tasks has so tired them that they have foregone their promised dinner-visit with the Fontans. They talk of their regret at not having gone. In scene three we are back at the

Fontans' place the next morning. There is no wine left, Fontan having drunk all by himself the three bottles he had brought for his good-bye drink with the narrator. He insists on going to the place where he keeps his wine, about a mile away. The narrator accompanies him. Scene four takes place outside the house, which they have found locked. The woman who is supposed to be there is absent, and Fontan's key will not unlock the door. Fontan wants to dig his way in, but is dissuaded from doing so. They can see Fontan's wine inside but they cannot get at it (just as the tough who narrates "After the Storm" cannot get at what is inside the sunken liner). Bitterly disappointed, Fontan agrees to return home without the wine. Scene five, back at the Fontans' place, briefly creates the sense of Fontan's "disgrace" and "ruin" because his plans for drinking the wine with his friend, the narrator-writer, have gone to smash. Present are Fontan, his wife, the narrator and his wife. In the sixth (and final) scene, the latter two are driving along in their car, enjoying the scenery and the wildlife and talking about what will happen to the country and the game, to the Fontans and their boy André. "'We ought to have gone last night,'" she says. "'Oh, yes,' I said. 'We ought to have gone.'" End of play.

Probably more so than any other story by Hemingway, "Wine of Wyoming" depends for its effect upon the sheer transparency of what happens and what is said. No one speaks indirectly or even suggestively. There appears to be nothing that is left unsaid. For once Hemingway's famous iceberg theory—in which in a story, as in an iceberg, seven-eighths of it is hidden below the surface—appears to have been put aside. Whatever depths, psychological or sociological, the Fontans possess (and "Wine of Wyoming" is their story: they are the true "wine" of Wyoming, transplanted from rural France), those "depths" are right there at the surface, to be expressed fully in conversation. That Fontan could feel that he is "ruined" and "disgraced" because he cannot get at his wine and therefore has failed to provide his friend with wine for his journey measures both his forthrightness and his profundity of feeling. Of an evening he may get stone drunk on three bottles of wine, but he is also the person who can appreciate the qualities of a wine sauce prepared by Madame Fontan. She tells it: "Fontan, il est crazy pour le vin. One time he killed a jack-rabbit and he wanted me to cook it with a sauce with wine" and "butter and mushrooms and onion and everything in it, for the jack. My God, I make the sauce all right, and he eat it all and said. 'La sauce est meilleure que le jack.'" Then Madame Fontan adds, "Dans son pays c'est comme ça. Il y a beaucoup de gibier et de vin. Moi, j'aime les pommes de terre, le saucisson, et la bière. C'est bon, la bière. C'est très bon pour la santé."

If "Wine of Wyoming" constitutes an experiment in narration based closely on actuality unadorned by the invention of character or incident (as it seems to do), within it there takes place another kind of experimentation. Hemingway tries to create a literary equivalent for the Franco-English spoken by the two immigrants. He succeeds exceedingly well. Their speech is a mixture of French, English, and a concoction of the two. It is a large part of their charm that their speech so clearly mirrors the intercultural and international truths about their situation. Hemingway had something more than a good ear for such patois, he had an artist's ability to replicate it in a thoroughly literary way. But such speech—or at least the hearing of it—was not for every occasion or at all times. When the narrator and his wife find themselves too tired at suppertime to return to the Fontans, the narrator tells us, "We did not want a foreign language. All we wanted was to go early to bed." From that point on in the story, in a writer's audacious trick, the Fontans speak no more Franco-English or French. They slip into perfectly common English speech.[96]

13. *Notre Dame and the Good Sister*: "The Gambler, the Nun, and the Radio"

Discovering that her patient is an author, Sister Cecilia asks him to write a story. "I wish you'd write something sometime for Our Lady. You could do it," she implores in "The Gambler, the Nun, and the Radio"; "you know you could do it, Mr. Frazer." "I don't know anything about her that I could write. It's mostly been written already," he explains. "You wouldn't like the way I write. She wouldn't care for it either." But Sister Cecilia is not a whit discouraged. "You'll write about her sometime," she predicts; "I know you will. You must write about Our Lady."

Whether or not Frazer resisted the temptation to write directly about the Virgin is not known, but the young nun's prediction for Mr. Frazer had already been fulfilled by Hemingway. His much acclaimed story "A Clean, Well-Lighted Place" had ended with an account of an insomniac's restive relationship with the Virgin.[97] It is not likely, however, that Hemingway's story about the Virgin would please the Virgin, let alone Sister Cecilia.

The story that would come closer to pleasing them, of course, was "The Gambler, the Nun, and the Radio." Largely autobiographical, the story focuses on a writer, Frazer, whose experience parallels that of the author. While returning from hunting on the first of November, 1930, Hemingway was in an automobile accident. Blinded by the headlights of an oncoming car that had pulled out to pass a second car, Hemingway managed to avoid hitting it, but in doing so he overturned his own car in a ditch at the side of the road. His passengers (Floyd Allington and John Dos Passos) were unhurt, but Hemingway suffered a severely broken right arm. He was admitted to St. Vincent's Hospital, a Catholic hospital staffed by the Sisters of Charity of Leavenworth. Hemingway would spend seven weeks in this Billings, Montana, hospital before being discharged just before Christmas. As he would later write of that stay, "I could remember ... my right arm broken off short between the elbow and the shoulder, the back of the hand hung down against my back, the points of the bone having cut up the flesh of the biceps until it finally rotted, swelled, burst, and sloughed off in pus. Alone with the pain in the night in the fifth week of not sleeping,"[98] he found his "nerves," like Frazer's, going "bad." That stay in hospital, with its legacy of insomnia, was the principal source of Hemingway's story, "The Gambler, the Nun, and the Radio."

> At first the story was called "Give Us a Prescription, Doctor," a title that linked it too obviously, perhaps, to Mr. Frazer's first "message" in this highly autobiographical story: "Religion is the opium of the people." But Marx is only a starting place, for he goes on: "And music is the opium of the people.... And now economics ... along with patriotism ... sexual intercourse ... drink ... radio ... gambling ... ambition ... liberty.... What was the real, the actual, opium of the people? He knew it very well.... What was it? Of course; bread was the opium of the people." This litany of opiates leads Frazer to ask, "Why should the people be operated on without an anaesthetic.... Why are not all the opiums of the people good?" For, as Robert Frost put it bluntly, "All Marxism is—a prescription—medicine."[99]

Hemingway based each of his fictional principals on an actual person at St. Vincent's Hospital. Besides the writer Frazer, who is based on Hemingway himself, Sister Cecilia, the nun who prays for Notre Dame—both Virgin and college football team—has her prototype in Hemingway's nurse, Sister Florence. "By all odds his [Hemingway's] favorite visitor was Sister Florence," writes his biographer Carlos Baker, "a gentle nun who loved baseball and believed strongly that the Lord could be persuaded to intercede in human affairs. Her prayers had been answered during the World Series of October. Ernest loved to see her and to hear her breathless talk."[100]

In "The Gambler, the Nun, and the Radio" Hemingway presents Sister Cecilia as an engaging, well-meaning naif. She constantly bubbles confidence, wonderfully impervious all the while to Frazer's mounting anxiety. If Sister Florence had actually become Hemingway's "chief consolation" for his "endless hours of lying in bed,"[101] then Sister Cecilia, as a well-intentioned, hard-to-dislike optimist, is faithfully portrayed. Indeed, in choosing to call her Cecilia, Hemingway calls attention to the blind Saint who is the patron of both music and the blind. Sister Cecilia has credentials in both areas. Before the Mexicans sent by the police to visit the gambler will be allowed to return with their music, they must have the good Sister's permission. And when she prays for the success of her favorite baseball teams, she works a little white magic for the Athletics by praying for their sight ("Oh, Lord, direct their batting eyes!") and against the Cardinals, their opponents, by praying for their blindness ("Oh, Lord, may they not see it! Oh, Lord, don't let them even catch a glimpse of it!"). It should be noted that it was Hemingway's temporary "blindness" that had initially landed him in St. Vincent's Hospital.

Since the story's point of view is undeniably Frazer's, however, it might be of interest to examine the real-life Sister Florence's own comments on Hemingway's hospital stay in Montana. Those comments survive at secondhand, in a review of Sister Mariella Gable's collection in 1942 of *Great Modern Catholic Short Stories*. Containing stories by Katherine Mansfield, Frank O'Connor, Elizabeth Madox Roberts, F. Scott Fitzgerald, and Morley Callaghan, as well as "The Gambler, the Nun, and the Radio," this book was reviewed by one Sister Mary Mark in *Books on Trial*, a Catholic periodical published by the Thomas More Library and Book Shop of Chicago, Illinois. The review contains an account—not entirely devoid of embroidery and, less fortunately, misinformation—of the biographical basis of the story. "Knowing how Ernest Hemingway came to write *The Gambler, The Nun[,] and the Radio* may delight readers of the collection," promises the editor.

> The incident was related four or five years ago by the Sister whom he calls Sister Cecilia. Mr. Hemingway (Mr. Frazer in the story) was vacationing on one of Montana's dude ranches where he met with an accident while horse-back riding. In the hospital, the great bone surgeon, finding a seriously broken hip, warned the Sisters that the man must be kept very quiet if he was to recover complete use of his limb. Sister Cecilia took him his mail and endeavored daily to keep his spirits up. She had learned that he had a book coming off the press, so that she was not surprised one day to see a copy of the bright new book lying in one of the hollows of the bed. Eagerly, she picked it up; at once he jerked his head off the pillow and thrust out his hand for it saying, "Don't open that book, Sister; don't open that book. I didn't write that book for you."

The editor continues:

> But he did not know Sister "Cecilia" whose black eyes flashed as she firmly asked, "You wrote it for the reading public...." She opened the book at random and began reading aloud with the first lines, many of them conversation flecked with the strong words usual to the writer's grim realism: all the while his protests became more violent, and more likely to turn into action. Mindful of the doctor's warning that the man must remain quiet, Sister closed the book and placed it in his hands.
> "Sister, you can't read this book. I didn't write it for you. But some day—I will write a story just for you." In *The Gambler, the Nun, and the Radio*, Mr. Hemingway fulfilled his promise.[102]

Hemingway had suffered a broken arm, as we have seen, not a broken hip, and the accident involved an automobile, not a horse. No Hemingway book appeared during his hospital stay though he did have in progress the long manuscript about Spanish bullfighting that would appear in 1932 as *Death in the Afternoon*. Despite these inaccuracies, however, we cannot dismiss the entire account as a fabrication, for, as we have seen, Hemingway's affection for the good sister has been amply documented.

> When "The Gambler, the Nun, and the Radio" was reprinted in *Great Modern Catholic Stories*, the editor of the collection had observed, not quite accurately, that the story was "almost the only instance in all Hemingway's fiction where the author comments on values." Having made that observation she ventured further that the reason for this departure from custom was that "Perhaps the impact of Sister Cecilia's personality carried farther than to Frazer and the Mexican [gambler]."[103]

Perhaps. On the other hand, it is possible that Sister Cecilia, named for the patron saint of the blind, it will be recalled, but who is high on the opiate of her overwhelming desire for sainthood, was viewed by the author as merely the second opiate of the three opiates listed in the title of the story. For the "gambler" (code), the "nun" (faith), and the "radio" (soporific)— each apparently offering the "writer" (nerves) an appealing "opiate"—cannot assuage the less than clean, less than well-ordered mind of Mr. Frazer.[104] It is not coincidental, I think, that in naming his Prufrock-like character Hemingway evokes the author of *The Golden Bough*, brought to renewed attention by Eliot in his notes to *The Wasteland* (1922) or that "The Gambler, the Nun, and the Radio" was written in the wake of T. S. Eliot's self-serving announcement that he had converted to Anglo Catholicism.

Hemingway had written a "religious" story for Sister Florence, but it was a story intended to dramatize the chasm between Frazer's state of mind as a skeptic and Sister Cecilia's unexamined faith. Indeed in this respect Sister Cecilia can be seen as Ernest Hemingway's version of William Faulkner's Dilsey. Functioning perfectly within an orderly, if severely limited, religious ambience, Sister Cecilia, like Dilsey, can be admired and loved; but her behavior, ethics, and religious being, like those of the fundamentalist Dilsey, offer neither palliative nor example to the writer whose great fear—"his nerves had become tricky"—is that he has begun to think "a little too well."

And yet might not Hemingway's story also serve as a skeptic's act of homage to the Virgin Mother? Might it not serve in the way, somewhat, that in the Middle Ages those jugglers, and jongleurs, so celebrated by Henry Adams, who did not know how to honor the Virgin in traditional prayer successfully performed instead their artistic tricks before the Queen of Heaven? In that sense, it is possible to regard "The Gambler, the Nun, and the Radio" as Hemingway's story about "Our Lady," one that has the additional merit of being an apologia to Sister Florence in explanation for the author's nervous acedia in the fifth week of his confinement in St. Vincent's Hospital. As such, it would be unwise to see in Frazer's litany of negation a key to the author's own prevailing spiritual state. Indeed, the story tells us "how it was" during a fixed period during which nothing was going well with the author or his fictional surrogate.

14. *Hostages to Fortune*: "Fathers and Sons"

Three months before the appearance of *Winner Take Nothing* Hemingway was still revising the last story for the collection. It carried, then, the title "The Tomb of My Grandfather."[105] When he finished his revisions of this story based on a trip to Arkansas in the company of his son John (Bumby), a trip taken the previous November (1932), he was certain that it should be placed fourteenth and last in the volume.[106] After considering other titles, he settled on "Fathers and Sons," a direct borrowing from Turgenev, always one of Hemingway's favorite writers. The story was about Nick Adams, aged thirty-eight, his young son, and Nick's own father, the boy's deceased grandfather.

The story starts out in Nick's mind as he drives across the South seemingly in late fall. He is traveling with his son, who is asleep on the seat beside him. Nick watches the landscape as it goes by, noting all the salient features of a tree-shaded town and the harvested cotton and corn fields. Stimulated by what he sees with his sportsman's practiced eye, he hunts in his imagination through the terrain and the cover suitable for birds. If he sees with a sportsman's eye, however, it is with a writer's mind that he confronts the memories that the drive through the landscape evokes, which are memories of his father and his childhood. The structure of the story, then, grows out of the associational logic in a person's thoughts and their interaction with a moving landscape. "Hunting the country in his mind as he went by," Nicholas Adams silently "lectures" on the subject of shooting quail, which leads him to thoughts about the father who taught him how to hunt. This is just the beginning, for Nick who has not yet been able to write about his father, a suicide, thinks out much of the fiction that we are reading. (In this story, too, Hemingway was first able to write, after four years, about his father's suicide.) Whenever Nick first thinks of his father his first thought, he tells us, is always about his eyes.

> The big frame, the quick movements, the wide shoulders, the hooked, hawk nose, the beard that covered the weak chin, you never thought about—it was always the eyes. They were protected in his head by the formation of the brows; set deep as

though a special protection had been devised for some very valuable instrument. They saw much farther and much quicker than the human eye sees and they were the great gift his father had. His father saw as a big-horn ram or as an eagle sees, literally.

Nick recalls that he is most grateful for what his father has taught him about shooting and fishing. "His father was as sound on those two things," reveals Nick, "as he was unsound on sex, for instance, and Nick was glad that it had been that way." After all, reasons Nick, someone has to give you your first gun and furnish you with a place to live where there is game. As for sex, that "other, that his father was not sound about," Nick decides, "all the equipment you will ever have is provided and each man learns all there is for him to know about it without advice; and it makes no difference where you live." All the sexual education given to him by his father, a doctor (a fact never mentioned in this story), Nick tells us, adds up to very little. He defined one "heinous" crime. "A bugger is a man who has intercourse with animals." (Silently Nick runs down the possibilities but finds no animal that seems "attractive or practical.") And the doctor says in answer to Nick's question about "mashing" only that "it is one of the most heinous of crimes." In fact, he "had summed up the whole matter [of sex] by stating that masturbation produced blindness, insanity, and death, while a man who went with prostitutes would contract hideous venereal diseases and that the thing to do was to keep your hands off of people." Nick slides from these thoughts into the more haunting thoughts about his father's death and the cosmetic job the undertaker had done on his father's face. It was all a good story, but one he was not yet ready to write.

Nick turns to other thoughts, pleasant thoughts about his own education in sex. He thinks of Trudy Gilby, the young Ojibway girl, and he couches his memories of this sexual partner who "did first what no one has ever done better" in the details of the northern Michigan woods where it all took place. He thinks of Trudy, her brother Billy, their older brother Eddie and Eddie's threat, reported to Nick at second hand, that some night he will make love to Nick's sister Dorothy, along with Nick's vehement reaction and threat in return that he will kill Eddie if he goes near his sister.

Nick stops thinking about Trudy and his Indian friends. As he rides along the highway, it gets dark and Nick thinks: now he's "all through thinking about his father." But "Fathers and Sons" resumes the account of Nick's relationship to his father. He never thinks of his father at the end of the day, though his father does come into his thoughts in the fall of the year, and in early spring, and when he sees shocks of corn, a lake, a horse and buggy, or when he sees or hears wild geese. His father returns to him, too, in deserted orchards, newly-plowed fields, in thickets or on small hills, when going through dead grass, when he is splitting wood, hauling water, standing by grist mills, cider mills, dams—"and always with open fires." Yet, as much as he loved his father, he had shared nothing with him after he turned fifteen. And he hated the smell of his father. The anecdote he tells about having to wear his father's underwear, deliberately losing it, and then being punished for it leads to the revelation that, like Huck Finn's determination to shoot Pap if need be, he, too, after the beating over the underwear, "sat inside the woodshed with the door open, his shotgun loaded and cocked, looking across at his father sitting on the screen porch reading the paper," and thinking, "'I can blow him to hell. I can kill him.'" It is not coincidental that this scene recalls the scene in Mark Twain's *Adventures of Huckleberry Finn*, chapter 6, in which Huck's drunken father dozes off. "By and by I got the old split-bottom chair and clumb up as easy as I could," writes Huck, "not to make any noise, and got down the gun. I slipped the ramrod down it to make sure it was loaded, and then I laid it across the turnip-barrel, pointing toward pap, and set down behind it to wait for him to stir." Unlike Huck, however, when Nick's anger abates, however, he feels a little sick about the fact that the shotgun was the one his father had given him. It is curious that Nick has not inherited his father's keen animal eye sight but does possess a preternatural sense of smell. It is that very sense that makes repugnant the smell of the members of his own family—except for Dorothy, the sister to whom Eddie Gilby is a sexual threat. As Nick concludes, his sense of smell was "good for a bird dog but it did not help a man."

All the while the child at his side has been asleep ostensibly. The child asks him to tell him what it was like to hunt with the Indians when he was a boy. Nick is startled to find, not having noticed, deeply immersed as he was in his own memories, that the boy has been awake. Nick tells him about Trudy and Billy Gilby and their hunting black squirrels. He says nothing, of course, about his sexual education. Then the boy asks about his grandfather, Nick's father, who also lived with the Indians. The boy wants to know when he will be given a shotgun. He is told that he will get one, if he shows himself to be careful, when he is twelve. He asks, "'What was my grandfather like?'" Nick tells him only about his essential qualities, those, one can safely infer, Nick himself wants to remember: "'He's hard to describe. He was a great hunter and fisherman and he had wonderful eyes.'" The boy decides that he should pray at the tomb of his grandfather, something he has never done. He doesn't feel good, not having done that. "'We'll have to go,' Nick said. 'I can see we'll have to go.'"

Hemingway had opened his first collection of stories *In Our Time* (1925) with "Indian Camp," the story of the young Nick's initiation into a world of pain, traumatic birth, and violent death when his doctor-father enrolls him as his "interne" during the delivery of a baby by Caesarean section performed in the field, so to speak, under primitive conditions. A good deal about the quality of his father's role in Nick's education is told there. Much of the rest of the story gets told in "Fathers and Sons."

Hemingway's earlier title for the story, "The Tomb of *My* Grandfather" (emphasis added), suggests that in its earlier stages Hemingway saw his story as being more of the boy's story than the finished story turned out to be. But the impulse to turn the reader's focus in such stories away from Nick's son and toward Nick was already present in a story such as "A Day's Wait." The gravitational pull in both that story and "Fathers and Sons" is toward the realization of Nick's specific reactions and overall consciousness. Not until *Islands in the Stream* (1970), the first novel to be fashioned (with mixed success) out of unfinished materials left behind at Hemingway's death, do we find Hemingway again delving as deeply into intimacies between fathers and sons of his and Nick Adams's generation.

10

The Mercenary's Call

To the first issue of Ernest Walsh's journal *This Quarter* (Spring 1925), which Walsh dedicated to Ezra Pound, Ernest Hemingway contributed a piece entitled "Homage to Ezra." To establish that Pound was "a major poet just as Yeats is and Browning and Shelley and Keats were," Hemingway found it necessary to define what he meant by "minor poet." "Minor poets do not fail because they do not attempt the major thing. They have nothing of major importance to say. They do a minor thing with perfection and the perfection is admirable." Thus, while Whitman is a major poet, T. S. Eliot is not. "All of Eliot's poems are perfect and there are very few of them. He has a very fine talent and he is very careful of it. He never takes chances with it and it is doing very well thank you." Hemingway's example of "the perfect case of the minor poet," however, is A. E. Housman: "He did it once and did it perfectly with the *Shropshire Lad*, but when he tried to do [it] again it wouldn't come off and the trick of mind all showed through and it imperiled the poems in the first book. One more book would have killed off all the poems. They proved to be unimportant."[1] Housman's *Last Poems* in 1922 was unimportant to Housman's literary reputation, perhaps, but the book was not as unimportant to Hemingway as he implied.

Given Hemingway's acknowledged admiration for *A Shropshire Lad*, it is surprising that Housman has figured so little in Hemingway scholarship. There are exceptions, of course. Paul Smith cites parallels between "A Shropshire Lad" itself and "Big Two-Hearted River."[2] "The Capital of the World" is called "a fine story on the 'athlete-dying-young' theme," by Carlos Baker, while Joseph Flora sees in the image of "far blue hills" ("Big Two-Hearted River") an echo of Housman's image of "blue remembered hills" of "Into My Heart an Air That Kills" in *A Shropshire Lad*.[3] To these suggestions I should like to add the suggestion that the fallen pastoral world of Hemingway's Upper Peninsula has its closest antecedent in Housman's Shropshire, a notion that warrants closer investigation and more elaborate treatment than I wish to give it here. Instead I shall focus on more specific parallels and affinities to support my contention that Hemingway profited in various ways from specific poems in Housman's *Shropshire Lad* as well as his *Last Poems*.

Hemingway's "Today is Friday," a play first published in pamphlet form in 1926, "To Will Davies," an unpublished poem, and "Chapter XV," the vignette on Sam Cardinella's hanging first published in (the lower-case) *in our time* (1924), can be viewed either together or separately as a realist's corrective to Housman's "The Carpenter's Son" from *A Shropshire Lad*. In Housman's poem we hear the young man's voice just before he is hanged:

> "Here the hangman stops his cart:
> Now the best of friends must part.
> Fare you well, for ill fare I:
> Live, lads, and I will die.
>
> "Oh, at home had I but stayed
> 'Prenticed to my father's trade,
> Had I stuck to plane and adze,
> I had not been lost, my lads.
>
> "Then I might have built perhaps
> Gallows-trees for other chaps,
> Never dangled on my own,
> Had I but left ill alone.
>
> "Now, you see, they hang me high,
> And the people passing by
> Stop to shake their fists and curse;
> So 'tis come from ill to worse.
>
> "Here hang I, and right and left
> Two poor fellows hang for theft:
> All the same's the luck we prove,
> Though the midmost hangs for love.
>
> "Comrades all, that stand and gaze,
> Walk henceforth in other ways;
> See my neck and save your own:
> Comrades all, leave ill alone.
>
> "Make some day a decent end,
> Shrewder fellows than your friend.
> Fare you well, for ill fare I:
> Live, lads, and I will die."[4]

These remorseful words from one about to hang, addressing the "lads" and "comrades" who constitute his audience offer cold comfort. Housman employs Christian symbols and allusions—his lad is a carpenter's son, his hanging evokes the Crucifixion, and he is to die between two thieves. S. G. Andrews has observed that "Housman's repeated allusions to Christ do not help us to understand the carpenter's son or his fate." Instead, "they encourage us to transfer the speech of the carpenter's son to the mouth of Christ and to search for a sense in which the speech might apply to Him."[5] More literally and naturalistically, in Hemingway's "Today is Friday," the Roman soldiers who have executed Jesus offer an epilogue to his crucifixion. Jesus does not speak in Hemingway's story. Instead we infer his emblematic courage from the effect his behavior on the cross has had on the soldiers. In Housman's poem, "the words of the carpenter's son are the means by which the poet reinterprets the significance of the Crucifixion."[6] In "Today is Friday" the words of the Roman soldiers offer a way to reinterpret the humanistic significance of what otherwise would have been to them just one more crucifixion.

The second Hemingway text to be read against the backdrop of Housman's "The Carpenter's Son" is Hemingway's own poem about hanging. "To Will Davies," a less moralistic account which reads, in part, "There were two men to be hanged / To be hanged by the neck until dead / A judge had said so. / A judge with a black cap." The poem now turns its focus on the men:

> One of them had to be held up
> Standing on the drop in the high corridor of the county jail.
> He drooled from his mouth and slobber ran down his chin
> And he fell all over the priest who was talking fast into his ear.
> In a language he didn't understand.

The poem concludes with the poet's confession: "I was glad when they pulled the black bag over his face."[7]

This description of the condemned man's involuntary reactions just before he is hanged anticipates Hemingway's later depiction, in Chapter XV of *In Our Time*, of Sam Cardinella's hanging "at six o'clock in the morning in the corridor of the county jail."

> They came out onto the gallows through a door in the wall. There were seven of them including two priests. They were carrying Sam Cardinella. He had been like that since about four o'clock in the morning.
> While they were strapping his legs together two guards held him up and the two priests where whispering to him. "Be a man, my son," said one priest. When they came toward him with the cap to go over his head Sam Cardinella lost control of his sphincter muscle. The guards who had been holding him up both dropped him. They were both disgusted. "How about a chair, Will?" asked one of the guards. "Better get one," said a man in a derby hat.

The vignette concludes with something of a final tableau:

> When they all stepped back on the scaffolding back of the drop, which was very heavy, built of oak and steel and swung on ball bearings, Sam Cardinella was left sitting there strapped tight, the younger of the two priests kneeling beside the chair. The priest skipped back onto the scaffolding just before the drop fell.

If Housman permits his condemned man to speak clearly to an unseen audience in precautionary terms, Hemingway allows his reader to infer the terror taking place in his condemned man's brain by describing his loss of bodily control, culminating in incontinence. This is how, Hemingway shows us, a condemned man will die.

Housman did not participate directly in the wars of his time—not the Boer War, not the Great War—but nevertheless wrote a number of poems about soldiers in wartime. So did Hemingway, who did go to the Great War. One of Hemingway's first attempts to use his wartime materials focuses on the victorious warrior's return to his welcoming home. "Soldier's Home," a story Hemingway described in 1924 as "the best story I ever wrote,"[8] has a "confessional note," suggests Paul Smith, that "could have been elicited" by the news of "Mussolini's recent honoring of Gabriele D'Annunzio," a ceremony that reminded Hemingway "of how he had drawn on some of the exploits of that flamboyant Italian in his own inventions for the home folks in 1919."[9]

Written against the background of an America putatively grateful to its returning soldiers, "Soldier's Home" stands as a corrective to the lyrics of songs such as those of "When Johnny Comes Marching Home." Hemingway tells the story of a veteran's return from the war only to find a home far different from the one he had left. The dream of returning to a safe place, to be feted for his exploits in a war in which he has acquitted himself honorably, lies behind this story of a fantasy and a life gone thoroughly sour. "Soldier's Home" gives the lie to the sentiments expressed in an untitled poem by Housman:

> Soldier from the wars returning,
> Spoiler of the taken town,
> Here is ease that asks not earning;
> Turn you in and sit you down.

After all, Housman continues:

> Peace is come and wars are over,
> Welcome you and welcome all,
> While the charger crops the clover
> And his bridle hangs in stall.
>
> Now no more of winters biting,
> Filth in trench from fall to spring,
> Summers full of sweat and fighting
> For the Kesar or the King.

The poet enhances the irony of his poem with the false comforting sentiments of final lines:

> Rest you, charger, rust you, bridle;
> Kings and kesars, keep your pay;
> Soldier, sit you down and idle
> At the inn of night for aye.[10]

Tell it to the marines, or, better still, tell it, in "Soldier's Home," to Krebs's mother, who, unlike the narrator of Housman's poem, harangues her son: "We want you to enjoy yourself," she says. "But you are going to have to settle down to work, Harold. Your father doesn't care what you start in at. All work is honorable as he says." Later Hemingway transposed the individual terms of the returning soldier's situation into the sweeping terms of the epigraph he composed for *Winner Take Nothing* (1933): "Unlike all other forms of lutte or / combat the conditions are that the / winner shall take nothing; neither / his ease, nor his pleasure, nor any / notions of glory; nor, if he win far / enough, shall there be any reward / within himself."[11]

In an important essay on Housman, Cleanth Brooks posits several analogies between Housman's "doomed young soldiers" and Hemingway's "hero as man-at-arms during the First World War."[12] Acknowledging that there are "surface differences" in the "idioms used," Brooks argues that "the situation, the stance taken, the attitude assumed" in the two writers "may not be different at all."[13] Curiously, Brooks does not bring up Hemingway's Frederic Henry, who can be compared with the soldier in Housman's "The Deserter," a poem that takes up the same ethos of war and love—loyalty, desertion, and treason—questioned in *A Farewell to Arms* (1929). When Lieutenant Henry flees with his lover, making for himself what Hemingway elsewhere calls "a separate peace," he also deserts the Italian army. Housman's unnamed soldier, tempted to desert the army, finds, at the last, that he cannot evade "all that croaks for war." In this dialogue between soldier and lover Housman's soldier speaks first:

> "Hark, I heard the bugle crying,
> And where am I?
> My friends are up and dressed and dying,
> And I will dress and die."

This evokes this response from his lover:

> "Oh love is rare and trouble plenty
> And carrion cheap,
> And daylight dear at four-and-twenty:
> Lie down again and sleep."

The soldier persists:

> "Reach me my belt and leave your prattle:
> Your hour is gone;
> But my day is the day of battle,
> And that comes dawning on."

The lover chides him:

> "They mow the field of man in season:
> Farewell, my fair,
> And, call it truth or call it treason,
> Farewell the vows that were."

And then she gives way to the claims of a "leaden lover":

> 'Ay, false heart, forsake me lightly:
> 'Tis like the brave.
> They find no bed to joy in rightly
> Before they find the grave.
>
> "Their love is for their own undoing,
> And east and west
> They scour about the world a-wooing
> The bullet to their breast."

The ship has sailed, she underscores, with final last lines:

> "Sail away the ocean over,
> Oh sail away,
> And lie there with your leaden lover
> For ever and a day."[14]

Housman's lines "Call it truth or call it treason, / Farewell the vows that were" expressed succinctly one of the major themes of *A Farewell to Arms*.[15]

But linking the deserter Frederic Henry to Housman's "deserter" would not do for Cleanth Brooks, so he turns instead to Housman's "Epitaph on an Army of Mercenaries," a defense of the professional, paid soldier:

> These, in the day when heaven was falling,
> The hour when earth's foundations fled,
> Followed their mercenary calling
> And took their wages and are dead.

But to them is owed the fighting that "saved" the day:

> Their shoulders held the sky suspended;
> They stood, and earth's foundations stay;
> What God abandoned, these defended,
> And saved the sum of things for pay.[16]

Brooks notes that "this brilliant little poem commemorates the small British professional army which heroically took its beating in the early days of the First World War, and which, in spite of terrible losses, managed to slow down and finally to stop the German advance, and so held the Channel ports."[17] Housman, well aware that his poem could be used as propaganda in support of the Allied war efforts and ever vigilant against the easy use (or misuse) of his work, released the poem to the London *Times* for its issue of 31 October 1917 (and, exactly a year later, allowed the *Times* to reprint it).[18] Its placement was strategic, just below an editorial commemorating

English heroism at the 1914 battle of Ypres originally perceived as a disastrous defeat for England. "This day, October 31, will in future, we trust, always be held sacred to the memory of the officers and men of our Regular Army," runs the editorial, "the Army which in 1914, in the glowing words of the Prime Minister, 'gathered the spears' of 'the Prussian legions into his breast,' and in 'perishing saved Europe,' pledging 'to hold for ever in remembrance the immortal valour of the "Old Contemptibles"—that is, "the Old Army.""[19] This was an important thing to say because some considered the soldiers of Britain's professional army to be mercenaries who fought not out of patriotism and loyalty but merely for their pay. The same charge was leveled at the French poilu whose wages were a pittance even for the times, as well as at any soldier anywhere, regular or recruit, who received pay for his service. The trick of Housman's poem is that in order to honor Britain's army he returns the term "mercenary" to its original meaning in the Hellenistic and Roman World, reminding his readers that a "mercenary soldier who fought for hire was not a dishonourable figure."[20]

Housman's poem on the virtues of the mercenaries had long held an honored place in English literary history when Cleanth Brooks concluded that it celebrates "the tough professional soldier who fights for his country, not because of some high-sounding ideal but because fighting is his profession—because that is the way he makes his living."[21] Moreover, Brooks continues, the poem makes the point that "the courage to stand and die rather than to run away usually comes from something like esprit de corps or professional pride or even from a kind of instinctive manliness rather than from adherence to the conventional rubrics of patriotism and duty."[22] It is this "manliness," concludes Brooks, that places the poem "in the general realm of Hemingway's fiction, for the mercenaries' gesture is completely consonant with the Hemingway ethos."[23] This brings us now to "The Mercenaries," a Hemingway story (whose title seems to draw on Housman's poem) that was unknown to Brooks, as it did not achieve print until twenty-four years after Hemingway's death.[24]

Some of Hemingway's most responsive interpreters have misled readers about what constitutes the essential story of "The Mercenaries," which contains a narrative within a narrative. These critics have read the embedded personal narrative of the American mercenary, Perry Graves, about the way he romantically vanquished the famous Italian war ace "Il Lupo" in a duel over a woman as the whole of Hemingway's story. For example, Paul Smith suggests that Hemingway has taken "a plot from Byron's Don Juan," capping it off with "a Western shoot-out."[25] Michael Reynolds recognizes that it is Rinaldi Renaldo who "tells the reader a war story" told to him in a Chicago bar by "an American mercenary on his way to Peru to sell his military skills in the war with Chile."[26] But Reynolds misrepresents "The

Mercenaries" by saying that it "takes place in Taormina, Sicily, late in the war," and then beginning his summary of the story this way:

> Graves, an American sergeant, has a passionate love affair with the wife or mistress of a famous Italian air ace, Il Lupo, whose picture decorated numerous magazine covers. Caught in compromising conditions, Graves faces a duel with Il Lupo. The courageous Graves, who fears death not at all, takes the challenge stoically. Facing each other with drawn pistols, their left hands touching across the table, the two soldiers wait as a servant counts to three. Il Lupo, under pressure to maintain his reputation, falters. At the count of two he tries to fire, but Graves is too quick for him, shooting the pistol out of his hand.[27]

Reynolds's shift in outlook leads him to apply the title "The Mercenaries," without textual authority, to the anecdote narrated by Graves when it belongs only to the story as a whole, to Rinaldi Renaldo's story.

If Hemingway's title directs us to his subject (the mercenary) and his theme (the mercenary's courage in facing death), it is unfortunate that most of the story is spent on the (tall) tale of a romantic duel with, in Reynolds' words, "overtones of the aging Italian poet/war-hero Gabriele d'Annunzio"—a figure who, for Hemingway at the time, was everything he "wanted to be: a famous writer, a warrior beloved by his country."[28] Perhaps Hemingway thought a story like D'Annunzio's could be used to illustrate a mercenary's wartime courage, but the tale of the romantic duel serves only to undermine Hemingway's intended effect (shared with Housman)—to emphasize the mercenary's virtuous calling and underscore his courage in warfare.

To bring this in—the realities of battle facing these "camp followers of fortune"[29]—Hemingway hit upon the device of using a pertinent quotation from Shakespeare. Thus, when Graves finishes telling his tale, the second mercenary—the Frenchman Ricaud—offers up a self-serving moral: "I wish I have it [courage without imagination]. I have died a thousand times, and I'm not a coward. I will die many more before I am buried, but it is, what you call it, Graves, my trade. We go now to a little war. Perhaps a joke war, eh? But one dies as dead in Chile as on Monfaucon."[30] These words echo Shakespeare's sententious emperor Julius Caesar, who boasts that "cowards die many times before their deaths; the valiant never taste of death but once" (II.ii.33–34). But "The Mercenaries" ends abruptly, truncated, failing to provide the precise balance (so often accomplished through pointed dialogue) that is the hallmark of the Hemingway story at its best. In 1919 he had not yet invented "the spare and additive Hemingway sentence," let alone "the peculiarly resigned sense of life that required it."[31] The tacked-on quotation from Shakespeare about courage and death fails to establish the author's sympathy for the mercenary and his ethos.

Still the device of the Shakespearean allusion-by-quotation, employed bluntly and less-than-successfully, in "The Mercenaries," remained available to Hemingway and would reappear in "The Short Happy Life of Francis Macomber," a story published in 1936.[32] There the quotation is voiced by the professional hunter Robert Wilson, a sort of "mercenary" whose trade is to steer amateur sportsmen to big game. Wilson says with self-satisfaction: "'By my troth, I care not; a man can die but once; we owe God a death and let it go which way it will, he that dies this year is quit for the next.' Damned fine, eh?" He does not attribute the quotation to *Henry IV*, Part II (III.ii.239–243), where Francis Feeble, a woman's tailor presented to Falstaff as a possible conscript, speaks the lines. And Wilson omits some of what Feeble actually says: "By my troth, I care not; a man can die but once; we owe God a death. I'll ne'er bear a base mind. An't be my destiny, so; an't be not, so. No man's too good to serve's Prince; and, let it go which way it will, he that dies this year is quit for the next." Feeble's words echo the theme introduced in Shakespeare's *Henry IV*, Part I, where Prince Hal reminds Falstaff, "Why, thou owest God a death," and Falstaff answers, "'Tis not due yet; I would be loath to pay him before his day" (V.i.127–29). Significantly, in *Henry IV*, Part II, Falstaff impugns Feeble's courage: "for a retreat—how swiftly will this Feeble, the woman's tailor, run off!" (III.ii.272–273). Thus when Wilson, himself a bit of a Falstaff, quotes Shakespeare's Francis Feeble to Hemingway's Francis Macomber, just after Macomber's boast—"You know, I'd like to try another lion…. I'm really not afraid of them now. After all, what can they do to you?"—his is a gut response to Macomber's show of confidence in an encounter with an animal—not in any showdown with another human being. Despite what Wilson subsequently says to Margot—that Macomber would have left her, too—the question of whether the "new" Francis would have stood up to Margot or Wilson is left open.[33]

And here, with the Shakespearean dialogue distributed among Feeble, Prince Hall, and Falstaff in mind, we can see an ironic foreshadowing of "The Short Happy Life of Francis Macomber" in "The Day of Battle," a final Housman poem that echoes the self-same Shakespearean lines but with greater authorial irony:

> "But since the man that runs away
> Lives to die another day,
> And cowards' funerals, when they come,
> Are not wept so well at home,"

Concluding this single-sentence poem:

> "Therefore, though the best is bad,
> Stand and do the best, my lad;
> Stand and fight and see your slain,
> And take the bullet in your brain."[34]

Macomber may never have posed such specific questions about cowardice and death to himself, but perhaps Wilson might believe it was better for Macomber to "take a bullet in the brain" than to live, a coward, only "to die another day." The lion and the Cape buffalo, it turns out, are not the only agents for testing male character in the wilds of Hemingway's Africa.

11

Memory and Experience

Of Ernest Hemingway it can be said that more successfully than any other major writer of his time he was able to communicate with a mass public without betraying his own sense of literary integrity. Time and again he discovered subjects, themes, and characters that attracted to his writings an enormous readership drawn from both the more literate and the wider popular sectors. One way in which he brought his otherwise largely discrete audiences together was through focusing upon shared, if sometimes unrecognized, cultural myths that appealed to the various segments of his total readership. Over and over, we have learned, he celebrated—sometimes darkly—his public's most persistent myths. Although much has been written about the many recognizable types that populate Hemingway's fiction—the lost-generation expatriate, the antihero at home and at war, the athlete dying young, and the triumphant professional—the intent here is to identify and to examine one of the more important, though seldom recognized, of the cultural types that bind Hemingway's work to the psychic needs of his audience: that of the aging, disabled, or apostate professional. He was particularly taken with the possibility for his professionals of what he considered a form of secular redemption. It is to such professionals, who would achieve one more unexpected triumph—something more than an empty, Pyrrhic victory—that Hemingway would turn and return many times.

Born in 1899, Hemingway aged in step with the twentieth century. Yet already in the 1920s, he had begun to write the annals of "aging" athletes such as the thirty-five-year-old boxer Jack Brennan and the apparently even older matador Manuel Garcia. It is true that Hemingway's interest at that time was that of a sensitive observer and careful writer, that of a young man sympathetic to the agonizing difficulties of the aging athlete. But a quarter of a century later, when he published *The Old Man and the Sea*, it was obvious that the young sympathetic observer had himself aged sufficiently to effect his own melding into the heroic character of his aging hero, Santiago. In this one sense *The Old Man and the Sea* can be read as the author's autobiography, allegorized and re-imagined in the life of a Cuban fisherman. Santiago's triumph, despite the Christian-ness of Hemingway's references and images, is a secular triumph. It is a triumph in and for this world, not for the next. It is a triumph defined by Santiago's knowledge that he has gone to the limit of his possibilities and beyond them, perhaps, and that he has done this when almost no one else believes that he can still do it. This triumph is of the same order as that recognized in Jesus by the most knowing of the Roman soldiers Hemingway depicts in his short play, "Today is Friday," when he remarks that Jesus "was pretty good in there today." It is Jesus' performance on the cross when it seems that no one believes in his efficacy that the professional Roman soldier admires.

That Hemingway often tended to see such unexpected triumphs by professionals debilitated by age in their enactment of the rituals of athletics cannot be taken to mean that he saw the experience of the athlete as merely a convenient metaphor for more profound human experiences. Like the conduct of war and the practice of writing, participation in certain sports, following concentrated and stylized forms, enables the dramatization of human truths as Hemingway would see them. Consequently, Hemingway could not only see that type embodied in that ancient, seemingly superannuated fisherman who would achieve one more unexpected victory, but he could also see it embodied in an aging professional baseball player. In this sense Santiago's reverence for the "great" DiMaggio meshes fully with what we know about Hemingway's convictions on courage and professionalism. Although Hemingway often saw the myth of the redeemed professional operating through the codes of sport—particularly those of prizefighting, bullfighting, and baseball—he saw it at work in other areas as well. One of the more important of those areas, of course, was art. And by art—the important late example of Thomas Hudson in *Islands in the Stream* notwithstanding—Hemingway usually meant writing. But even art he could not always accept directly in its own terms, for he tended to present its tensions and pressures in the codes and language of sport. If life was like a baseball game, writing was like championship prizefighting. One stepped into the ring with Maupassant, he would say, taking him on as he would successive challengers and winning his way, if possible, to a last match with Tolstoy. And even champions—tragically aging champions—must defend their championship turf. It was not enough, Hemingway insisted, to have won once (for which, one can read "to have once written at the very top of one's form"), but one must bring off this driving notion again and again. In point is the short story "The Snows of Kilimanjaro," in which a writer emerges as a particularly illuminating case of the aging professional in extremis: namely, the dying professional who not only has failed to live up to his conception of an essential self, but has actually come to discover that he has betrayed both trust and vocation.

In many ways "The Snows of Kilimanjaro" is highly autobiographical. It lays out in narrative form what might have happened had one particular possibility, out of many deriving from one autobiographical incident, event, or fantasy, been carried through. Written in the mid-1930s during the Great Depression, just after Hemingway and his second wife had luxuriated through an expensive African safari bankrolled by Pauline's family, "The Snows of Kilimanjaro" addressed itself to one of the probable fates awaiting the writer, kept by the rich, whom Hemingway feared he might have already become.

To measure the career of the dying writer in his mid-thirties (approximately Hemingway's own age, which was thirty-six in 1935), Hemingway again draws on the professional's code. This time, however, he crosses that code with the notion of the writer as priest, and he affirms that writing itself is, in the purer sense of the word, a vocation. Other writers had already made those equations, of course, notably James Joyce. Of particular interest to Hemingway, however, may have been F. Scott Fitzgerald's decision to cast Dick Diver, his psychiatrist-hero, as both a "spoiled priest" and failed writer.

Tender Is the Night was one of Hemingway's principal literary sources when he went about composing his elegiac account of a writer whose sickness unto death derives from apostasy and self-betrayal. That Harry Walden is at once Hemingway's surrogate for himself, the fictional Dick Diver, and even his friend Scott Fitzgerald, will surprise no one. Nor will anyone be surprised at the observation that Hemingway and Fitzgerald were much taken with metaphors of vocation and profession. Yet, if Fitzgerald chooses to dramatize the slow moral slippage of his psychiatrist-writer—Fitzgerald's key term is lesion, a wonderfully precise word, employed only at crucial moments—Hemingway chooses to dramatize his writer-priest's eleventh-hour recapitulation of a life, that though well enough begun, has undeniably soured along the way. Hemingway's writer, who "never infects," is nevertheless dying of an infection. He numbers his time now not in days, but in minutes. There are only two important activities left to him: to remember and to write. To remember so as to write. But writing, in any physical sense, is no longer a possibility. Not even dictation, he reminds Helen, matters. Yet at a crucial moment in the story he insists, in an answer to one of Helen's questions, that he is writing. Beyond the point when writing would require the physical act of transcribing composed thoughts on paper, Harry radically redefines writing as an act of pure composition. He now composes—that is, he now writes—as the pure Romantic would write, disdaining the written word itself. And it is Hemingway's intention that we see that Harry at the very end of his life is writing well, that is, to use Hemingway's most honorific term, writing truly. Only at the eleventh hour, perhaps, and only for hours and minutes, but Harry, Hemingway would tell us, has earned the fantasy of his final journey, that apocalyptic rescue that would lead not to the healing of his infected leg but to redemption for his infected spirit. Because the writer has recovered his capacity to write, this "spoiled priest" has managed at the last to "work the fat off his soul."

In "The Snows of Kilimanjaro" Hemingway draws upon the permeating codes of vocation and profession in two other ways: first, in Harry's obsession with the terms trade and talent; and second, in Hemingway's penchant for seeing Harry's life as if it were the life of another apostate professional, Milton's Samson. Harry's true trade is writing. But he has long ago betrayed that trade, as he puts it, by trading on his talent. Harry has done this, he admits, by lying and by adopting lesser trades such as loveless lovemaking. Indeed, he has sold out his talent, as he says, for the "blood money" that came with that "rich bitch" he had married, that destroyer of his talent.

> The steps by which she had acquired him and the way in which she had finally fallen in love with him were all part of a regular progression in which she had built herself a new life and he had traded away what remained of his old life.
> He had traded it for security, for comfort too, there was no denying that, and for what else? He did not know.

Whatever his reasons and elaborate rationalizations, it cannot be denied, however, that Harry had married into the world of the rich: Helen's "goddamned Old Westbury, Saratoga, Palm Beach people." The land of the rich, to Harry the priest-writer, is his land of the Philistines. Like Milton's Samson, whose betrayal of his priestly vocation, his "Heav'n-gifted strength," began when he married a woman "of another people," Harry dates his apostasy from his marriage to Helen. Even as Delilah was traditionally associated with the hyena, as a deceiver and devourer, Helen herself, as an emblematic reminder of Harry's spiritual decay, is abetted by the hyena that stands as the obscene omen of Harry's physical death. If imprisoned, blind, ridiculed Samson meditates sorrowfully on the way in which he came to betray his priestly vocation, gangrenous, embattled, cynical Harry rides his reason through his memories to a just assessment of the way in which he has betrayed his talent. In a deeply personal sonnet Milton himself had marveled bitterly at his fate in having been implicitly commanded to employ his innate talent in the service of his God but afflicted with the blindness that would seem to prevent the fulfillment of that talent. Harry's affliction has not been physical blindness, but it has involved another kind of blindness. Afflicted by self-deception, Harry has told himself that having married money he would someday write well about the rich, which is to say, write truly about them, and that he has not traded on his talent. Like Milton, Hemingway draws on the parable of the talents in Matthew, which charges the lord's steward with failure to increase the fortune entrusted to him. A hard fate it is to be endowed with God-given talent and then to be ordered to exercise that talent to the fullest, regardless of the personal risk or ultimate cost involved. For Milton and Hemingway, writing itself was a great gamble. It is in that sense that at the end of his allotted time Harry once again functions as a writer. His eleventh-hour triumph over his apostasy allies him to Milton, the Samson who tears down the pillars of the temple, the Santiago who survives his arrogance in daring to go out too far, and all other redeemed professionals, in literature, life, and myth.

Hemingway found those cultural types that would link him to his audience. He was true to the subjects and characters that would reach his larger mass audience even as his disciplined, artful style appealed to that more literate audience that would insure his continuing literary reputation. Yet Hemingway's accomplishment was due less to his shrewdness, assuredly, than to the necessities of his personality and character. What emerges clearly is that Hemingway himself deeply believed in the validity of the types that characterized his culture in its broadest reaches.

12

Standing Alone

Out of field notes taken for an unwritten dispatch for the North American News Alliance (NANA), Ernest Hemingway's wrote "Old Man at the Bridge," a work of fiction that first appeared, not as a story but as a dispatch, in the news journal *Ken* on May 29, 1938.[1] In first-person narration, Hemingway tells a soldier's story. While he looks out at what he calls "the African looking country of the Ebro Delta," this loyalist soldier listens for "the first noises" of the enemy "that would signal that ever mysterious event called contact." Before that "contact" takes place, however, he experiences a different sort of contact. He comes upon an old man, a civilian dressed in "black dusty clothes" and wearing "steel rimmed spectacles" who sits exhausted by the side of the nearly empty road. The implied contrast between these two "contacts"—the one expected and probably imminent and the other unexpected and present—gives Hemingway's Spanish Civil War story its emotive strength.

The soldier-narrator discovers that this old man who has lived a half a dozen years beyond his three score and ten is without family or politics. But he has been the last one evacuated from San Carlos because he was caring for two goats, a cat, and four pairs of pigeons. Now all of them have been left behind and he fears for their safety, though the cat will be all right, he thinks, for "a cat can look out for itself." The old man is too tired to go on. When he struggles to his feet and tries to move on, he sways from "side to side" and sits "down backwards in the dust." "There was nothing to do about him," concludes the narrator, for "the Fascists were advancing toward the Ebro." It was overcast, a gray day in which the low ceiling kept the Fascist planes on the ground. "That and the fact that cats know how to look after themselves was all the good luck that old man would ever have."

When the narrative ends the moment of contact with the enemy is still in the offing. What has taken place is that in a different sort of "mysterious moment" two human beings have come into minimal but humane contact even if the soldier can do nothing for the old man, even as the old man could do nothing at the end for his animals and birds. Yet there is a connection to be made here between the narrator's observation about the moment of contact with enemy forces during battle and the incidental contact between soldiers and civilians in the context of the war overall. Both kinds of contact remain mysterious, but it is the mystery of humane contact that Hemingway dramatizes in "Old Man at the Bridge," a contact that also epitomizes the effect the war was having on the Spanish people at large. Of that other kind of contact, signaled in this story by the advancing sounds of the enemy, there would be more than plenty in the events surrounding the blowing-up of the Fascist-held bridge depicted in Hemingway's 1940 Spanish Civil War novel, *For Whom the Bell Tolls*.

13

The Hemingway Ending

Literary historians and critics today mention Hemingway and O. Henry in the same breath only to contrast their stories, particularly the endings of those stories, and they do so, invariably, to O. Henry's disadvantage.[1] While O. Henry is customarily offered up as the facile contriver of ingenious plots, Hemingway is invoked as the architect of the virtually plotless story.[2] O. Henry's stories work toward surprising, sometimes astonishing endings—so runs the argument—but Hemingway's stories often seem to stop without really finishing. Indeed, so evidently radical was Hemingway's departure from the received conventions of the short story, that on one occasion his friends Scott Fitzgerald and Christian Gauss actually accused him of having constructed in "Big Two-Hearted River" a story "in which nothing happened."[3]

Hemingway himself had something to do with the terms of the comparison of his stories with those of O. Henry. To his Shandyean interlocutor in *Death in the Afternoon* he explained that as for himself it had been a long time since he had "added the wow to the end of a story."[4] If he did not have his predecessor precisely in mind, he was at least referring to his predecessor's kind of story. In short, although he had once been an imitator of O. Henry's work,[5] Hemingway would now have us believe that he had long since elected to compose what he took to be a different, less traditional kind of story than the one advocated by the day's "handbooks" on short-story writing.[6]

Critics have so totally accepted Hemingway's word that he spurned the surprise ending that they have failed to acknowledge that Hemingway was wont to employ his own brand of the surprise ending. At first look, the ending of the typical Hemingway story may appear to be radically muted, its effect more oblique than that of the typical O. Henry story. But like O. Henry's, those endings are unexpected and highly ironic. One need look only at "A Clean, Well-Lighted Place" with the older waiter's dismissal of his despair as "probably only insomnia," "Indian Camp" with the child's conviction that as for himself, despite the suicide he has just witnessed, he will never die, and the revelation in "A Canary for One" that the American couple, who have just been subjected to a long disquisition on the superiority of American husbands, are about to get a divorce—one need only sample Hemingway's characteristic endings to see that in his own way Hemingway was as addicted to the "wow" as was O. Henry. What he did do, in reality, was adapt the surprise ending to his own quite different view of human experience. To see how he did this and to measure just how his practice both approximates and diverges from O. Henry's, it is instructive to examine Hemingway's "The Snows of Kilimanjaro" and O. Henry's "The Last Leaf." Both stories are based on an individual's vigil in the face of impending death.

A New York story about artists, "The Last Leaf" turns on the idea of heroic sacrifice. The aging artist Behrman's sacrifice of his life in order to paint a life-sustaining image of a leaf on the wall opposite the window of a dying young woman is the stuff of open-faced sentimentality. At the cost of life the old artist paints the masterpiece he has talked about for a lifetime. But Behrman's character has no depth, no complexity, nor does his author intend him to have any. Neither, for that matter, do the story's other principals, the two young girls who share the flat above Behrman's. But then the author does not intend anyone to take on life at the expense of the plot. His total interest is in the turn his incident takes. His characters are counters to be maneuvered toward the surprising irony, which scoops out the plot. Evidently the characters have been invented to serve the pure plot line of the incident the author has devised. Recognizing this, we must agree that they serve their function well. They say their lines but never get in the way of the action. There is no evidence in "The Last Leaf" that O. Henry was interested in what Henry James once called the prime function of fiction: to convey "a direct impression of life." What interests O. Henry is an action that surprisingly and ironically reveals a moment in which death and sacrifice work ironically to sustain youth and life. In fact, O. Henry moves quickly through the exposition necessary to crack out his denouement. One even senses that the author is impatient to get the preliminary terms of his story squared away so that he can uncover his particular irony. As a result, there is one ironic moment in the story and that one is, in characteristic O. Henry fashion, saved for the end. The dying girl has been deceived into choosing life over death and it has been a failed artist who has at last found an occasion and a purpose worthy of his modest art. The irony remains locked in the incident. Above all, it is not adequate to suggest that O. Henry's vision of life is ironic. Indeed, despite O. Henry's use of the universal themes of sacrifice and death, the story offers us no sense of universal fate or timeless psychology. The author's vision of human experience never breaks out of the incident he has devised. Only the sentimentality of the surprisingly happy ending remains. It is of course a tribute to O. Henry's inventiveness that for multitudes of readers that has sufficed.

In 1934, Hemingway offered the readers of *Esquire* his considered opinion of O. Henry in comparison with the French master of the short story Guy de Maupassant: "They taught us in high-school how when someone compared O. Henry to DeMaupassant," he starts out. "O. Henry was indignant, saying that he had never written a dirty word or a dirty song in his life. O. Henry was a wonderful fellow too."

> They put him in jail once it is true but everybody agreed, when he died, that he was a prince. Now Guy DeMaupassant was not a wonderful fellow. He spent a lot of time getting girls into trouble and he died violently after living some time with syphilis of the brain. But he was a great writer. Sometimes he was a great hack writer but, along with his poor stories, he wrote more truly great short stories than any other man except Rudyard Kipling whose work it is now fashionable to disparage because he was a fool about politics and had the misfortune to outlive his talent.

Then he returns to Maupassant and his commitment to using only the "real" words: "When DeMaupassant wrote about prostitutes he used the true words and wrote literature," Hemingway concludes. "O. Henry was morally superior to the committing of literature."[7]

Such write-offs were typical of Hemingway, especially at that time. But the timing of this one is particularly interesting. Within two years, oddly enough, Hemingway would write and publish two of his most complexly plotted and, in some ways, most O. Henry–like stories: "The Short Happy Life of Francis Macomber" with its surprise "ending"—the sudden violent death of the hero—sprung on the reader only to have the story fall away in ironic dialogue, and "The Snows of Kilimanjaro."

Most readers will agree that Hemingway's "The Snows of Kilimanjaro" is a more complex performance than O. Henry's "The Last leaf." Its mosaic of retrospectives and its shifts between the writer Harry's inner reality and the outward reality he shares with his wife have no parallel in O. Henry's story. Nevertheless, the stories deal with the same basic situation: a disabled artist facing death. And both stories depend upon a "wow" ending. Indeed, the fate of Hemingway's hero, complete with the presentation of his apocalyptic translation to the "House of God" at the top of Kilimanjaro, succeeded by his wife's shrieking recognition that—all-too-naturalistically— Harry is dead, provides us with Hemingway's complicated version of the surprise ending. If we do not know whether or not Harry has undergone an eleventh-hour redemption, we have nevertheless had the surprise of learning of his death even as we have first experienced his "rescue." Hemingway's "second" ending exactly reverses that of O. Henry's story "the Last Leaf" but only after his "first" ending has paralleled it.

That O. Henry himself was one of the writers Hemingway had in mind when writing "Snows" is suggested by the exchange between the husband and wife, Harry and Helen. "You can't die if you don't give up," encourages the rich woman; to which the writer replies, "Where did you read that? You're such a bloody fool." As the doctor in "Last Leaf" says of his patient, "She has one chance in—let us say, ten.... And that chance is for her to want to live.... [W]henever my patient begins to count the carriages in her funeral procession I subtract 50 per cent, from the curative powers of medicines."[8]

While subscribing implicitly to the critical theories of Edgar Allan Poe and following the sometime practice of Nathaniel Hawthorne in that he would invent the incidents which would convey the single, predetermined effect of his tale, O. Henry works out everything toward his "wow" ending; but Hemingway tries to make every detail of the story release that "wow" gradually. Perhaps it is only in retrospect that we perceive how Hemingway defines the nature of contradictory human experience by so arranging his stories through a sequence of ironies; but there can be no doubt that Hemingway's faith in his kind of resonant ending—the ending without the single O. Henry "wow"—was justified. It is after one has finished the story that one sees the purposes of the earlier details and scenes, and the fact that those details unfold a series of quiet, decentralized ironies gives us a sense that the author is revealing something about the nature of human life. Not an ironic incident only does he present us with, but the felt sense that life itself is grained with irony. In O. Henry's "The Last Leaf" we are left with an incident that concludes ironically; in Hemingway's "The Snows of Kilimanjaro" we are left with a chapter in the author's assessment of the ironic nature of human experience. The difference, of course, is one of total outlook. Fascinated by the small ironies of human experience, O. Henry heightened the drama of life to an artificially precise final effect, but Hemingway, seeing the whole of human life as itself inherently and inescapably ironic, worked to move the reader toward his own discovery that irony is at the core of human experience. Despite the essential differences, however, and all public disclaimers notwithstanding, in practice Hemingway never did forsake the "wow" or surprise ending. He merely placed it somewhere else.

Chapter Notes

Preface

1. Leo Spitzer, "Linguistic Perspectivism in 'Don Quijote,'" in *Linguistics and Literary History: Essays in Stylistics* (Princeton, N. J.: Princeton University Press, 1948), p. 42.
2. Ford Madox Ford, Introduction, *A Farewell to Arms* (New York: Modern Library, 1932), p. ix.
3. Ernest Hemingway, *A Moveable Feast* (New York: Scribner's, 1964), p. 75.
4. Unless otherwise noted, quotations from Hemingway's stories refer to *The Complete Short Stories of Ernest Hemingway*, The Finca Vigía Edition (New York: Scribner's, 1991).
5. George Plimpton, "An Interview with Ernest Hemingway," *Writers at Work: The Paris Review Interviews*, Second Series, intr. Van Wyck Brooks (New York: Viking, 1963), p. 235. This interview was first published in *The Paris Review*, 18 (Spring 1958). Hemingway's formulation of the iceberg theory occurs in *Death in the Afternoon* (New York: Scribner's 1932), p. 192.
6. Ernest Hemingway, *Selected Letters, 1917–1961*, ed. Carlos Baker (New York: Scribner's, 1981), p. 867.
7. Mary Welsh Hemingway, *How It Was* (New York: Knopf, 1976), p. 352.
8. When the Old Lady asks Hemingway about the meaning of the phrase "talking horseshit," his answer is: "we apply the term now to describe unsoundness in an abstract conversation or, indeed, any over-metaphysical tendency in speech" (*Death in the Afternoon*, 95).
9. Hemingway, *Selected letters*, 780. Hemingway described *The Old Man and the Sea* (New York: Scribner's, 1952) as "the prose that I have been working for all my life that should read easily and simply and seem short and yet have all the dimensions of the visible world and the world of a man's spirit" (738).
10. Hemingway, *Selected Letters*, 837.

Introduction

1. *Selected Letters of John O'Hara*, ed. Matthew J. Bruccoli (New York: Random House, 1978), p. 348. In 1950 O'Hara had evoked a flurry of protest when he wrote: "The most important author living today, the outstanding author since the death of Shakespeare, has brought out a new novel. The title of the novel is *Across the River and Into the Trees*. The author, of course, is Ernest Hemingway, the most important, the outstanding author out of the millions of writers who have lived since 1616" ("The Author's Name is Hemingway," *New York Times Book Review*, Sept. 10, 1950, 1, 30).
2. D. H. Lawrence, Review of *In Our Time*, *Calendar of Modern Letters*, 4 (Apr. 1927), 72–73.
3. Scribner's followed Philip Young's plan for the book, but decided not to use his critical introduction, preferring a much shorter preface; see Young, "Big World Out There: The Nick Adams Stories," *Novel: A Forum on Fiction*, 6 (Fall 1972), 5–19, and "Posthumous Hemingway, and Nicholas Adams," in *Hemingway In Our Time*, eds. Richard Astro and Jackson J. Benson (Corvallis: Oregon State University Press, 1974), pp. 13–23. As early as 1930 Granville Hicks asserted that any study of Hemingway's portrayal of the "spiritual history" of the hero must start with Nick Adams ("The World of Hemingway," *New Freeman*, 1 [Mar. 1930], 40–42).
4. This epigraph appears on the title-page of editions of *Winner Take Nothing* but is absent from the collective editions of Hemingway's stories.
5. It is Maxwell Perkins' warning that Carlos Baker quotes in *Ernest Hemingway, A Life Story* (New York: Scribner's, 1969), p. 241.
6. Typical of Harry Walden's final "stories," echoing the content and style of the sketches Hemingway first published as part of *in our time* and incorporated into *In Our Time*, is the following:

He remembered long ago when Williamson, the bombing officer, had been hit by a stick bomb some one in a German patrol had thrown as he was coming in through the wire that night and, screaming, had begged every one to kill him. He was a fat man, very brave, and a good officer, although addicted to fantastic shows. But that night he was caught in the wire, with a flare lighting him up and his bowels spilled out into the wire, so when they brought him in, alive, they had to cut him loose. Shoot me, Harry. For Christ sake shoot me. They had had an argument one time about our Lord never sending you anything you could not bear and some one's theory had been that meant that a certain time the pain passed you out automatically. But he had always remembered Williamson, that night. Nothing passed out Williamson until he gave him all his morphine tablets that he had always saved to use himself and then they did not work right away [53].

7. Two additional stories, "Philip Haines Was a Writer" and "Lack of Passion," edited from manuscript, appeared in *The Hemingway Review*, 9 (Spring 1990), 1–93.
8. *Moveable Feast*, v.
9. Glauco Ortolano, "An Interview with Ana Maria Machado," *WLT: World Literature Today*, 76 (Spring 2002), 112.

Chapter 1

1. See, for example, Edmund Wilson, *Apologies to the Iroquois* (New York: Farrar, Straus and Cudahy, 1960), and *O Canada: An American's Notes on Canadian Culture* (New York: Farrar, Straus and Giroux, 1965).
2. Lionel Trilling, *Matthew Arnold* (New York: Columbia University Press, 1949), and *E. M. Forster* (Norfolk, Conn.: New Directions, 1943).
3. Lionel Trilling, *A Gathering of Fugitives* (Boston: Beacon Press, 1956), p. 86.
4. Talcott Parsons, *The Social System* (Glencoe, Ill. and London: Free Press, 1964), p. 445.
5. F. Scott Fitzgerald, *Tender Is the Night* (New York: Scribner's, 1934), p. 185.
6. William Faulkner, *The Wild Palms* (New York: Random House, 1939), pp. 51–52.
7. Philip Young, *Ernest Hemingway* (New York and Toronto: Rinehart, 1952), pp. 3–4; and, revised, *Ernest Hemingway: A Reconsideration* (University Park, Pennsylvania: Pennsylvania State University Press, 1966), pp. 31–32.
8. Ben Raeburn, Foreword, *Treasury for the Free World*, ed. Ben Raeburn (New York: Arco, 1946), p. xv.

Chapter 2

1. Herman Melville, *Moby-Dick or, The Whale* (New York: Hendricks House, 1952), pp. 393–96.
2. Melville defines "waif" as "a pennoned pole," which is "inserted upright into the floating body of a dead whale, both to mark its place on the sea, and also as token of prior possession, should the boats of any other ship draw near" (*Moby-Dick*, 389).
3. Melville, *Moby-Dick*, 395.
4. Hemingway's disapproval of the Christian Scientist surfaces in a letter to Maxwell Perkins in 1929: "But the Xian Science business *was* something to worry over I can see. Though I don't think *they* will make any trouble for A Farewell—They arent smart—They are simply wonderfully organized—If they were more intelligent they wouldnt be Xstian Scientists maybe. Anyway I hope you have luck with the book [Fraden Dakin's *Mrs. Eddy: The Biography of a Virginal Mind*]—The next 2 times that you would in your plans devote a large space to A Farewell please use ½ the space and the other ½ for the Eddy Book—I would be damned pleased if you would—" (*The Only Thing That Counts: The Ernest Hemingway/ Maxwell Perkins Correspondence, 1925–1947*, ed. Matthew J. Bruccoli [New York: Scribner's, 1996], p. 135).
5. For an early psycho-sexual interpretation of the father's "fondling of the gun," see Robert Murray Davis, "Hemingway's 'The Doctor and the Doctor's Wife,'" *The Explicator*, 25 (Sept. 1966), 1.
6. Larry E. Grimes employs William James's categories of religious experience to read the story as a conflict between the physician and his wife—his is of the "sick-soul" variety, hers of the "healthy-minded" ("William James and 'The Doctor and the Doctor's Wife,'" in *Hemingway: Up in Michigan Perspectives*, ed. Frederic J. Svoboda and Joseph J. Waldmeir [East Lansing: Michigan State University Press, 1995], pp. 47–57).
7. See Young, *Hemingway: A Reconsideration*, 33.
8. Carlos Baker, "A Search for the Man As He Really Was," *New York Times Book Review* (July 26, 1964), BR14.
9. Hemingway, *Selected Letters*, 153.

Chapter 3

1. *The Forum*, 74 (Aug. 1925), 227.
2. In Chapter 32 of *A Farewell to Arms* (New

York: Scribner's, 1929), Frederic Henry proves he is adept at "riding" the freights by skillfully mounting a passing train, where he will pass the night nestled among the guns being carried to the front.

3. Paul Smith, A *Reader's Guide to the Short Stories of Ernest Hemingway* (Boston: G. K. Hall, 1989), p. 116, and Frederic Joseph Svoboda, "Inventing the Experience in 'The Battler,'" *Up in Michigan: Proceedings of the First National Conference of the Hemingway Society*, ed. Joseph J. Waldmeir (East Lansing: Michigan State University Press, 1983), p. 44. Even Nick Adams does not always ride the freights. In "Big, Two-Hearted River," for instance, it is apparent that he has paid for his ticket to Seney (where, as it turned out, "there was no town, nothing but the rails and the burned-over country") because he has been allowed to "check" his stuff: "Nick sat down on the bundle of canvas and bedding the baggage man had pitched out of the door of the baggage car" (163).

4. *American Fiction, American Myth: Essays by Philip Young*, ed. Sandra Spanier (University Park, PA: Pennsylvania State University Press, 2000), p. 99.

5. In "Miss Stein Instructs," Hemingway riffs on what he could have told Stein about his "prejudices against homosexuality" but did not at the time:

> I knew its more primitive aspects. I knew it was why you carried a knife and would use it when you were in the company of tramps when you were a boy in the days when wolves was not a slang term for men obsessed by the pursuit of women. I knew many *inaccrochable* terms and phrases from Kansas City days and the mores of different parts of that city, Chicago and the lake boats. Under questioning I tried to tell Miss Stein that when you were a boy and moved in the company of men, you had to be prepared to kill a man, know how to do it and really know that you would do it in order not to be interfered with. That term was *accrochable*. If you knew you would kill, other people sensed it very quickly and you were let alone; but there were certain situations you could not allow yourself to be forced into or trapped into. I could have expressed myself more vividly by using an *inaccrochable* phrase that wolves used on the lake boats. "Oh gash may be fine but one eye for mine." But I was always careful of my language with Miss Stein even when true phrases might have clarified or better expressed a prejudice. (*Moveable Feast*, 18–19)

Sure he could have, but it's sure as certain that Miss Stein would have seen through this invention of personal experience, borrowed from the tramp literature of his youth.

6. See Peter Griffin, *Along with Youth: Hemingway, the Early Years* (New York: Oxford University Press, 1985), p. 40; Nicholas Gerogiannis, "Nick Adams on the Road: 'The Battler' as Hemingway's Man on the Hill," in *Critical Essays on Ernest Hemingway's "In Our Time*," ed. Michael Reynolds (Boston: G. K. Hall, 1983), pp. 178–79.

7. These titles are not represented in Hemingway's library at Finca Vigía or listed among other books Hemingway is known to have read (Michael S. Reynolds, *Hemingway's Reading, 1910–1940: An Inventory* [Princeton, NJ: Princeton University Press, 1981], and "A Supplement to Hemingway's Reading: 1910–1940," *Studies in American Fiction*, 14 [Spring 1986], 99–108). But as records of Hemingway's reading are incomplete, and given the widespread popularity of London's books at the time, it is plausible that the young Hemingway was acquainted with them. Surely such stuff, along with the Davies and Flynt autobiographies, would have appealed to a schoolboy of Hemingway's adventurous temperament. Few if any of the books surviving at Finca Vigía can be traced to Hemingway's boyhood years in Oak Park.

8. Joseph Flynt, *Tramping with Tramps* (New York: Century, 1900), p. 313.

9. Nowhere (except perhaps in the staged photograph of the young Hemingway hanging from a box car), does Hemingway romanticize the hobo's feeling for riding the trains, epitomized by this passage from Glen H. Mullin:

> To the genuine hobo, a train is a thing compounded of magic and beauty, just as a bravely trimmed vessel is to a mariner. It arouses within him a latent mysticism. The rattle and swank of a long freight pulling out of the yards, the locomotive, black and eager, shoving her snorting muzzle along the rails, this is a spectacle and a challenge which only the wanderer who loves train riding can understand. To him at such a moment, a train is not harnessed to the sordid, uncouth uses of commercial transport. She is an enchanted caravan moving into the mysterious beyond, hailing with bells and song the blue distance that fades forever as she moves. As a hobo sits on a tie-pile, perhaps, and watches her go by, there is a lure in the cars themselves individually. He moves his lips unconsciously repeating the sonorous names that lilt past: Père Mar-

quette, Burlington, Chicago Great Western, Lake Shore and Michigan Southern, Grand Trunk, Iron Mountain, Canadian Pacific, Santa Fé, C. C. C. and St. L., Lehigh Valley, Lackawanna. He hears the grind of the cars as they pound and jostle each other, the wheels spinning faster and faster. Box-cars, oil-tanks, cattle-cars odorous and packed with clamorous stock, coal-cars, bulging fruit-cars—a motley-colored procession—squeal by. He must make her now, for in a moment she will be too fast for him. Out he bounds, picking his car with a practiced eye, and swings himself exultingly to a flying stirrup. On the Road again!" [*Adventures of a Scholar Tramp* (New York & London: Century, 1925), pp. 105–06].

10. William H. Davies, *The Autobiography of a Super-Tramp* (New York: Knopf, 1924), pp. 29–30.
11. Flynt, *Tramping*, 355–56.
12. Clark G. Spence, "Knights of the Fast Freight," *American Heritage Magazine* (Aug. 1976). www.americanheritage.com/articles/magazine/ah
13. Mullin, *Adventures*, 259.
14. Mullin, *Adventures*, 259, 260.
15. Mullin, *Adventures*, 139, 181.
16. Davies, *Autobiography*, 175.
17. Flynt, *Tramping*, 119.
18. Jack London, *The Road* (Santa Barbara and Salt Lake City: Peregrine, 1970), pp. 134–35.
19. Mullin, *Adventures*, 123.
20. Todd DePastino, Introduction, to Jack London, *The Road*, ed. Todd DePastino (New Brunswick, NJ, and London: Rutgers University Press, 2006), pp. xxvii–xxviii, and Harold Wentworth and Stuart Berg Flexner, eds. *Dictionary of American Slang*, Second Supplemented Edition (New York: Crowell, n.d.).
21. DePastino, *The Road*, xxvii.
22. DePastino, *The Road*, xxvii.
23. Davies, *Autobiography*, 183.
24. Possibly Alice is related to a generous and charitable fat woman that Mullin met on his travels: "An enormous woman blond as Brunhild rocked to the door, all chins, and pinkness, and smiling dimples. I immediately put her in my pocket (figuratively speaking) with a hard-luck story that was principally the truth." After she feeds him and gives him some of her husband's cast-off garments, he pleads "with that fat woman to give me some work of some sort to repay her for her kindness, but she insisted that there was nothing." May the benisons of Fortunatus descend upon all fat women, now and forever. Amen!" (Mullin, *Adventures*, 228–29).

25. Cleveland Amory, Introduction, *The Lawrenceville Stories* (New York: Simon and Schuster, 1967), p. ix.
26. Owen Johnson, *The Varmint* (New York: Baker & Taylor, 1910), p. 200.
27. Owen Johnson, *The Lawrenceville Stories* (New York: Simon and Schuster, 1967), p. 7.
28. Johnson also touches on one of Hemingway's great passions, the Spanish bullfight. His observation in *The Varmint* that the "nag had that superiority which one sacrificial horse in a Spanish bullfight ring has over another" (252) prefigures, specifically, Hemingway's disquisition on the bullfight horse in *Death in the Afternoon*.
29. Arthur Mizener, *The Far Side of Paradise: A Biography of F. Scott Fitzgerald* (Boston: Houghton Mifflin, 1951), p. 97; Henry Dan Piper, *F. Scott Fitzgerald: A Critical Portrait* (London: Bodley Head, 1966), pp. 51–52: and Matthew J. Bruccoli, *Some Sort of Epic Grandeur: The Life of F. Scott Fitzgerald* (New York and London: Harcourt Brace Jovanovich, 1981), pp. 32, 43.
30. Hemingway, *Selected Letters*, 695.
31. F. Scott Fitzgerald, *This Side of Paradise* (New York: Scribner's, 1920), p. 26.
32. John Updike, "Basically Decent," *New Yorker* (Mar. 9, 2009), p. 75.
33. Diana Warwick, "Life and Letters," *Life*, 83 (Mar. 6, 1924), 24.
34. Young, *American Fiction*, 116.
35. "Dale Wasserman, Playwright, Dies at 94," New York *Times* (Dec. 27, 2008), 18.

Chapter 4

1. Nagrom Notpoh, "In praise of M. Barkers excellent Book of Angling," in Thomas Barker, *Barker's Delight: or, The Art of Angling* (London: Humphrey Moselye, 1659); the second (enlarged) edition is reprinted in *Three Books on Fishing (1599–1659) Associated with The Complete Angler (1653) by Izaak Walton*, intr. J. Milton French (Gainesville, Florida: Scholars' Facsimiles and Reprints, 1962). The poem appears in *Three Books*, 145.
2. "Proclamation 5817—National Fishing Week, 1988," *Public Papers of the Presidents of the United States: Ronald Reagan 1988, Book I—January 1 to July 1, 1988* (Washington: United States Government Printing Office, 1990), p. 569.
3. Izaak Walton, *The Complete Angler 1653–1676*, ed. Jonquil Bevan (Oxford: Clarendon Press, 1983), p. 59.
4. Izaak Walton's name has only infrequently been paired with Hemingway's. When Carlos Baker did so, in 1952, he wrote only: "If

we read the river-story singly, looking merely at what it says, there is probably no more effective account of euphoria in the language, even when one takes comparative account of *The Compleat Angler*, Hazlitt on the pleasures of hiking, Keats on the autumn harvest, Thoreau on the Merrimack, Belloc on 'The Mowing of a Field,' or Frost on 'Hyla Brook.' It tells with great simplicity of a lone fisherman's expedition after trout" (*Hemingway: The Writer as Artist*, 4th ed. [Princeton, New Jersey: Princeton University Press, 1972], p. 125). But, of course, Baker did not read the story "singly," any more than he looked further into *The Compleat Angler*'s relevance to "Big Two-Hearted River." Even Gregory S. Sojka, who focuses on the figure of the angler, makes only fleeting references to Walton (*Ernest Hemingway: The Angler as Artist* [New York: Peter Lang, 1985]). Gerry Brenner, on the other hand, suggests that Walton was a (silent) influence on *Death in the Afternoon*, though he does not choose to extend his thesis to Hemingway's other work. His failure to do so is explained, perhaps, by his footnote: "Fatal though it may be to my argument in the following few pages, I, well, take the bull by the horns here to admit that none of the existing records of Hemingway's reading or libraries has turned up a copy of Walton's *Compleat Angler*. I find it hard to believe, however, that he had not encountered it at one time or another. And the resemblances that I discuss seem to me to be too strong for them to be merely coincidental" (*Concealments in Hemingway's Works* [Columbus: Ohio State University Press, 1983], pp. 4, 65-70, and 247n). Brenner does not mention that Hemingway refers to Walton and his book in two pieces of journalism: "The Best Rainbow Trout Fishing," *Toronto Star Weekly* (Aug. 28, 1920), reprinted in *Dateline: Toronto: The Complete Toronto Star Dispatches, 1920-1924*, ed. William White (New York: Scribner's, 1985), pp. 50-52; and "Out in the Stream: A Cuban Letter," *Esquire* (Aug. 1934), 19, 156, 158, reprinted in *By-line: Ernest Hemingway, Selected articles and Dispatches of Four Decades*, ed. William White (New York: Scribner's, 1967), pp. 172-78.

5. Edmund Wilson, "Ernest Hemingway: Bourdon Gauge of Morale," *Atlantic Monthly*, 164 (July 1939) 36-46; Malcolm Cowley, Introduction to the *Viking Portable Library Hemingway* (New York: Viking, 1944), pp. vii-xxiv; and Young, *Ernest Hemingway*, 15-20.

6. "Big Two-Hearted River," *Field & Stream*, 59 (May 1954), 45-48, 96-105.

7. Ernest Hemingway, "The Art of the Short Story," *Paris Review*, 23 (Spring 1981), 85-102; and *Moveable Feast*, 76-77. At the time Scribner's gave up the idea for the new story collection, and Hemingway's essay was not published during his lifetime.

8. This student is in agreement with Stephen Miko, a "hiker" who asks rhetorically "did anyone ever go on a hiking or fishing trip *not* to escape whatever else his life is?" ("The River, the Iceberg, and the Shit-detector," *Criticism*, 33 [Fall 1991], 513). He also concludes that "the action, especially in part two of the story, can be organized as a series of deliberate 'how to' lessons: how to catch, store, and use grasshoppers for bait; how to make flapjacks, including what tools to use and how to tell when they are done; how to prepare the fly-rod, with special attention to gut leaders; how to carry all that you need to the stream" (521).

9. Kenneth Lynn, "Hemingway's Private War," *Commentary*, 72 (July 1981), 24-33; reprinted in Lynn, *The Air-Line to Seattle: Studies in Literary and Historical Writing about America* (Chicago: University of Chicago Press, 1983), pp. 108-31. Cowley's reply, "Hemingway's Wound—And Its Consequences for American Literature," appeared in the *Georgia Review*, 38 (Summer 1984), 223-39. See also Sanford Pinsker, "Revisionism With Rancor: The Threat of the Neoconservative Critics," *Georgia Review*, 38 (Summer 1984), 255-56; R. W. B. Lewis, "Who's Papa?" *New Republic*, 193 (Dec. 2, 1985), pp. 33-34; Lynn, "Hemingway's Wars," *New Republic*, 194 (Jan. 20, 1986), 6, 40; "Readers' Forum [letters from Lynn, Philip Young, and Malcolm Cowley]," *Georgia Review*, 38 (Fall 1984), 668-72; and Kenneth S. Lynn, *Hemingway* (New York: Simon and Schuster, 1987), pp. 102-08.

10. Robert Paul Lamb's view of the situation is that "the Young and Lynn interpretations only seem incompatible.... More interesting are the similarities: both see a severe psychological disturbance; both believe that once this problem is recognized and the fiction read in light of it then the meaning of the texts will become clear; and both acknowledge that the fiction, especially this story, is difficult to decipher without searching outside of the text" ("Fishing for Stories: What 'Big Two-Hearted River' is Really About," *Modern Fiction Studies*, 32 [Summer 1991], 163n.).

11. Hemingway, *Selected Letters*, 122.

12. Carlos Baker, *Hemingway: The Writer as Artist* (Princeton, N.J.: Princeton University Press, 1952), p. 125.

13. F. Scott Fitzgerald, "How to Waste Material, A Note on My Generation" *Bookman*, 63 (May 1926), 262-65; reprinted in *Ernest Hemingway: The Critical Reception*, ed. Robert O. Stephens (New York: Burt Franklin, 1977), pp. 17-19.

14. Allen Tate, "Good Prose," *The Nation*, 122

(Feb. 10, 1926), 160–62; reprinted in Stephens, *Critical Reception*, 14.

15. Michael Reynolds, *Hemingway: The Paris Years* (Oxford and New York: Basil Blackwell, 1989), p. 282. See also Constance Cappel Montgomery, *Hemingway in Michigan* (New York: Fleet, 1966), pp. 141–58.

16. Hemingway, "Best Rainbow Trout Fishing," *Dateline*, 50.

17. Hemingway, "Art of the Short Story," 88.

18. Bevan, Preface, *Compleat Angler*, v.

19. Walton, *Compleat Angler*, 59.

20. Walton borrowed much from *The Arte of Angling*, including, apparently, the two characters, Piscator and Viator (as Walton called Venator in the first edition of *The Complete Angler*). The author of *The Arte of Angling* 1577 is unknown (ed. Gerald Eades Bentley, intr. Carl Otto v. Kienbusch [Princeton, New Jersey: Princeton University Library, 1956]).

21. Walton, *Compleat Angler*, 59.

22. Walton, *Compleat Angler*, 170.

23. John R. Cooper, *The Art of The Compleat Angler* (Durham: Duke University Press, 1968), pp. 75–76.

24. Smith Palmer Bovie, Introduction to *Virgil's Georgics: A Modern English Verse Translation* (by Bovie) (Chicago: University of Chicago Press, 1956), p. xv.

25. *Princeton Encyclopedia of Poetry and Poetics*, Enlarged Edition, ed. Alex Preminger, Frank J. Warnke and O. B. Hardison, Jr. (Princeton, New Jersey: Princeton University Press, 1974).

26. Joseph Addison, "An Essay on Virgil's Georgics," in *Works*, ed. Richard Hurd (London: Henry G. Bohn, 1854–1885), I (1872), 154–55; quoted in Cooper, *Art*, 35.

27. Quoted in *Princeton Encyclopedia*, 311.

28. *Princeton Encyclopedia*, 311. In sixteenth-century Italy there were even several poems—readers of "Now I Lay Me" take notice—on the silk-worm, which was also the subject of a 1599 poem entitled *The Silkwormes*, the first conscious imitation of Virgil's *Georgics* published in England (Cooper, *Art*, 39–40).

29. Cooper, *Art*, 36–37.

30. Cooper, *Art*, 55.

31. Cooper, *Art*, 55.

32. Cooper, *Art*, 56. Moving beyond the narrowly "piscatorial georgic" to other kinds of prose georgics, Cooper fittingly calls attention to Thoreau's *Walden*, the cetological chapters of *Moby-Dick*, and the hunting lore of William Faulkner's "The Bear" (*Art*, 56). *The Compleat Angler* is one of the major sources of Thoreau's *Walden*.

33. James Burnham later wrote books such as *The Managerial Revolution* and *The Coming Defeat of Communism* and was a founding editor of the conservative journal *National Review*.

34. James Burnham, "Incompleat Angler," *New International*, 4 (Mar. 1938), 92–93.

35. Burnham, "Incompleat Angler," 92.

36. Burnham, "Incompleat Angler," 93.

37. Walton, *Compleat Angler*, 246.

38. Walton, *Compleat Angler*, 288. In a letter to William Dean Howells, Constance Fenimore Woolson alludes to the same passage in Walton: "I like thy tender, half-relenting way of showing her up [Mrs. Farrell, a character in Howells's 'Private Theatricals'], like Izaak putting the frog on the hook 'as if you loved him'" (*Selected Letters of W. D. Howells*, ed. George Arms and Christoph K. Lohmann [Boston: Twayne, 1979], II, p. 110n).

39. Walton, *Compleat Angler*, 355. The author of *A Moveable Feast* (not to mention "Big Two-Hearted River") would not have missed the point of Walton's talk about hunger: "I now remember and find that true which devout *Lessius* says, *That poor men, and those that fast often, have much more pleasure in eating than rich men and gluttons, that always feed before their stomachs are empty of their last meat, and call for more: for by that means they rob themselves of that pleasure that hunger brings to poor men*" (253).

40. It may be worth noting that the *New York Times* has appropriated the spelling Hemingway made famous. For an example of its own "moveable feast" advertisement, see the *Times* for July 9, 1993 (p. D26).

41. Walton, *Compleat Angler*, 96.

42. Cooper, *Art*, 58.

43. Cooper, *Art*, 59.

44. Cooper, *Art*, 65–66.

45. Cooper, *Art*, 143.

46. Cooper, *Art*, 79. "Piscator must not only teach; he must persuade. He must not only pass on information; he must also communicate the special quality of the information, its dignity, its interest, its total moral and human significance. Much of Piscator's display of bookish learning has this rhetorical function" (Cooper, *Art*, 156).

47. "Out in the Stream," in Hemingway, *Byline*, 173–74.

48. These rejected pages first achieved print as "On Writing," in *The Nick Adams Stories*, pref. Philip Young (New York: Scribner's, 1972). For a study of the surviving manuscript at the Humanities Research Center, the University of Texas, Austin, see Max Westbrook, "Text, Ritual, and Memory: Hemingway's 'Big Two-Hearted River,'" *North Dakota Quarterly*, 60 (Summer 1992), 14–25.

49. Barker advises: "You must angle alwayes

with the point of the rod down the stream, for trouts have not quickness of sight so perfect up the stream as they have opposite against them" (*Barker's Delight*, in *Three Books*, 153).

50. Walton, *Compleat Angler*, 255.

51. Cooper, *Art*, 141. The conventional wisdom on the matter of fishing downstream or upstream is displayed in David Foster's *The Scientific Angler: Being a General and Instructive Work on Artistic Angling*: "the rodster should invariably fish up stream, as by that means not only will his bait act as herald in advance, but he has the additional advantage of being able to take note carefully of the particular position tenanted by the fish, and to regulate his cast accordingly" (compiled by his Sons, and edited by Wm. C. Harris [New York: Orange Judd, 1883], p. 93). Andrew Lang, whose introduction to the Everyman's Library edition of *The Compleat Angler* appears in all seven editions published from 1906 to 1925, writes: "Both men [Barker and Walton] insist on fishing down stream, which is, of course, the opposite of the true art, for fish lie with their heads up stream, and trout are best approached from behind" (London: J. M. Dent/ New York: E. P. Dutton, 1906; p. xxxii). In Zane Grey's story, "A Trout Fisherman's Inferno," which begins as a realistic treatment of a bit of trout fishing, a solitary fisherman begins "to fish downstream" (his "mind in harmony with the racing current"), hooks a big fish, that pulls him further and further downstream until he lands in Hell. It's all a dream, of course, but it is as if the angler must pay for this transgression of what Lang calls the "true art" of fishing (*Field and Stream* [Apr. 1910]; reprinted in *Zane Grey: Outdoorsman*, ed. George Reiger [Englewood Cliffs, NJ: Prentice-Hall, 1972], pp. 282–91). Hemingway owned several of Zane Grey's fishing books, three of which are now in Cuba at Finca Vigía (see Reynolds, *Hemingway's Reading*, 132, and Brasch and Sigman, *Hemingway's Library*, 155).

52. Walton, *Compleat Angler*, 176–77.

53. Cooper, *Art*, 75.

54. Cooper, *Art*, 75.

55. Cooper, *Art*, 122.

Chapter 5

1. "Although the term 'rehabilitation' has taken on many different meanings, in its widest sense it 'signifies the whole process of restoring a disabled person to a condition in which he is able, as nearly as possible, to resume a normal life'" (P. J. R. Nichols, *Rehabilitation Medicine: The Management of Physical Disabilities* [London: Butterworth, 1976], p. 2).

2. Glenn Gritzer and Arnold Arluke, *The Making of Rehabilitation: A Political Economy of Medical Specialization, 1890-1980* (Berkeley: University of California Press, 1985), pp. 40–41.

3. Nichols, *Rehabilitation*, 3.

4. *A Farewell to Arms*, 117.

5. Hemingway, *The Sun Also Rises* (New York: Scribner's, 1926), p. 31.

6. Published originally in *Scribner's Magazine*, 81 (Apr. 1927), 355–57, "In Another Country" was collected first in *Men Without Women* (New York: Scribner's, 1927) and then in *The Fifth Column and the First Forty-Nine Stories* (New York: Scribner's, 1938).

7. After reading "In Another Country" in *Scribner's Magazine*, F. Scott Fitzgerald told Hemingway that the story opened with "one of the most beautiful prose sentences I've ever read" (*The Letters of F. Scott Fitzgerald*, ed. Andrew Turnbull [New York: Scribner's, 1963], p. 300). *A Farewell to Arms* opens: "In the late summer of that year we lived in a house in a village that looked across the river and the plain to the mountains."

8. Friedrich Nietzsche, *Twilight of the Idols* (1888) in *The Portable Nietzsche*, ed. and trans. by Walter Kaufmann (New York: Viking Press, 1954), p. 483.

9. In *A Farewell to Arms* the "Cova" is mentioned by Frederic Henry's friend Rinaldi as the place in Milan to meet women. It is also at the "Cova" that Lieutenant Henry buys chocolates for Catherine Barkley.

Chapter 6

1. *Death in the Afternoon*, 192.
2. *Moveable Feast*, 75.
3. *Moveable Feast*, 75.
4. *Moveable Feast*, 76.
5. Philip Young and Charles W. Mann, *The Hemingway Manuscripts: An Inventory* (University Park and London: Pennsylvania State University Press, 1969), p. 118.
6. H. E. Bates, *The Modern Short Story: A Critical Survey* (Boston: The Writer, 1972), p. 173.
7. *Death in the Afternoon*, 122.
8. Quoted by George Plimpton, "An Interview with Ernest Hemingway," Baker, *Hemingway and His Critics*, 34.
9. Robert McAlmon, *Being Geniuses Together* (London: Seeker & Warburg, 1938), p. 159; quoted in Baker, *Life Story*, 595.
10. Young and Mann, *Manuscripts*, 43.
11. Quoted by Baker, *Life Story*, 595; emphasis added.
12. Robert McAlmon, *Being Geniuses Together 1920-1930*, revised and with supplemen-

tary chapters by Kay Boyle (Garden City: Doubleday, 1968), p. 277.

Chapter 7

1. George Plimpton, "An Interview with Ernest Hemingway," in Baker, *Hemingway and His Critics*, 31.
2. Young and Mann, *Manuscripts*, 46.
3. Originally Hemingway's fighter's name was Neroni, not Anderson (Baker, *Life Story*, 169).
4. Cleanth Brooks and Robert Penn Warren, *Understanding Fiction* (New York: Crofts, 1943), pp. 303–12.
5. Edmund Wilson complained about Max and Al: "I like 'The Killers' too," he wrote to Hemingway, "but I thought you gave the thugs a line of banter which sounded a little too much like the hero of your novel and his friend on their fishing trip [Jake and Bill in *The Sun Also Rises*], that is to say, a little too sophisticated" (*Letters on Literature and Politics, 1912–1972*, ed. Elena Wilson [New York: Farrar, Straus and Giroux, 1977], p. 140).

Chapter 8

1. Hemingway: *Selected Letters*, 470, and Baker, *Life Story*, 137.
2. Working from a manuscript in the *Little Review* files and a letter to Jane Heap, Phillip R. Yannella dates the composition of "Banal Story" as falling "between 28 January and 30 January [1925]" ("Notes on the Manuscript, Date, and Sources of Hemingway's 'Banal Story,'" *Fitzgerald / Hemingway Annual 1974*, ed. Matthew J. Bruccoli and C.E. Frazer Clark, Jr. [Englewood: Microcard, 1975], p. 176).
3. Hemingway, *Selected Letters*, 245.
4. *The Forum* described itself, in the words of Henry Goddard Leach, its editor at the time: "A Non-Partisan Magazine of Free Discussion. What Is Praised in This Issue May Be Attacked in the Next. The Forum Aims to Interpret the New America That Is Attaining National Consciousness in the Decade in Which We Live" (74 [Aug. 1925], 161).
5. "Frush Knocked Out by Mascart in 2D," *New York Times* (Jan. 28, 1925), 11. Yannella says that Hemingway misspelled the fighter's name, the correct spelling being "Muscart." ("Notes on … 'Banal Story'": 176). If so, so did the New York Times.
6. "Test Cricket Game Stirs All London," *New York Times* (Jan. 23, 1925), 16.
7. *Forum*, 73 (Feb. 1925), 209.
8. *Forum*, 73 (Feb. 1925), 214.
9. *The Great Gatsby* (New York: Charles Scribner's Sons, 1925), p. 5.
10. *Forum*, 72 (Oct. 1924), 433.
11. *Forum*, 73 (June 1925), 769–83. The debate, with spirited reactions from, among others, Frank Jewett Mather, Jr., and John Sloan, continued in the letters columns of the issues for July (146–50) and August (296–98).
12. *Forum*, 74 (Aug. 1925), 227. The author is Towne Nylander. Incidentally, one also thinks of Robert Frost's poem "Two Tramps in Mud-Time" when the author observes that "many housewives are inconsiderate enough to suggest the wood-pile [to a tramp] as a preliminary to eating" (236).
13. *Forum*, 72 (Oct. 1924), 455.
14. *Forum*, 73 (Feb. 1925), preliminary pages, unnumbered.
15. For another look at the contents of *The Forum* in 1924-25, see Wayne E. Kvam, "Hemingway's 'Banal Story,'" *Fitzgerald / Hemingway Annual 1974*, pp. 181–91.
16. *Death in the Afternoon*, 82–83.
17. *Death in the Afternoon*, 82.
18. See Audre Hanneman, *Ernest Hemingway: A Comprehensive Bibliography* (Princeton: Princeton University Press, 1967), p. 6.
19. *in our time* (Paris: Three Mountains Press, 1924) 27; facs. ed. Bloomfield Hills: Bruccoli Clark Books, 1977.

Chapter 9

1. Bruccoli, *Only Thing*, 322.
2. Lionel Trilling, "Hemingway and His Critics," in *The Moral Obligation to be Intelligent: Selected Essays*, ed. Leon Wieseltier (New York: Farrar, Straus and Giroux, 2000), p. 12; and Marvin Mudrick, "A No-Good Self-Righteous Bragging Boasting Chickenshit Character," *Hudson Review*, 24 (Spring 1981), 455.
3. Quoted in George Monteiro, Introduction, *Critical Essays on Ernest Hemingway's A Farewell to Arms*, ed. George Monteiro (New York: G. K. Hall, 1994), p. 6.
4. The first edition of *Winner Take Nothing* (New York and London: Scribner's, 1933) is used throughout this study unless otherwise indicated. Its fourteen stories, in the same order, appear as the last fourteen stories in *The Fifth Column and the First Forty-nine Stories* (New York: Scribner's, 1938) and in subsequent printings, which drop *The Fifth Column*, as *Short Stories of Ernest Hemingway*. In *Complete Short Stories of Ernest Hemingway* (1987) they appear as the last fourteen stories of Part II.
5. Hanneman, *Bibliography*, 35, 37.
6. Hemingway, *Selected Letters*, 399.

7. Quoted in A. Scott Berg, *Maxwell Perkins: Editor of Genius* (New York: Dutton, 1978), p. 218.
8. Hemingway, *Selected Letters*, 401.
9. Unless otherwise indicated quotations from reviews of *Winner Take Nothing* come from those collected in *Ernest Hemingway: The Critical Reception*, ed. Robert O. Stephens (New York: Burt Franklin, 1977), pp. 135–47.
10. Harvey Curtis Webster, "An Annotated Bibliography of Contemporary Literature for 1933: A Partial List," *English Journal*, 23 (Oct. 1934), 668.
11. John Chamberlain, "Books of the Times," *New York Times* (Oct. 27, 1933), 17.
12. Selden Rodman, "Books," *Common Sense*, 3 (Jan. 1934), 28.
13. Bruccoli, *Only Thing*, 202–03.
14. Bruccoli, *Only Thing*, 203.
15. Bruccoli, *Only Thing*, 191–92.
16. Bruccoli, *Only Thing*, 195.
17. Bruccoli, *Only Thing*, 194.
18. There were two other changes. "A Day's Wait" and "One Reader Writes" also changed places, the former now becoming the tenth story, the latter the eighth; and "Fathers and Sons" was added to the collection as the fourteenth and final story.
19. Bruccoli, *Only Thing*, 187.
20. Bruccoli, *Only Thing*, 190.
21. Hemingway, *Selected Letters*, 393. William Barrett employs Hemingway's title as the rubric for his chapter on Hemingway in *Time of Need: Forms of Imagination in the Twentieth Century* (New York: Harper & Row, 1972), pp. 64–95.
22. John Kieran, "A Wicked Sham Report on Sports," *New York Times* (Jan. 23, 1930), 21. Two examples of the many uses of the phrase "winner take nothing" in print after Kieran and Hemingway are Thomas F. Brady, "Quine and Asher to Turn Out Film: Complete Deal with Columbia to Produce and Direct 'Winner Take Nothing,'" *New York Times* (Jan. 28, 1948) ("'Winner Take Nothing,' a film to be based on a 1946 magazine story by Richard English about prize fighting"); and "Television," *New York Times* (Nov. 28, 1958), 55 ("Winner Take Nothing," an episode of *Lineup* about San Francisco police detectives). That it's right up to date, moreover, is suggested by the use put to the shibboleth by *The Economist*, which captions its Mar. 26-Apr. 1, 2016 cover "Winners Take All."
23. Turnbull, *Letters of Fitzgerald*, 308.
24. Reynolds, *Paris Years*, 62.
25. Michael Reynolds, "Ernest Hemingway 1899-1961: A Brief Biography," in *A Historical Guide to Ernest Hemingway*, ed. Linda Wagner-Martin (New York: Oxford University Press, 2000), pp. 32–33.
26. Hemingway, *Selected Letters*, 443.

27. Turnbull, *Letters of Fitzgerald*, 307. One can only imagine the satisfaction it gave Fitzgerald, at least for the moment, to hear from Edmund Wilson just after he had read *Winner Take Nothing*: "I have just read Hemingway's new stories, and though the best of them are excellent, now is your time to creep up on him" (Wilson, *Letters on Literature and Politics*, 231).
28. Hemingway, *Selected Letters*, 409.
29. Turnbull, *Letters of Fitzgerald*, 308.
30. Hemingway, *Selected Letters*, 397.
31. Hemingway, *Selected Letters*, 401.
32. Philip Rahv, Review of *Winner Take Nothing*, *Partisan Review*, 1 (Feb.–Mar. 1934), 58–59.
33. V. S. Pritchett, *Fortnightly Review*, 135 (Mar. 1934), 381–82.
34. Reprinted in *Hemingway: The Critical Heritage*, ed. Jeffrey Meyers (London: Routledge & Kegan Paul, 1982), pp. 183–85. The quotation comes from page 185.
35. Maurice Edgar Coindreau, "La Autobiografía de Gertrude Stein," *Sur*, 4 (July 1934), 173. (My translation.) Coindreau's comment on the inadequacy of Hemingway's words takes on additional interest when one recalls that for the French translation of *A Farewell to Arms* Hemingway supplied his translator—Coindreau—with the words his publisher had deleted from the original. See James B. Meriwether, "The Dashes in Hemingway's *A Farewell to Arms*," *Papers of the Bibliographical Society of America*, 58 (Oct.–Dec. 1964), 449–57.
36. Maurice Edgar Coindreau, "Panorama de la Actual Literatura Joven Norteamericana," *Sur*, 7 (Mar. 1927), 61.
37. Henry Seidel Canby, *Seven Years' Harvest: Notes on Contemporary Literature* (New York: Farrar & Rinehart, 1936), pp. 151–53.
38. Quoted in Halford E. Luccock, *American Mirror: Social, Ethical and Religious Aspects of American Literature 1930-1940* (New York: Macmillan, 1940), pp. 98–100.
39. Oscar Cargill, *Intellectual America: Ideas on the March* (New York: Macmillan, 1941), p. 363.
40. Malcolm Cowley, "*Winner Take Nothing*: Editor's Preface," in *Viking Portable Library Hemingway*, 525.
41. Maxwell Geismar, "Was 'Papa' a Truly Great Writer?" *New York Times* (July 1, 1962), p. 16.
42. Jackson R. Bryer, "Ernest Hemingway," in *Sixteen Modern American Authors, Volume 2: A Survey of Research and Criticism Since 1972*, ed. Jackson R. Bryer (Durham and London: Duke University Press, 1990), p. 473.
43. Brian Harding, "Ernest Hemingway: Men With, or Without, Women," in *American Dec-*

larations of Love, ed. Ann Nassa (New York: St. Martin's Press, 1990), p. 116.

44. Peter L. Hays, *Ernest Hemingway* (New York: Continuum, 1990), p. 67.

45. Matthew J. Bruccoli, *Fitzgerald and Hemingway: A Dangerous Friendship* (New York: Carroll & Graf, 1994), p. 170. Jeffrey Meyers, calling *Winner Take Nothing* "uneven," describes "One Reader Writes" and "A Day's Wait" as "thin sketches," but considers "A Way You'll Never Be," "A Clean, Well-lighted Place" and "Fathers and Sons" to be "three of his finest works in this genre" (*Hemingway: A Biography* [New York: Harper & Row, 1985], p. 258).

46. Joseph M. Flora, *Ernest Hemingway: A Study of the Short Fiction* (Boston: Twayne, 1989), p. 74.

47. "The Rime of the Ancient Mariner" was on the English I reading list at Oak Park High School when Hemingway took the course (Reynolds, *Hemingway's Reading*, 40).

48. Arthur Power, *Conversations with James Joyce*, ed. Clive Hart (New York: Barnes & Noble, 1974), p. 107.

49. *Farewell to Arms*, 184–85.

50. *New Baltimore Catechism No. 1*, Official Revised Edition (New York: Benziger Brothers, n.d.), p. 3.

51. See Baker, *Life Story*, 238. Dashiell's rejection of "The Light of the World" continued to nettle Hemingway, as evidenced in his letter to Perkins on Apr. 9, 1936: "I would like to get a good idea from her [Nancy Hale] sometime for a story to be called Sea Change and then Dashiel [sic] to publish it" (Hemingway, *Selected Letters*, 444). "The Sea Change" was included in *Winner Take Nothing* (1933).

52. "Boston Police Bar Scribner's Magazine," *New York Times* (June 21, 1929), 2, and "Boston Bans Scribner's for July," *New York Times* (June 29, 1929), 8.

53. See Hemingway's letter to Perkins, June 7, 1929, in Hemingway, *Selected Letters*, 296–98. The resulting suppression of words and other changes in the text are studied by Meriwether, "Dashes," 449–57.

54. Baker, *Life Story*, 241.

55. Ernest Hemingway, Preface, *The Fifth Column and the First Forty-nine Stories* (New York: Scribner's, 1938), p. v; Hemingway, *Selected Letters*, 393.

56. In "Banal Story" (*Men Without Women*, 1927) Hemingway refers to "Tramps and Hoboes," an article by Towne Nylander in *The Forum* in August 1925.

57. Baker, *Life Story*, 606.

58. Hemingway's "truthful" Alice harks back to Chaucer's two married women named Alison (the young wife of "The Miller's Tale" and the Wife of Bath) in *The Canterbury Tales*.

59. John Bunyan, *The Pilgrim's Progress from This World to That Which Is to Come* (1728). Its two parts had been published in 1678 and 1684, respectively.

60. *Hawthorne's Short Stories*, ed. Newton Arvin (New York: Vintage, 1946), p. 212.

61. Baker, *Life Story*, 51–52; DeFalco, *Hemingway's Short Stories*, 55; and Peter L. Hays, "Hemingway and the Fisher King," *University Review* (Mar. 1966), 32: 225–28.

62. Baker, *Life Story*, 51–52.

63. Quotations from the story follow the text of *God Rest You Merry Gentlemen* (New York: House of Books, Ltd., 1933). I have chosen this first and now scarce publication of the story because its subsequent printings, in which, incidentally, Hemingway re-punctuated the title—"God Rest You Merry, Gentlemen"—reflect Hemingway's publisher's own principles of censorship in the 1930s.

64. Hays, "Fisher King," 226.

65. Julian Smith, "Hemingway and the Thing Left Out," *Journal of Modern Literature*, 1 (1970–71), 180–82.

66. Quoted in Hugh Ford, *Published in Paris: American and British Writers, Printers, and Publishers in Paris, 1920–1939* (New York: Macmillan, 1975), p. 164.

67. Hemingway, "Art of the Short Story," 88. Hemingway's explanation might have been intended to counter the suggestion that his story was indebted to Morley Callaghan's novella *No Man's Meat*. Hugh Ford, who finds Hemingway's story "remarkably similar" to Callaghan's, describes Callaghan's plot: "Teresa's husband Bert, who, unaware of Jean's homosexuality, has shamefacedly made love to her after she had lost a wager in which she staked 'her virtue' against his fifty dollars. That experience, traumatic for both, is partly repaired by Teresa who, after she comforts Jean, tells Bert that Jean had left her husband, not for another man, but for a young woman with whom she had fallen in love, and that now 'she can hardly stand to be touched by a man.' The full import of Lucretias's maxim ('One man's meat is another man's poison.') along with Callaghan's twist descends on Bert the morning after. Having spent the night with Jean, Teresa obligingly drives her to the station, but not, it appears, with the intention of saying goodbye to a friend. At noon, a stranger, a 'townman,' delivers a note from Teresa informing Bert that she had never known how much she had loved Jean herself and that she could not return to him for a long time" (*Published in Paris*, 164, 157).

68. *Clothes for a Summer Hotel: A Ghost Play* (New York: New Directions, 1983), p. 67.

69. *Death in the Afternoon*, 180–182.

70. *The Works of Alexander Pope*, notes by

Dr. Warburton (Philadelphia: James B. Smith, n.d.), p. 108.

71. Robert E. Fleming, "Perversion and the Writer in 'The Sea Change,'" *Studies in American Fiction*, 4 (Autumn 1986), 215–20.

72. *Works of Alexander Pope*, 109.

73. *Moveable Feast*, 181.

74. Jacqueline Tavernier-Courbin, *Ernest Hemingway's A Moveable Feast: The Making of Myth* (Boston: Northeastern University Press, 1991), pp. 22–23.

75. Tavernier-Courbin, *Making of Myth*, 129–30.

76. Tavernier-Courbin, *Making of Myth*, 239, 17n.

77. Robert E. Fleming does not consider Fitzgerald in this context, but his reading of "The Sea Change" as a tale about the moralities and immoralities of writing readily fits the Fitzgeralds as well as the McAlmons (*The Face in the Mirror: Hemingway's Writers* [Tuscaloosa and London: University of Alabama Press, 1994], pp. 48–53). That Hemingway's "Phil" stories cut deeply and personally is further suggested when "The Sea Change" and "Get Yourself a Seeing-Eyed Dog" are seen to be linked to the untitled story about the writer Philip Haines, his lover, and the wife he is divorcing in order to marry his lover (reminiscent of the Hadley, Pauline, and Ernest situation in the late 1920s). When he published the story for the first time, Donald Junkins assigned it the title: "Philip Haines Was a Writer..." (*Hemingway Review*, 9 [Spring 1990], 2–9. Incidentally, in his "Sea Change" stories Hemingway may also have had the Robert McAlmon—Bryher marriage in mind.

78. Bruccoli, *Only Thing*, 194.

79. Lynn, *Hemingway*, 408.

80. Sheldon Grebstein, *Hemingway's Craft* (Carbondale and Edwardsville: Southern Illinois University Press, 1973), pp. 57–59.

81. For a reading in which the "mother" of the title is interpreted as the male narrator, see Charles Stetler and Gerald Locklin, "Beneath the Tip of the Iceberg in Hemingway's 'The Mother of a Queen,'" *Hemingway Review* (Fall 1982), 2: 68–69.

82. James R. Mellow, who finds Roger's "precise relationship to Paco ... purposely shadowy," suggests that both characters are linked to the American bullfighter Sidney Franklin (*Hemingway: A Life Without Consequences* [Boston: Houghton Mifflin, 1992], pp. 411–13).

83. *Nathanael West: A Collection of Critical Essays*, ed. Jay Martin (Englewood Cliffs, N.J.: Prentice-Hall, 1971), p. 171.

84. Hanneman, *Bibliography*, 35.

85. Hemingway, *Selected Letters*, 400.

86. Baker, *Life Story*, 227. At the time of Dr. Clendenning's death, the *Kansas City Star* editorialized (Feb. 1, 1945) that he "took his profession seriously, but not too seriously. In his writings he occasionally poked fun at people who were overanxious about their health. 'What's the use?' he would inquire. 'By giving yourself infinite trouble you may prolong your life perhaps a fortnight. Why not enjoy things as you go along?' His friends would accuse him of setting out in his writings to rationalize his own way of life, which was to do about as he pleased without regard to health consequences. And he would smile that charming smile of his and say, 'Well? And then what?'" (14) Clendenning offers his view of sex and venereal disease in "Sex Madness," *Forum and Century*, 84 (Oct. 1930), 208–12. See also Paul Smith, "The Doctor and the Doctor's Friend: Logan Clendenning and Ernest Hemingway," *Hemingway Review*, 8 (Fall 1988), 37–39; and Smith, *Reader's Guide*, 297–301.

87. Gertrude Stein, *Three Lives* (New York: Modern Library, 1936), p. 215.

88. Ernest Hemingway, *To Have and Have Not* (New York: Scribner's, 1937), pp. 257–61.

89. Baker, *Life Story*, 238.

90. Hemingway, *Selected Letters*, 367.

91. Baker, *Life Story*, 236.

92. In "Up and Down: Making Connections in 'A Day's Wait,'" Linda Gajdusek writes that the story is about "the need to reconcile opposites" with "the hero-father engaged in the healing task of establishing vital connections" (in Susan F. Beegel, ed., *Hemingway's Neglected Short Fiction: New Perspectives* [Ann Arbor, Michigan: UMI Research Press, 1989], p. 300).

93. *The Letters of Robert Frost to Louis Untermeyer* (New York: Holt, Rinehart and Winston, 1963), p. 236.

94. That the story as published in *Winner Take Nothing* is all of a piece is John Portz's argument in "Allusion and Structure in Hemingway's 'A Natural History of the Dead,'" *Tennessee Studies in Literature*, 10 (1964), 27–41. Sheldon Grebstein disagrees: "The work ... is a personal essay, with a tack-on fictional episode as conclusion" (*Hemingway's Craft*, 77).

95. *To Have and Have Not*, 221.

96. For a bio-critical interpretation in which the authenticity of Hemingway's own conversion to Catholicism is emphasized, see H. R. Stoneback, "'Mais Je Reste Catholique': Communion, Betrayal, and Aridity in 'Wine of Wyoming,'" in Beegel, *Neglected Short Fiction*, 209–24.

97. See George Monteiro, "The Education of Ernest Hemingway," *Journal of American Studies*, 8 (Apr. 1974), 96–98.

98. Hemingway, *Green Hills of Africa* (New York: Scribner's, 1935), p. 148.

99. Quoted in Louis Mertins, *Robert Frost: Life and Talks-Walking* (Norman: University of Oklahoma Press, 1965), p. 397.
100. Baker, *Life Story*, 218, 602.
101. Baker, *Life Story*, 218.
102. "As Others See Us," *Books on Trial*, 1 (Dec. 1942-Jan. 1943), 15.
103. Sister Mariella Gable, *Great Modern Catholic Short Stories* (New York: Sheed & Ward, 1942), p. 99.
104. "The parallelism of the series of nouns [in the title] is broken by an unparalleled third term. One would expect *writer* to balance *gambler* and *nun* rather than *radio*," writes Marion Montgomery ("Hemingway's 'The Gambler, the Nun, and the Radio': A Reading and a Problem," *Forum*, 3 [Winter 1961], 36n.). Actually, it can be argued that the parallelism is *not* broken, for its basis is not character but theme.
105. Hemingway, *Selected Letters*, 395.
106. Baker, *Life Story*, 241.

Chapter 10

1. Ernest Hemingway, "Homage to Ezra," in *Ernest Hemingway: A Literary Reference*, ed. Robert Trogdon (New York: Carroll & Graff, 1999), p. 41.
2. Paul Smith, *A Reader's Guide to the Short Stories of Ernest Hemingway* (Boston: G. K. Hall, 1989), p. 88.
3. Baker, *Writer as Artist*, 119, and Joseph M. Flora, *Hemingway's Nick Adams* (Baton Rouge and London: Louisiana State University Press, 1982), pp. 155-56.
4. A. E. Housman, *The Collected Poems of A. E. Housman* (New York: Holt, Rinehart and Winston, 1965), pp. 70-71.
5. S. G. Andrews, "Housman's 'The Carpenter's Son,'" *The Explicator*, 19 (October 1960): 3.
6. Andrews, "Housman's 'The Carpenter's Son,'" 3.
7. Ernest Hemingway, "To Will Davies," in *88 Poems*, ed. Nicholas Gerogiannis (New York and London: Harcourt Brace Jovanovich / Bruccoli Clark, 1979), p. 21.
8. Hemingway, *Selected Letters*, 139.
9. Hemingway also exploited D'Annunzio's self-attributed derring-do in "The Mercenaries," written shortly after his return to Oak Park in 1919.
10. Smith, *Reader's Guide*, 68-69.
11. Hemingway, *Winner Take Nothing* (New York: Scribner's, 1933), p. [iii].
12. Cleanth Brooks, *A Shaping Joy: Studies in the Writer's Craft* (New York: Harcourt Brace Jovanovich, 1971), p. 292.
13. Brooks, *Shaping Joy*, 292.
14. Housman, *Collected Poems*, 112-13.
15. The theme of treason and loyalty is taken up in my essay, "Patriotism and Treason in *A Farewell to Arms*," *WLA: War, Literature & the Arts*, 9 (Spring/Summer 1997): 27-38.
16. A. E. Housman, *Last Poems* (New York: Henry Holt, 1922), p. 71.
17. Brooks, *Shaping Joy*, 293.
18. This is a crucial matter because it speaks to Housman's intentions. In my opinion any attempt to read the poem ironically as an anti-war poem misses the mark. The poets have not been fooled. See Hugh MacDiarmid's "Another Epitaph on an Army of Mercenaries" and Edwin Morgan's "A Third Epitaph on an Army of Mercenaries," both of which take issue with Housman's pro-war stance.
19. "The Anniversary of Ypres," *London Times* (31 October 1917), 7.
20. John Bayley, *Housman's Poems* (Oxford: Clarendon Press, 1992), p. 125.
21. Brooks, *Shaping Joy*, 293.
22. Brooks, *Shaping Joy*, 293-94.
23. Brooks, *Shaping Joy*, 294.
24. Griffin, *Along with Youth*, 108-12.
25. Paul Smith, "Hemingway's Apprentice Fiction: 1919-1921," in *New Critical Approaches to the Short Stories of Ernest Hemingway*, ed. Jackson J. Benson (Durham: Duke University Press, 1998), p. 140.
26. Michael Reynolds, *The Young Hemingway* (Oxford: Basil Blackwell, 1986), p. 125. The name "Rinaldi" surfaces as well in *A Farewell to Arms* and elsewhere.
27. Reynolds, *Young Hemingway*, 125.
28. Reynolds, *Young Hemingway*, 126.
29. Griffin, *Along with Youth*, 104.
30. Griffin, *Along with Youth*, 112.
31. Richard Wilbur, *Responses: Prose Pieces, 1953-1976* (New York: Harcourt Brace Jovanovich, 1976), pp. 166-67.
32. The cuckold theme from "The Mercenaries" also reappears in "The Short Happy Life of Francis Macomber." The guide, Wilson, sleeps with Margot, Macomber's wife.
33. In his 1942 introduction to *Men at War* (New York: Avon, 1952), Hemingway stated that he was in Italy in 1918 when he first heard these lines from Shakespeare: "I was very ignorant at nineteen and had read little and I remember the sudden happiness and the feeling of having a permanent protecting talisman," he wrote, "when a young British officer I met when in the hospital first wrote out for me, so that I could remember them, these lines: 'By my troth, I care not; a man can die but once; we owe God a death ... and let it go which way it will, he that dies this year is quit for the next'" (xi).
34. Housman, *Collected Poems*, 82.

Chapter 12

1. *Ken*, 1 (May 19, 1938), 36. That from the outset Hemingway considered the piece to be a story, not a news dispatch, is argued by William Brasch Watson in "'Old Man at the Bridge': The Making of a Short Story," *Hemingway Review*, 7 (Spring 1988), p. 164, 14n.

Chapter 13

1. Philip Young and Charles Mann, for example, identify O. Henry as "a writer of short stories, whose 'surprise' endings Hemingway's stories did much to outmode" ... ("Fitzgerald's Sun Also Rises: Notes and Comment," *Fitzgerald / Hemingway Annual 1970* [Washington, D.C.: NCR/Microcard Editions, 1970], p. 1. Sheldon Grebstein suggests that Hemingway was influenced by Chekhov's technique of the "zero ending," a response to "the kind of ending O. Henry carried almost to parody: the surprise-resolution neatly knotting up separate strands of plot and by an ingenious twist of plot or revelation of character" (*Hemingway's Craft*, 2).

2. Early if minor comparisons of Hemingway with O. Henry occur in Henry Seidel Canby, "Farewell to the Nineties," *Saturday Review of Literature*, 10 (Oct. 28, 1933), 217; and Edith Mirrielees, "Those College Writing Courses," *Saturday Review of Literature*, 17 (Jan. 15, 1938), 3–4, 16. On O. Henry's reputation and periodic revaluation, see Eugene Current-Garcia, *O. Henry (William Porter)* (New York: Twayne, 1965), pp. 156–66.

3. Quoted in Baker, *Writer as Artist*, 4th ed., p. 125. Their charge accords with Brander Matthews's pronouncement in 1884 that "a Short-story in which nothing happens at all is an absolute impossibility.... [I]n a Short-story there must be something done, there must be an action" (*The Philosophy of the Short-story* [New York: Peter Smith, 1931], p. 35). Later critics have redefined the concept of what constitutes action in fiction.

4. *Death in the Afternoon*, 182.

5. See Charles A. Fenton, *The Apprenticeship of Ernest Hemingway: The Early Years* (New York: Farrar, Straus and Young, 1954), p. 17.

6. See Fred Lewis Pattee, *The Development of the American Short Story: An Historical Survey* (New York: Harper and Brothers, 1923), especially "O. Henry and the Handbooks" (Chapter 16).

7. "Defense of Dirty Words: A Cuban Letter," *Esquire*, 2 (Sept. 1934), 158B. Yet it should be noted that in 1920 upon learning that a friend had not yet read O. Henry, Hemingway presented her with a copy of *Cabbages and Kings*, inscribing it: "To the Negative from the Affirmative" (Baker, *Life Story*, 69).

8. *The Complete Works of O. Henry* (Garden City, N.Y.: Doubleday, Page, 1927), pp. 1131–32.

Bibliography

Addison, Joseph. "An Essay on Virgil's Georgics," *Works*, ed. Richard Hurd. London: Henry G. Bohn, 1854–1885), I (1872), 154–55.

Amory, Cleveland. Introduction. *The Lawrenceville Stories*. New York: Simon & Schuster, 1967.

Andrews, S.G. "Housman's 'The Carpenter's Son.'" *The Explicator*, 19 (Oct. 1960).

"The Anniversary of Ypres." London *Times* (31 Oct. 1917), 7

"As Others See Us." *Books on Trial*, 1 (Dec. 1942–Jan. 1943), 15.

Astro, Richard, and Jackson J. Benson (eds.). *Hemingway in Our Time*. Corvallis: Oregon State University Press, 1974.

Baker, Carlos. *Ernest Hemingway, a Life Story*. New York: Scribner's, 1969.

———. *Hemingway: The Writer as Artist*. Princeton, N.J.: Princeton University Press, 1952.

———. *Hemingway: The Writer as Artist*, 4th ed. Princeton, N.J.: Princeton University Press, 1972.

———. "A Search for the Man as He Really Was." *New York Times Book Review* (July 26, 1964). Pp. BR4–5, 14

Barker, Thomas. *Barker's Delight: Or, the Art of Angling*. London: Humphrey Moselye, 1659.

Barrett, William. *Time of Need: Forms of Imagination in the Twentieth Century*. New York: Harper & Row, 1972.

Bates, H.E. *The Modern Short Story: A Critical Survey*. Boston: The Writer, 1972.

Bayley, John. *Housman's Poems*. Oxford: Clarendon Press, 1992.

Beegel, Susan F. (ed.). *Hemingway's Neglected Short Fiction: New Perspectives*. Ann Arbor, Michigan: UMI Research Press, 1989; also Tuscaloosa and London: University of Alabama Press, 1991.

Benson, Jackson J. (ed.). *New Critical Approaches to the Short Stories of Ernest Hemingway*, Durham: Duke University Press, 1998.

Berg, A. Scott. *Maxwell Perkins: Editor of Genius*. New York: Dutton, 1978.

"Boston Bans Scribner's for July." New York *Times* (June 29, 1929), 8.

"Boston Police Bar Scribner's Magazine." New York *Times* (June 21, 1929), 2.

Bowie, Smith Palmer. Introduction. *Virgil's Georgics: A Modern English Verse Translation* (by Bovie). Chicago: University of Chicago Press, 1956.

Brady, Thomas F. "Quine and Asher to Turn Out Film: Complete Deal with Columbia to Produce and Direct 'Winner Take Nothing.'" New York *Times* (Jan. 28, 1948).

Brasch, James D., and Joseph Sigman. *Hemingway's Library: A Composite Record*. New York & London: Garland, 1981.

Brenner, Gerry. *Concealments in Hemingway's Works*. Columbus: Ohio State University Press, 1983.

Brooks, Cleanth. *A Shaping Joy: Studies in the Writer's Craft*. New York: Harcourt Brace Jovanovich, 1971.

Brooks, Cleanth, and Robert Penn Warren. *Understanding Fiction*. New York: Crofts, 1943.

Brooks, Van Wyck (ed.). *Writers at Work: The Paris Review Interviews*, Second Series. Intr. Van Wyck Brooks. New York: Viking, 1963.

Bruccoli, Matthew J. *Fitzgerald and Hemingway: A Dangerous Friendship*. New York: Carroll & Graf, 1994.

———. *Some Sort of Epic Grandeur: The Life of F. Scott Fitzgerald*. New York and London: Harcourt Brace Jovanovich, 1981.

Bryer, Jackson R. "Ernest Hemingway," *Sixteen Modern American Authors, Volume 2: A Survey of Research and Criticism Since 1972*. Ed. Jackson R. Bryer. Durham: Duke University Press, 1990.

Burnham, James. "Incompleat Angler." *New International*, 4 (Mar. 1938), 92–93.

Canby, Henry Seidel. "Farewell to the Nineties." *Saturday Review of Literature*, 10 (Oct. 28, 1933).

———. *Seven Years' Harvest: Notes on Contem-*

porary Literature. New York: Farrar & Rinehart, 1936.

Cargill, Oscar. *Intellectual America: Ideas on the March*. New York: Macmillan, 1941.

Chamberlain, John. "Books of the Times." *New York Times* (Oct. 27, 1933), 17.

Clendenning, Logan. "Sex Madness." *Forum and Century*, 84 (Oct. 1930), 208–12.

Coindreau, Maurice Edgar. "La Autobiografia de Gertrude Stein." *Sur*, 4 (July 1934).

Cooper, John R. *The Art of the Compleat Angler*. Durham: Duke University Press, 1968.

Cowley, Malcolm. "Hemingway's Wound—And Its Consequences for American Literature." *Georgia Review*, 38 (Summer 1984), 223–39.

———. Introduction. *Viking Portable Library Hemingway*. Ed. Malcolm Cowley. New York: Viking, 1944. Pp. vii–xxiv.

———. "*Winner Take Nothing*: Editor's Preface." In *Viking Portable Library Hemingway*.

Current-Garcia, Eugene. *O. Henry (William Porter)*. New York: Twayne, 1965.

"Dale Wasserman, Playwright." Dies at 94." *New York Times* (Dec. 27, 2008), 18.

Davies, William H. *The Autobiography of a Super-Tramp*. New York: Knopf, 1924.

Davis, Robert Murray. "Hemingway's 'The Doctor and the Doctor's Wife.'" *The Explicator*, 25 (Sept. 1966), 1.

DeFalco, Joseph. *The Hero in Hemingway's Short Stories*. Pittsburgh: University of Pittsburgh Press, 1963.

DePastino, Todd. Introduction. Jack London, *The Road*. Ed. Todd DePastino. New Brunswick, N.J.: Rutgers University Press, 2006.

Eades, Gerald (ed.). *The Arte of Angling (1577)*. Intr. Carl Otto v. Kienbusch. Princeton, NJ: Princeton University Library, 1956.

Editorial on Logan Clendenning's Death. *Kansas City Star* (Feb. 1, 1945), 14.

Faulkner, William. *The Wild Palms*. New York: Random House, 1939.

Fenton, Charles A. *The Apprenticeship of Ernest Hemingway: The Early Years*. New York: Farrar, Straus and Young, 1954.

Fitzgerald, F. Scott. *The Great Gatsby*. New York: Charles Scribner's Sons, 1925.

———. "How to Waste Material, a Note on My Generation." *Bookman*, 63 (May 1926), 262–65. In Stephens, *Hemingway: Critical Reception*. Pp. 17–19.

———. *The Letters of F. Scott Fitzgerald*. Ed. Andrew Turnbull. New York: Scribner's, 1963.

———. *Tender Is the Night*. New York: Scribner's, 1934.

———. *This Side of Paradise*. New York: Scribner's, 1920.

Fleming, Robert E. *The Face in the Mirror: Hemingway's Writers*. Tuscaloosa: University of Alabama Press, 1994.

———. "Perversion and the Writer in 'The Sea Change.'" *Studies in American Fiction*, 4 (Autumn 1986), 215–20.

Flora, Joseph M. *Ernest Hemingway: A Study of the Short Fiction*. Boston: Twayne, 1989.

———. *Hemingway's Nick Adams*. Baton Rouge: Louisiana State University Press, 1982.

Flynt, Joseph. *Tramping with Tramps*. New York: Century, 1900.

Ford, Ford Madox. Introduction. *A Farewell to Arms*. New York: Modern Library, 1932.

Ford, Hugh. *Published in Paris: American and British Writers, Printers, and Publishers in Paris, 1920–1939*. New York: Macmillan, 1975.

The Forum, 74 (Aug. 1925).

Foster, David. *The Scientific Angler: Being a General and Instructive Work on Artistic Angling*. Ed. Wm. C. Harris. New York: Orange Judd, 1883.

French, J. Milton (ed.). *Three Books on Fishing (1599–1659) Associated with the Complete Angler (1653) by Izaak Walton*. Gainesville, Florida: Scholars' Facsimiles and Reprints, 1962.

Frost, Robert. *The Letters of Robert Frost to Louis Untermeyer*. New York: Holt, Rinehart and Winston, 1963.

"Frush Knocked Out by Mascart in 2d." *New York Times* (Jan. 28, 1925), 11.

Gable, Sister Mariella. *Great Modern Catholic Short Stories*. New York: Sheed & Ward, 1942.

Gajdusek, Linda. "Up and Down: Making Connections in 'A Day's Wait.'" In Beegel, *Neglected Short Fiction*.

Geismar, Maxwell. "Was 'Papa' a Truly Great Writer?" *New York Times* (July 1, 1962), 16.

Gerogiannis, Nicholas. "Nick Adams on the Road: 'The Battler' as Hemingway's Man on the Hill." In Reynolds, *Critical Essays*. Pp. 178–79.

Grebstein, Sheldon. *Hemingway's Craft*. Carbondale and Edwardsville: Southern Illinois University Press, 1973.

Grey, Zane. "A Trout Fisherman's Inferno." *Field and Stream* (Apr. 1910). In Reiger, *Zane Grey*. Pp. 282–91.

Griffin, Peter. *Along with Youth: Hemingway, the Early Years*. New York: Oxford University Press, 1985.

Grimes, Larry E. "William James and 'The Doctor and the Doctor's Wife.'" In *Hemingway: Up in Michigan Perspectives*. Pp. 47–57.

Gritzer, Glenn, and Arnold Arluke. *The Making of Rehabilitation: A Political Economy of Medical Specialization, 1890–1980*. Berkeley: University of California Press, 1985.

Hanneman, Audre. *Ernest Hemingway: A Comprehensive Bibliography*. Princeton, NJ: Princeton University Press, 1967.

Harding, Brian. "Ernest Hemingway: Men With, or Without, Women." In Nassa, *American Declarations of Love.*

Hart, Clive (ed.). *Conversations with James Joyce.* New York: Barnes & Noble, 1974.

Hawthorne, Nathaniel. *Hawthorne's Short Stories.* Ed. Newton Arvin. New York: Vintage, 1946.

Hays, Peter L. *Ernest Hemingway.* New York: Continuum, 1990.

———. "Hemingway and the Fisher King." *University Review* (Mar. 1966), 32: 225–28.

Hemingway, Ernest. *Across the River and into the Trees.* New York: Scribner's, 1950.

———. "The Art of the Short Story." *Paris Review*, 23 (Spring 1981), 85–102.

———. "The Best Rainbow Trout Fishing," *Toronto Star Weekly* (Aug. 28, 1920). In *Dateline.* Pp. 50–52.

———. "Big Two-Hearted River. *Field & Stream*, 59 (May 1954), 45–48, 96–105.

———. *By-Line: Ernest Hemingway, Selected Articles and Dispatches of Four Decades.* Ed. William White. New York: Scribner's, 1967.

———. *The Complete Short Stories of Ernest Hemingway.* The Finca Vigía Edition. New York: Scribner's, 1991.

———. *Dateline: Toronto: The Complete Toronto Star Dispatches, 1920–1924.* Ed. William White. New York: Scribner's, 1985.

———. *Death in the Afternoon.* New York: Scribner's, 1932.

———. "Defense of Dirty Words: A Cuban Letter." *Esquire*, 2 (Sept. 1934).

———. *A Farewell to Arms.* New York: Scribner's, 1929.

———. *The Fifth Column and the First Forty-Nine Stories.* New York: Scribner's, 1938.

———. *God Rest You Merry Gentlemen.* New York: House of Books, Ltd., 1933.

———. *Green Hills of Africa.* New York: Scribner's, 1935.

———. "Homage to Ezra." In Trogdon, *A Literary Reference.*

———. "In Another Country." *Scribner's Magazine*, 81 (Apr. 1927), 355–57.

———. *in our time.* Paris: Three Mountains Press, 1924.

———. *In Our Time.* New York: Boni & Liveright, 1925.

———. Introduction. *Men at War.* New York: Avon, 1952.

———. "Lack of Passion." *The Hemingway Review*, 9 (Spring 1990), 1–93.

———. *Men Without Women.* New York: Scribner's, 1927.

———. *A Moveable Feast.* New York: Scribner's, 1964.

———. *The Old Man and the Sea.* New York: Scribner's, 1952.

———. "Old Man at the Bridge." *Ken*, 1 (May 19, 1938), 36.

———. "On Writing." In *The Nick Adams Stories.* Pref. Philip Young. New York: Scribner's, 1972.

———. "Out in the Stream: A Cuban Letter." *Esquire* (Aug. 1934), 19, 156, 158. In *By-Line.* Pp. 172–78.

———. "Philip Haines Was a Writer." *The Hemingway Review*, 9 (Spring 1990), 1–93.

———. Preface. In Hemingway, *Fifth Column and the First Forty-Nine Stories.*

———. *Selected Letters, 1917–1961.* Ed. Carlos Baker. New York: Scribner's, 1981.

———. "The Short Happy Life of Francis Macomber." In *Complete Stories.*

———. "The Snows of Kilimanjaro," In *Complete Stories.*

———. *The Sun Also Rises.* New York: Scribner's, 1926.

———. *To Have and Have Not.* New York: Scribner's, 1937.

———. "To Will Davies." In Gerogiannis, *88 Poems.* P. 21.

———. *Winner Take Nothing.* New York: Scribner's, 1933.

Hemingway, Ernest, and Maxwell Perkins. *The Only Thing That Counts: The Ernest Hemingway/ Maxwell Perkins Correspondence, 1925–1947.* Ed. Matthew J. Bruccoli. New York: Scribner's, 1996.

Hemingway, Mary Welsh. *How It Was.* New York: Knopf, 1976.

Henry, O. *The Complete Works of O. Henry.* Garden City, N.Y.: Doubleday, Page, 1927.

Hicks, Granville. "The World of Hemingway" *New Freeman*, 1 (Mar. 1930), 40–42.

Housman, A.E. *The Collected Poems of A.E. Housman.* New York: Holt, Rinehart and Winston, 1965.

———. *Last Poems.* New York: Henry Holt, 1922.

Howells, William Dean. *Selected Letters of W. D. Howells.* Eds. George Arms and Christoph K. Lohmann (Boston: Twayne, 1979).

Johnson, Owen. *The Lawrenceville Stories.* New York: Simon & Schuster, 1967.

———. *The Varmint.* New York: Baker & Taylor, 1910.

Kieran, John. "A Wicked Sham Report on Sports." *New York Times* (Jan. 23, 1930), 21.

Kvam, Wayne E. "Hemingway's 'Banal Story.'" *Fitzgerald / Hemingway Annual 1974.* pp. 181–91

Lamb, Robert Paul. "Fishing for Stories: What 'Big Two-Hearted River' Is Really About." *Modern Fiction Studies*, 32 (Summer 1991).

Lang, Andrew. Introduction. *The Compleat Angler.* London: J.M. Dent / New York: E.P. Dutton, 1906.

Lawrence, D.H. Review of *In Our Time*. *Calendar of Modern Letters*, 4 (Apr. 1927), 72–73.

Leach, Henry Goddard. "A Non-Partisan Magazine of Free Discussion." *The Forum*, 74 (Aug. 1925), 161.

Lewis. R.W.B. "Who's Papa?" *New Republic*, 193 (Dec. 2, 1985), pp. 33–34.

London, Jack. *The Road*. Santa Barbara and Salt Lake City: Peregrine, 1970.

Luccock, Halford E. *American Mirror: Social, Ethical and Religious Aspects of American Literature 1930–1940*. New York: Macmillan, 1940.

Lynn, Kenneth. *The Air-Line to Seattle: Studies in Literary and Historical Writing About America*. Chicago: University of Chicago Press, 1983.

———. *Hemingway*. New York: Simon & Schuster, 1987.

———. "Hemingway's Private War," *Commentary*, 72 (July 1981), 24–33. In Lynn, *Air-Line*, 108–31.

Martin, Jay (ed.). *Nathanael West: A Collection of Critical Essays*. Englewood Cliffs, N.J.: Prentice-Hall, 1971.

Matthews, Brander. *The Philosophy of the Short-Story*. New York: Peter Smith, 1931.

McAlmon, Robert. *Being Geniuses Together*. London: Secker & Warburg, 1938;

———. *Being Geniuses Together 1920–1930*, Rev. ed., supplemented by Kay Boyle. Garden City: Doubleday, 1968.

Mellow, James R. *Hemingway: A Life Without Consequences*. Boston: Houghton Mifflin, 1992.

Melville, Herman. *Moby-Dick Or, the Whale*. New York: Hendricks House, 1952.

Mertins, Louis. *Robert Frost: Life and Talks-Walking*. Norman: University of Oklahoma Press, 1965.

Meyers, Jeffrey. *Hemingway: A Biography*. New York: Harper & Row, 1985.

——— (ed.). *Hemingway: The Critical Heritage*, London: Routledge & Kegan Paul, 1982.

Mirrielees, Edith. "Those College Writing Courses." *Saturday Review of Literature*, 17 (Jan. 15, 1938), 3–4, 16.

Miko, Stephen. "The River, the Iceberg, and the Shit-Detector." *Criticism*, 33 (Fall 1991).

Mizener, Arthur. *The Far Side of Paradise: A Biography of F. Scott Fitzgerald*. Boston: Houghton Mifflin, 1951.

Montgomery, Marion. "Hemingway's 'The Gambler, the Nun, and the Radio': A Reading and a Problem." *Forum*, 3 (Winter 1961).

Monteiro, George. "The Education of Ernest Hemingway." *Journal of American Studies*, 8 (Apr. 1974), 96–98.

———. Introduction. *Critical Essays on Ernest Hemingway's A Farewell to Arms*. Ed. George Monteiro. New York: G.K. Hall, 1994.

———. "Patriotism and Treason in A *Farewell to Arms*." *WLA: War, Literature & the Arts*, 9 (Spring/Summer 1997), 27–38.

Montgomery, Constance Cappel. *Hemingway in Michigan*. New York: Fleet, 1966.

Mudrick, Marvin. "A No-Good Self-Righteous Bragging Boasting Chickenshit Character." *Hudson Review*, 24 (Spring 1981).

Mullin, Glenn H. *Adventures of a Scholar Tramp*. New York & London: Century, 1925.

Nassa, Ann (ed.). *American Declarations of Love*. New York: St. Martin's Press, 1990.

New Baltimore Catechism No. 1. Official Revised Edition. New York: Benziger Brothers, n.d.

Nichols, P.J.R. *Rehabilitation Medicine: The Management of Physical Disabilities*. London: Butterworth, 1976.

Nietzsche, Friedrich. *The Portable Nietzsche,*. Ed. and trans. Walter Kaufmann. New York: Viking Press, 1954.

———. *Twilight of the Idols* (1888). In *Portable Nietzsche*.

Notpoh, Nagrom. "In Praise of M. Barkers Excellent Book of Angling." In Barker, *Barker's Delight*.

Nylander, Towne. "Tramps and Hoboes." *The Forum*, 74 (Aug. 1925), 227–37.

O'Hara, John. "The Author's Name Is Hemingway." *New York Times Book Review*, Sept. 10, 1950, 1, 30.

———. *Selected Letters of John O'Hara*. Ed. Matthew J. Bruccoli. New York: Random House, 1978.

Ortolano, Glauco. "An Interview with Ana Maria Machado." *WLT: World Literature Today*, 76 (Spring 2002), 112.

Parsons, Talcott. *The Social System*. Glencoe, Ill.: Free Press, 1964.

Pattee, Fred Lewis. *The Development of the American Short Story: An Historical Survey*. New York: Harper and Brothers, 1923.

Pinsker, Sanford. "Revisionism with Rancor: The Threat of the Neoconservative Critics." *Georgia Review*, 38 (Summer 1984), 255–56;

Piper, Henry Dan. *F. Scott Fitzgerald: A Critical Portrait*. London: Bodley Head, 1966.

Plimpton, George. "An Interview with Ernest Hemingway." In Brooks, *Writers at Work*.

Plomer, William. Review of *Winner Take Nothing*. *Now and Then* (Spring 1934). In Meyers, *Critical Heritage*. Pp. 293–95.

Pope, Alexander. *The Works of Alexander Pope*. Notes by Dr. Warburton. Philadelphia: James B. Smith, n.d.

Portz, John. "Allusion and Structure in Hemingway's 'A Natural History of the Dead.'" *Tennessee Studies in Literature*, 10 (1964), 27–41.

Power, Arthur, in Hart. *Conversations with James Joyce.*
Preminger, Alex, Frank J. Warnke and O.B. Hardison, Jr. (eds.). *Princeton Encyclopedia of Poetry and Poetics.* Enlarged Edition. Princeton, NJ: Princeton University Press, 1974.
Pritchett, V.S. *Fortnightly Review,* 135 (Mar. 1934), 381–82.
"Proclamation 5817—National Fishing Week, 1988." *Public Papers of the Presidents of the United States: Ronald Reagan 1988, Book I—January 1 to July 1, 1988.* Washington: United States Government Printing Office, 1990.
Raeburn, Ben. Foreword. *Treasury for the Free World,* ed. Ben Raeburn. (New York: Arco, 1946.
Rahv, Philip. Review of *Winner Take Nothing. Partisan Review,* 1 (Feb.–Mar. 1934), 58–59.
"Readers' Forum [Letters from Lynn, Philip Young, and Malcolm Cowley]." *Georgia Review,* 38 (Fall 1984), 668–72.
Reagan, Ronald. "Proclamation 5817—National Fishing Week, 1988." *Public Papers of the Presidents of the United States: Ronald Reagan 1988, Book I—January 1 to July 1, 1988.* Washington: United States Government Printing Office, 1990.
Reiger, George (ed.). *Zane Grey: Outdoorsman.* Englewood Cliffs, NJ: Prentice-Hall, 1972.
Reynolds, Michael (ed.). *Critical Essays on Ernest Hemingway's "In Our Time."* Boston: G.K. Hall, 1983.
_____. "Ernest Hemingway 1899-1961: A Brief Biography." In Wagner-Martin, *Historical Guide.*
_____. *Hemingway: The Paris Years.* Oxford and New York: Basil Blackwell, 1989.
_____. *Hemingway's Reading, 1910-1940: An Inventory.* Princeton, NJ: Princeton University Press, 1981.
_____. "A Supplement to Hemingway's Reading: 1910-1940." *Studies in American Fiction,* 14 (Spring 1986), 99–108.
Rodman, Selden. "Books." *Common Sense,* 3 (Jan. 1934), 28.
Smith, Julian. "Hemingway and the Thing Left Out." *Journal of Modern Literature,* 1 (1970-71), 180–82.
Smith, Paul. "The Doctor and the Doctor's Friend: Logan Clendenning and Ernest Hemingway." *Hemingway Review,* 8 (Fall 1988), 37–39;
_____. "Hemingway's Apprentice Fiction: 1919-1921." In Benson, *New Critical Approaches.*
_____. *A Reader's Guide to the Short Stories of Ernest Hemingway.* Boston: G.K. Hall, 1989.
Sojka, Gregory S. *Ernest Hemingway: The Angler as Artist.* New York: Peter Lang, 1985.
Spanier, Sandra (ed.). *American Fiction, American Myth: Essays by Philip Young.* University Park, PA: Pennsylvania State University Press, 2000.
Spence, Clark G. "Knights of the Fast Freight." *American Heritage Magazine* (Aug. 1976). www.americanheritage.com/articles/magazine/ah
Spitzer, Leo. "Linguistic Perspectivism in 'Don Quijote.'" In Spitzer, *Linguistics.*
_____. *Linguistics and Literary History: Essays in Stylistics.* Princeton, NJ: Princeton University Press, 1948.
Stein, Gertrude. *Three Lives.* New York: Modern Library, 1936.
Stephens, Robert O. (ed.). *Ernest Hemingway: The Critical Reception.* New York: Burt Franklin, 1977.
Stetler, Charles, and Gerald Locklin. "Beneath the Tip of the Iceberg in Hemingway's 'The Mother of a Queen.'" *Hemingway Review,* 2 (Fall 1982), 68–69.
Stoneback, H.R. "'Mais Je Reste Catholique': Communion, Betrayal, and Aridity in 'Wine of Wyoming.'" In Beegel, *Neglected Short Fiction,* 209–24.
Svoboda, Frederic J. "Inventing the Experience in 'The Battler.'" In Svoboda and Waldheim, *Up in Michigan.*
Svoboda, Frederic J., and Joseph J. Waldmeir (eds.). *Hemingway: Up in Michigan Perspectives.* East Lansing: Michigan State University Press, 1995.
Tate, Allen. "Good Prose." *The Nation,* 122 (Feb. 10, 1926), 160–62. In Stephens, *Critical Reception.*
Tavernier Courbin, Jacqueline. *Ernest Hemingway's A Moveable Feast: The Making of Myth.* Boston: Northeastern University Press, 1991.
"Television." *New York Times* (Nov. 28, 1958), 55.
"Test Cricket Game Stirs All London." *New York Times* (Jan. 23, 1925), 16.
Trilling, Lionel. *E.M. Forster.* Norfolk, Conn.: New Directions, 1943.
_____. *A Gathering of Fugitives.* Boston: Beacon Press, 1956.
_____. "Hemingway and His Critics." In Trilling, *Moral Obligation.*
_____. *Matthew Arnold.* New York: Columbia University Press, 1949.
_____. *The Moral Obligation to Be Intelligent: Selected Essays.* Ed. Leon Wieseltier. New York: Farrar Straus and Giroux, 2000.
Trogdon, Robert (ed.). *Ernest Hemingway: A Literary Reference.* New York: Carroll & Graff, 1999.
Updike, John. "Basically Decent." *New Yorker* (Mar. 9, 2009).
Wagner-Martin, Linda (ed.). *A Historical Guide to Ernest Hemingway.* New York: Oxford University Press, 2000.

Waldmeir, Joseph J. (ed.). *Up in Michigan: Proceedings of the First National Conference of the Hemingway Society*. East Lansing: Michigan State University Press, 1983.

Walton, Isaak. *The Complete Angler (1653) by Izaak Walton*. In French, *Three Books on Fishing*.

———. *The Complete Angler 1653–1676*, ed. Jonquil Bevan. Oxford: Clarendon Press, 1983.

Warwick, Diana. "Life and Letters." *Life*, 83 (Mar. 6, 1924), 24.

Watson, William Brasch. "'Old Man at the Bridge': The Making of a Short Story." *Hemingway Review*, 7 (Spring 1988).

Webster, Harvey Curtis. "An Annotated Bibliography of Contemporary Literature for 1933: A Partial List." *English Journal*, 23 (Oct. 1934).

Wentworth, Harold, and Stuart Berg Flexner (eds.). *Dictionary of American Slang*, Second Supplemented Edition. New York: Crowell, n.d.

Westbrook, Max. "Text, Ritual, and Memory: Hemingway's 'Big Two-Hearted River.'" *North Dakota Quarterly*, 60 (Summer 1992), 14–25.

Wilbur, Richard. *Responses: Prose Pieces, 1953–1976*. New York: Harcourt Brace Jovanovich, 1976.

Williams, Tennessee. *Clothes for a Summer Hotel: A Ghost Play*. New York: New Directions, 1983.

Wilson, Edmund. *Apologies to the Iroquois*. New York: Farrar, Straus and Cudahy, 1960.

———. *O Canada: An American's Notes on Canadian Culture*. New York: Farrar, Straus and Giroux, 1965.

———. "Ernest Hemingway: Bourdon Gauge of Morale," *Atlantic Monthly*, 164 (July 1939) 36–46.

———. *Letters on Literature and Politics, 1912–1972*. Ed. Elena Wilson. New York: Farrar, Straus and Giroux, 1977.

"Winners Take All," *The Economist*, Mar. 26–Apr. 1, 2016, cover.

Yannella, Phillip R. "Notes on the Manuscript, Date, and Sources of Hemingway's 'Banal Story.'" *Fitzgerald / Hemingway Annual 1974*. Ed. Matthew J. Bruccoli and C.E. Frazer Clark, Jr. Englewood: Microcard, 1975.

Young, Philip. *American Fiction, American Myth: Essays by Philip Young*. Ed. Sandra Spanier. University Park, PA: Pennsylvania State University Press, 2000.

———. "Big World Out There: The Nick Adams Stories." *Novel: A Forum on Fiction*, 6 (Fall 1972), 5–19.

———. *Ernest Hemingway*. New York and Toronto: Rinehart, 1952.

———. *Ernest Hemingway: A Reconsideration*. University Park: Pennsylvania State University Press, 1966.

———. "Posthumous Hemingway, and Nicholas Adams." In *Hemingway in Our Time*. Eds. Richard Astro and Jackson J. Benson. Corvallis: Oregon State University Press, 1974. Pp. 13–23.

Young, Philip, and Charles W. Mann. *The Hemingway Manuscripts: An Inventory*. University Park: Pennsylvania State University Press, 1969.

———. "Fitzgerald's Sun Also Rises: Notes and Comment." *Fitzgerald/Hemingway Annual 1970*. Washington, DC: NCR/Microcard Editions, 1970.

Index

acedia 98, 134
Across the River and Into the Trees 5, 21, 50, 56–57
Adams, Henry 133
Addison, Joseph 54
Aesculapius 65
affective neutrality (neutralized affections) 28–29, 34, 67, 106–107, 127
Africa (African) 19, 21, 25, 81
"An African Story" 22
"After the Storm" 16, 24, 83, 85–86, 88, 93–97, 100
After the Storm, and Other Stories (abandoned title for *Winner Take Nothing*) 87
Allington, Floyd 130
American Medical Association 60
Amory, Cleveland 48
Anderson, Sherwood 7, 13
Andrews, S.G. 139–40
Anis del Toro 69
Antunes, Antonio Lobo 25
Arnold, Matthew 28
ars poetica 16, 109, 125
"The Art of the Short Story" 22, 108
"The Ash Heel's Tendon" 22
Associated Press 76
Atlantic Monthly (journal) 21–22, 111–12
Aton, James 78; "An Apostle of Thunder" 78; "Too Good to be True" 78

Babbitt, Irving 126
Baker, Carlos 2, 101, 118–19, 122–23, 131, 138
"Banal Story" 42, 75–80
Bar Basque 108
Barker, Thomas 58, 164–65*ch*4*n*49; *Barker's Delight* 58
Bates, H.E. 69
"The Battler" 9, 10, 14, 43, 45, 47–49, 77
Belasco, David 121
Bellevue Hospital 84
Berryman, John 10
Biddle, Francis 78; "Aunt Jane's Sofa" 78
"The Big Rock Candy Mountain" (song) 47
"Big Two-Hearted River" 11–12, 44, 68, 81–82, 138, 155, 161*ch*3*n*3

Bird, Bill 71
Bird, Sally 7
"Black Ass at the Crossroads" 22
Boni & Liveright 1, 10, 78, 86
Books on Trial (journal) 132
Britton, Jack 76
Bromfield, Louis 78; "Justice" 78
Brooks, Cleanth 142–44
Browne, Sir Thomas 35
Browning, Robert 138; *Men and Women* 13
Bruccoli, Matthew J. 93
Bryer, Jackson 93
Bunyan, John 102; *Pilgrim's Progress* 102
Burnham, James 55–56; "Incompleat Angler" 55
Butcher, Fanny 82
"The Butterfly and the Tank" 21–22
Byron, George Gordon Lord 144; *Don Juan* 144

Caldwell, Erskine 92
Callaghan, Morley 132, 168*ch*9*n*67
Canadian literature 27
"A Canary for One" 17, 156
Canby, Henry Seidel 83, 85, 91; *Seven Years' Harvest: Notes on Contemporary Literature* 91
Canfield, Dorothy 78; "Mr. Rooster Rebels" 78
"The Capital of the World" 6, 21, 138
Cardinella, Sam 139–40
Cargill, Oscar 93
Carver, Raymond 1, 25
"Cat in the Rain" 11, 15
Cervantes, Miguel 1
Chamberlain, John 84, 85
Charles Scribner's Sons 13, 21–22, 82, 100, 113
"Charlots" ("Charlie Chaplins") 73
Chicago 6, 14, 99
Chicago Daily Tribune (*Chicago Tribune*) 82, 108
Christian Science 38, 39
Christianity (Christian) 102–06, 139, 149
Cincinnati Enquirer 83

Index

"A Clean, Well-Lighted Place" 3, 18–19, 25, 50–59, 66, 81, 84–86, 89–90, 93, 97–100, 126, 155
Clendenning, Logan 118, 169ch9n86
Coindreau, Maurice Edgar 91
Coleridge, Samuel Taylor 94; "The Ancient Mariner" 94
The Complete Short Stories of Ernest Hemingway 22
confidenza (confidence) 98
Congleton, J.E. 54
Contact Publishing Company 7
Coolidge, Calvin 76
Cooper, John 53–55, 57–59, 164ch4n32, 164ch4n46, 164–165ch4n49; *The Art of the Compleat Angler* 53
Cosmopolitan (magazine) 14, 19, 21, 43, 88, 93–94, 122
Cowley, Malcolm 50–51, 54, 93, 100; *Viking Portable Hemingway* 100
"Cross Country Snow" 10–11
"Crossroads" 22
Cubism 77

Dahlberg, Edward 91
D'Annunzio, Gabriele 141, 145
Dashiell, Alfred 100
David (scripture) 98
Davies, W.H. 42–43, 45, 48–49; *The Autobiography of a Super-Tramp* 43–44
"A Day's Wait" 17, 24, 83, 86, 93, 123–124, 126, 137
Death in the Afternoon 16–17, 50, 57, 68–69, 79, 109, 125–26, 133, 155, 159pren8
"The Denunciation" 21–22
Depression *see* Great Depression
DiMaggio, Joseph Paul 149
"The Doctor and the Doctor's Wife" 10, 17, 36–41
The Doctor and the Doctor's Wife (Portuguese edition) 36
Dos Passos, John 25, 130

Eastman, Max 87
Eddy, Mary Baker 38
Einstein, Albert 77
Eliot, Ethel Cook 78; "Maternal" 78
Eliot, T.S. 3, 35, 133, 138; "The Love Song of J. Alfred Prufrock" 133; *The Wasteland* 133
"The End of Something" 10, 111
English Journal 83
Esquire (magazine) 14, 19, 57, 94, 157

Fadiman, Clifton 82–83, 85
"The Faithful Bull" 21–22
A Farewell to Arms 6, 9, 16–17, 60–61, 83, 91, 98–99, 100, 142–43, 165ch5n7, 165ch5n7, 165ch5n9
Farrell, James T. 91
"Fathers and Sons" 16, 17, 83–84, 86, 88–91, 134–37

Faulkner, William 25, 29, 31, 32, 84, 133; "Old Man" 29, 31–32; "Wild Palms" 29, 31; *The Wild Palms* 29, 31
Field & Stream (magazine) 51
The Fifth Column 6
The Fifth Column and Four Unpublished Stories of the Spanish Civil War 6, 21
The Fifth Column and the First Forty-Nine Stories 6, 21–22, 75, 82, 100
"Fifty Grand" 14, 25, 76, 148
Fisher King 103
Fitzgerald, F. Scott 1, 23, 25, 29–30, 32, 42, 49, 52, 76, 87–88, 108–09, 112–13, 121, 132, 150, 155, 165ch5n7; *The Great Gatsby* 76–77; *Tender Is the Night* 29–31, 150; *This Side of Paradise* 49
Fitzgerald, Zelda 23, 29, 112–13
Flora, Joseph 93, 138
Flynt, Josiah 42–43; *Tramping with Tramps* 43–44
For Whom the Bell Tolls 21, 154
Ford, Ford Madox 1, 8, 13, 23; *Women and Men* 13
Forster, E.M. 28
Fortnightly Review 89
Fortune (magazine) 21, 42
The Forum (magazine) 75–80
Frank E. Campbell (mortuary) 84
Frisbie, Robert Dean 78; "Palmleaf Gambling Hells" 78
Frost, Robert 42, 125–26, 131
Frush, Danny 76

Gable, Sister Mariella 132–33; *Great Modern Short Stories* 132–33
Gajdusek, Linda 169ch9n92
"The Gambler, the Nun, and the Radio" 18–19, 24, 83–84, 86, 89, 93, 126, 130–34
Garcia, Manuel 148
The Garden of Eden 21–22, 56
Gauss, Christian 52, 155
Geismar, Maxwell 92
Gellhorn, Martha 22
Georgics (georgics) 54, 57, 59
"Get a Seeing-Eyed Dog" 22, 111–12, 169ch9n77
Gibbs, Arthur Hamilton 77; *Soundings* 77
"Give Us a Prescription, Doctor" 18, 131
"God Rest You Merry, Gentleman" 17, 32, 83, 85–86, 88, 102–08, 126
"Golden Age of Sport" 87
The Golden Bough 133
"A Good Café on the Place St.-Michel" 23–24
"The Good Lion" 21–22
Great Depression 81, 87–88, 150
"Great News from the Mainland" 22
Grebstein, Sheldon 116, 169ch9n94
Green Hills of Africa 9, 19, 50, 57, 71, 81, 125, 127
Greene, Wade 125

Index

Gregory, Horace 83, 85
Griffin, Peter 22; *Along with Youth* 22

Halper, Albert 91
Harding, Brian 93
Harry's Bar (Venice) 21
Hartford Courant 83
Hawthorne, Nancy 77
Hawthorne, Nathaniel 102, 158; "The Celestial Railroad" 102
Hayes, Peter L. 93
Hemingway, Clarence 5, 32, 35, 41
Hemingway, Ernest 2, 3, 5–6, 9, 13, 16, 21–23, 24, 25, 31, 35, 41–43, 49–53, 57–58, 60, 68, 70, 81–82, 85, 87–89, 100, 108–09, 131, 138, 141, 148–149, 157, 169$ch2n$4, 170$ch10n$33
Hemingway, Grace Hall 5
Hemingway, Hadley Richardson 6, 23, 70, 75, 122
Hemingway, John (Bumby) 75, 123, 134
Hemingway, Mary Welsh 3, 22
Hemingway, Patrick 21, 123
Hemingway, Pauline Pfeiffer 6, 19, 70, 71
Hemingway Collection (John F. Kennedy Library) 8
The Hemingway Reader 21
Henderson, Archibald 77
Heywood, Du Bose 78; "Crown's Bess" 78
Hicks, Granvuille 159$intrn$6
Hijuelos, Oscar 25
"Hills Like White Elephants" 14–15, 17–18, 24–25, 68–71, 80–81, 89
Holy Ghost 97
"Homage to Ezra" 138
"Homage to Switzerland" 16–17, 82–83, 86, 90, 93, 120–23
homosexuality 88
Hot Springs (golf links) 49
Housman, A.E. 138–146, 170$ch10n$18; "The Carpenter's Son" 139–40; *Collected Poems* 146; "The Deserter" 142–43; "Epitaph on an Army of Mercenaries" 143; "Into My Heart an Air That Kills" 138; *Last Poems* 138–39; *A Shropshire Lad* 138–39; [Untitled poem] 141–42
Hudson, W.H. 125
Hughes, Richard 78; "Poor Man's Inn" 78
Hunt, Holman 101; "The Light of the World" (painting) 101

"I Guess Everything Reminds You of Something" 22
"In Another Country" 3, 14, 25, 61–67
in our time 1, 8–11, 13, 78–79, 139, 159–160In6
In Our Time 6–8, 10, 12, 16, 21, 23–24, 36, 43, 52, 78, 81–83, 86–88, 112, 126, 136, 140–41
"Indian Camp" 10, 14, 17, 25, 32–36, 80–81, 86, 126, 136, 155–56
"The Inquest" (book series) 8, 13
Iroquois 27

Islands in the Stream 17, 21, 50, 56, 137, 149
Italy (Italian) 8, 63, 65

James, Henry 156
Joan of Arc 77
John (scripture) 101
John the Baptist (scripture) 97
Johnson, Owen 42, 48, 49, 162$ch3n$28; *The Prodigious Hickey* 48; *Stover at Yale* 48–49; *The Tennessee Shad* 48; *The Varmint* 48
Joselito 79
Joyce, James 6, 76, 150
Junkins, Donald 113

Kalkaska 43
Kansas City 17, 83, 90, 105
Kansas City Star 5, 43, 83
Ken (magazine) 153
Kerouac, Jack 42; *On the Road* 42
Ketchel, Steve ("Stanley") 47, 101, 102
Ketchum, Idaho 6
Key West (The Keys) 16, 94
Kieran, John 87; "A Wicked Sham Report on Sports" 87
"The Killers" 14, 24–25, 72–74, 81, 90
Kronenberger, Louis 83

Lake Superior 59
Lamb, Paul 163$ch4n$10
"Landscape with Figures" 22
Lardner, Ring 1, 7
"The Last Good Country" 12, 22
Lausanne (France) 6
Lawrence, D.H. 12
Lawrence, T.E. 122
Lawrenceville School 48
Leopoldina (ship) 6
"The Light of the World" 16, 17, 25, 43, 45–48, 49, 81, 85–86, 88–89, 100–02, 126
Lish, Gordon 1
Little Review 75
Liveright, Horace 7–8
London 76, 112
London, Jack 42–43, 45–46, 48, 49; *On the Road* 43, 45–46
London *Times* 143–144
Lord's Prayer 97, 98; *nada* parody 18–19, 90, 99
Luke (scripture) 97, 104
Lynn, Kenneth 51, 113, 163$ch4n$9

Machado, Ana Maria 25
Macleish, Archibald 125
The Macomber Affair (movie) 20
Madrid 69, 72, 117
Maera, Manuel Garcis 78–80
Mailer, Norman 25
"A Man of the World" 22, 112
Mancelona 43
Mansfield, Katherine 132

Index

Mark, Sister Mary 132
Marx (Marxism) 27, 55, 131
Mascart, Edouard 76
"The Matadores" (early title for "The Killers") 14, 72
"A Matter of Measurements" 23
Matthew (scripture) 101, 105, 152
Matthews, Brander 171*ch*13*n*3
Matthews, T.S. 83
Maupassant, Guy de 16, 86, 100, 149, 157; "La Maison Tellier" 16, 86, 100
McAlmon, Robert 70–71
Mellow, James R. 169*ch*9*n*82
Melville, Herman 37–38, 98
Men Without Women 6, 13–14, 21, 75, 81–83, 87, 109
Mencken, H.L. 80
"The Mercenaries" 22, 144–46
Miko, Stephen 163*ch*4*n*8
Milan (Italy) 65, 90
Milton, John 151–52; *Samson Agonistes* 151–52; "Sonnet [on his blindness]" 151
"Miss Stein Instructs" 23
"Mr. and Mrs. Elliot" 11
Mizener, Arthur 49
Montana 85, 132
Montgomery, Marion 170*ch*9*n*104
"The Mother's of a Queen" 16, 24, 82, 86, 93, 116–18
A Moveable Feast 6, 22, 50, 56, 68, 112–13, 125, 161*ch*3*n*5, 164*ch*4*n*39
Mudrick, Marvin 81
Mullen, Kate 78; "Interval" 78
Mullin, Glenn H. 42, 44–45, 161–62*ch*3*n*9, 162*ch*3*n*24; *Adventures of a Scholar Tramp* 44–45
Mussolini, Benito 141
"My Old Man" 7, 11, 87

nada (parody) *see* "Lord's Prayer"
Nation (journal) 84
National Geographic Society 122
"A Natural History of the Dead" 17, 32, 82, 84, 86, 91, 125–27
New International (journal) 55
New Republic (journal) 83
New Testament (scripture) 104
New York 27, 84
New York Herald Tribune 83
New York Times 84, 87, 93, 125
New York Times Book Review 83
Nichols, P.J.R. 165*ch*5*n*1
The Nick Adams Stories 6, 12, 22, 23, 58
Nietzsche, Friedrich 66
"Night Before Battle" 21–22
Noble Prize for Literature 22
"Nobody Ever Dies!" 21–22
North American News Alliance (NANA) 153
Notpoh, Nagrom 50
Now and Then (journal) 90

"Now I Lay Me" 14, 98
Nylander, Towne 42; "Tramps and Hoboes" 42, 77

O. Henry 1, 10, 24, 124, 155–158, 171*ch*13*n*1, 171*ch*13*n*2, 171*ch*13*n*7; *Cabbages and Kings* 171*ch*13*n*7; "The Last Leaf" 156–58
Oak Park, Illinois 5, 48, 49, 123
Oates, Joyce Carol 25
O'Hara, John 5, 159*intro*n1
The Old Man and the Sea 3, 13, 21, 50, 56–57, 96, 148–49
"Old Man at the Bridge" 6, 21, 153–54
"On the Quai at Smyrna" 9
"One Reader Writes" 17, 24, 82, 84, 86, 93, 118–20
"One Trip Across" 14, 16, 22, 88, 94
Ospedale Maggiore 61
"Out in the Stream: A Cuban Letter" 57–58
"Out of Season" 2, 7–8, 11, 15, 68
Ovid 54; *Halieuticon* 54

Pamplona 25
Paris 6, 7, 22–23, 35, 75, 78, 112
Paris Review 22
Park, Mungo 125
Parsons, Talcott 28–29
Partisan Review 89
Perkins, Maxwell 75, 81–82, 86, 87–88, 100, 113
Philippians (scripture) 102
Picasso, Pablo 77
Plomer, William 90
Poe, Edgar Allan 158
Pope, Alexander 109; "Essay on Man" Epistle II 109–11
"The Porter" 22
Pound, Ezra 3, 6, 8, 13, 23, 138
Princeton Encyclopedia of Poetry and Poetics 164*ch*4*n*28
Princeton University 49, 76
Pritchett, V.S. 89–90
Prohibition 128
Proverbs (scripture) 38
Pulitzer Prize 21
Pyle, Howard 123–24; *Book of Pirates* 123–24

Quarterly (Christian Science) 38

Rahv, Philip 89
Rapallo (Italy) 70
Reagan, Ronald 50
Red Cross 5
Reisman, David 28; *The Lonely Crowd* 28
Renaissance 54
"The Revolutionist" 9, 11
Reynolds, Michael 52, 87–88, 144–45
Richardson, Anthony 78; "Old Mossy Face" 78
Roberts, Elizabeth Madox 132
Rodman, Seldon 84–85

Index

St.-Jean-de-Luz 108
St. Paul (scripture) 104, 105–06; I Corinthians (scripture) 104, 105–06
St. Vincent's Hospital 131, 134
Salinger, J.D. 25
San Francisco de Paula, Cuba 22–23
San Isidro (Spain) 72
Saturday Review of Literature 83, 91–93
Schruns (Austria) 75
Science and Health 38
Scribner's Magazine 18, 100
"The Sea Change" 17, 22, 24, 85, 108–13, 126, 169ch9n77
Seney 44
Seville (Spain) 79
Shakespeare, William 3, 110, 145–46; *Henry IV, Part II* 146; *Julius Caesar* 143; *The Tempest* 111
"Shakespeare and Company" 23
Sharkey, Jack 87
Shaw, George Bernard 77
Shelley, Percy Bysshe 138
"Short Happy Life of Francis Macomber" 2, 6, 19, 21, 25, 68, 71, 81, 146–7
Shropshire (England) 138
"A Simple Enquiry" 24, 109
Sister Florence 131–34
Sisters of Charity of Leavenworth 131
Smith, Alfred E. 128
Smith, Julian 107–08
Smith, Paul 138, 141, 144
"The Snows of Kilimanjaro" 2, 6, 9, 19–21, 25, 81, 149, 152, 156–58
Sociology 27–28
"Soldier's Home" 11, 25, 141–42
Spain (Spanish) 23, 65, 78, 90, 98, 109, 117
Spanish Civil War 6, 21, 153–154
Stein, Gertrude 6, 8, 23, 51, 58, 90, 119, 161ch3n5; *Autobiography of Alice B. Toklas* 90; *The Making of Americans* 8; *Three Lives* 8, 119–20
Steinbeck, John 25, 42; *The Grapes of Wrath* 42
"The Strange Country" 22
suicide 34–35, 88, 122, 134
"Summer People" 12, 22
Summit 72, 74
The Sun Also Rises 6, 13, 16, 23, 50, 61, 70, 76, 84, 91, 107, 125
Sur (journal) 90

Taine, Hippolyte 27
Tarkington, Booth 83
Tate, Allen 52
Tavernier-Courbin, Jacqueline 112–13
"Ten Indians" 14
This Quarter (journal) 52, 108, 138
"The Three Day Blow" 10, 23, 112
Three Mountains Press 1, 8, 78
Three Stories & Ten Poems 6, 7, 11
Time (magazine) 83

To Have and Have Not 14, 22, 50, 55–56, 94, 120
"To Will Davis" 139–40
"Today is Friday" 13, 139–40, 149
Toklas, Alice B. 51
Tolstoy, Leo 149
"The Tomb of His Grandfather" (abandoned title for "Fathers and Sons") 86, 134, 137
Toronto Star 52
Torrents of Spring 13, 76, 78
"The Tradesman's Return" 14, 16, 22, 94
"A Train Trip" 22
Transatlantic Review 10, 68
transition (journal) 68
triage 125, 127
Trilling, Lionel 27–28, 81
Troy, William 84
True at First Light 21
Turgenev, Ivan 17, 134; *Fathers and Sons* 134; *Sportsman's Sketches* 17
Twain, Mark 77, 136; *Adventures of Huckleberry Finn* 136
Twenty-Third Psalm (David's confidence in the Grace of God) (scripture) 97–98
"Two Titles of Darkness" (general title for "A Man of the World" and "Get a Seeing-Eyed Dog") 22

Ulysses 77
"The Undefeated" 13, 24–25
"Under the Ridge" 21–22
"*Une Génération Perdue*" 23
Untermeyer, Louis 125
"Up in Michigan" 6–9, 11, 15, 21, 77
Updike, John 25, 49
Upper Peninsula (Michigan) 11, 52, 138

Valhalla 52
Venice (Italy) 21, 35
"A Very Short Story" 9, 11
Virgil 54
Vorarlberg (Austria) 75

Walsh, Edward 138
Walton, Izaak 50, 52, 53–54, 56–59, 162–63ch4n4; *The Compleat Angler* 50, 52–59
"A Way You'll Never Be" 16, 25, 83, 85, 89–90, 113–16
Webster, Harvey Curtis 83
West, Nathanael 118, 120; *Miss Lonelyhearts* 118–20
"When Jonny Comes Marching Home" (song) 141
White, Gilbert 125
Whitman, Walt 138
Williams, Tennessee 108; *Clothes for a Summer Hotel: A Ghost Play* 108–09
Williams, Ursula Trainor 78; "Will Turner's Wife" 78
Williams, William Carlos 8
Wilson, Edmund 27, 50–51, 54, 166ch7n5

"Wine of Wyoming" 17, 24, 83–84, 86, 127–30
Winner Take Nothing 6, 16–17, 21, 43, 81, 137, 142
Woolson, Constance Fenimore 164*ch4n*38
World War I (First World War) 60, 65, 125, 127, 141–43
Wyoming 35, 90

Yale News 77
Yale University 76
Yeats, William Butler 138
Young, Philip 32, 43, 50–51, 54
The Young Doctor's Friend and Guide 103

www.ingramcontent.com/pod-product-compliance
Ingram Content Group UK Ltd.
Pitfield, Milton Keynes, MK11 3LW, UK
UKHW042013140426
5217IPUK00015B/1155